THE FORGOTTEN CITY

Rethinking Digital Living
for Our People and the Planet

Phil Allmendinger

First published in Great Britain in 2021 by

Policy Press, an imprint of Bristol University Press
University of Bristol
1-9 Old Park Hill
Bristol
BS2 8BB
UK
t: +44 (0)117 954 5940
e: bup-info@bristol.ac.uk

Details of international sales and distribution partners are available at
policy.bristoluniversitypress.co.uk

© Bristol University Press 2021

British Library Cataloguing in Publication Data
A catalogue record for this book is available from the British Library.

ISBN 978-1-4473-5601-1 hardcover
ISBN 978-1-4473-5604-2 ePub
ISBN 978-1-4473-5603-5 ePdf

Cover design: blu inc
Front cover image: Unsplash shade jay FkdpRnTjDLk

Bristol University Press and Policy Press use
environmentally responsible print partners

Printed in Great Britain by TJ Books, Padstow

MIX
Paper from
responsible sources
FSC® C013056

For Fleur and Florence

Contents

Acknowledgements

I'd like to acknowledge the huge support and input from Tina Gaw, Humbert Pang, Betty Man and Matthew Budden. Thank you all.

1

A tale of two stories

Humans love telling stories. We're really good at it. In fact, we've been telling stories for thousands of years, spreading them by word of mouth, then in writing, and latterly via our screens. Psychologists will tell you that stories follow recognisable patterns that fulfil a need to find meaning in the seemingly meaningless. Anthropologists say they are an integral part of our survival instinct, helping us understand and plan what to do when faced with danger and the need for quick decisions. And because we've been telling them for so long, our brains have adapted to look for stories or patterns, even when they don't exist. Stories let us feel as though we have control and allow us to share our understanding of the world and its history with others. But stories have another function too. They not only explain the past and the present; they also frame our actions and help shape the future.

Cities are the embodiment of why we tell stories. Our cities are unique, complex places that defy easy understanding or prediction. It's no surprise, then, that in order to comprehend cities we've made up stories about them throughout history. One popular narrative has cities as the springboard of civilisation, home to art, literature, drama and democracy. Another paints them as dens of iniquity and sin, or there is the story of the entrepreneurial city of trade and commerce, or the future city of Fritz Lang's *Metropolis*.[1] Whilst there are multiple different narratives, there have been two dominant stories of the city over the past 150 years or so, the 'city of the dreadful night' and the 'city of bright lights'.

The 'city of the dreadful night'

The first story of the city is one of deprivation, bleakness and misery. In 1929 the celebrated and controversial English writer D.H. Lawrence put pen to paper on one of his favourite topics, the state of the English city. 'The English are town-birds through and through', he opined, 'but they don't know how to build a city, how to think of one, or how to live in one'.[2] For Lawrence, the city was more than simply the physical – the state of the city reflected that of its inhabitants:

> The great city means beauty, dignity, and a certain splendour. This is the side of the Englishman that has been thwarted and shockingly betrayed. England is a mean and petty scrabble of paltry dwellings called "homes".... And the men inside these little red rat-traps get more and more helpless, being more and more humiliated, more and more dissatisfied, like trapped rats.[3]

Lawrence was by no means the first to condemn the city and imagine a better, alternative future, yet he reflected the dominant view of the time, a view that had emerged with the coming of the Industrial Revolution in the 19th century. It was during this period of rapid economic and urban growth that the city began to develop its dark reputation, what the justifiably long-forgotten Scottish poet James Thomson described in his 1880 poem as 'The City of the Dreadful Night', notable for its bleak, pessimistic view of the state of the Victorian city. But he captured the reality of urban living at the time, helping spread and reinforce the story of the city as a place dominated by slums, disease and poverty, where people were forced to live through economic necessity. For many – mainly the poor and the working class – the 'city of the dreadful night' was a daily reality.

This story of darkness wasn't just confined to the imagination of writers. From the 1930s onwards, developers and banks, keen to build and to loan money, played on the contrast between town and country, portraying the former as dark and polluted, and no place to bring up a family. Their aim was to help persuade the middle classes to take advantage of cheap finance and the rise in car ownership and spread out into the ever-expanding suburbs. Governments reinforced this bleak view, building new towns and cities and attempting to provide an 'escape' for skilled workers and the middle classes.

Despite concern over poverty, disease and crime, little was done for the cities themselves throughout the 19th and early 20th centuries beyond some half-hearted attempts to improve sanitation and impose building standards on new developments. In part, this lack of action was due to the conviction that the urban poor were largely to blame for their own situation. On the rare occasions when attempts were made to improve cities, they were motivated by self-interest, such as when the political and economic elites feared social unrest or the spread of radical ideas in the slums, or had concerns over the health of the workforce and the impacts on profits. The general attitude of the governing classes towards cities at the time is captured by what was known as 'slumming', a popular pastime in 19th-century Europe and the US, where wealthy residents would tour poor areas, marvelling at the horror of the lives of the destitute, accompanied by guides and pamphlets advertising the 'best spots' to visit.[4]

This dominant 'anti-city' attitude was by no means uniquely English: Germany, France and the US all had their own versions. If D.H. Lawrence was the novelist who spoke for the English, then Henry James was his US equivalent. James, renowned as one of the 20th century's greatest writers, couldn't have been more different to Lawrence in background, but they both shared a similar view of the city. Born into a wealthy, intellectual family, James was privately educated and travelled widely around Europe, living in France for some time. Between 1904 and 1905 he journeyed around the US and chronicled his experiences. Whilst no fan of the city in general, he focused particular disdain on New York, which he described as 'both squalid and gilded, to be fled rather than enjoyed'.[5] In his view, cities were where money was made, and the suburbs and the country were where it was spent and enjoyed. Like Lawrence, James wasn't alone in his denunciation of the city. In 1897 the *American Journal of Sociology* pointed to the 'popular belief' that 'large cities are great centres of social corruption and ... degeneration'.[6] That popular feeling extended to solutions too, summed up by the great industrialist Henry Ford when he said that 'we shall solve the city by leaving the city. Get the people into the countryside, get them into communities where a man knows his neighbors.'[7]

Nor was this belief confined to the 19th-century industrial city. In 1963 an assessment of North American cities came to the view that a visitor from Europe would 'justly reproach the US for being too hasty in its reliance on technology to solve every problem'.[8] The particular focus of concern was the impact of growing car use:

> For the expertly engineered automobiles are seen against a background of ramshackle slums, the winding rivers are dark with pollution, the waterfronts crowded with ancient factories and the spreading suburbs seem to have no centres of life or evidence of individual distinction.[9]

In this bleak story of the city, the 1970s were the nadir, yet the foundations of this low point were assembled a decade earlier. Cities in the 1960s had set the scene for what was to follow, acting as the backdrop for social unrest and growing discontent. In the US and many European cities there were protests against the war in Vietnam. German and Italian cities experienced the rise of domestic terrorism, whilst those in Northern Ireland felt the impact of growing sectarianism. Protests and riots against continued racial segregation and police violence dominated some US cities, whilst in Paris and other French cities civil unrest against social and economic convention, American imperialism, and the capitalist order sprang up. Cities were a place of strife, a focus of disharmony that matched the image of poverty and deprivation. In the UK there was a growing sense that the future wasn't urban, that the city had had its moment in history. The loss of manufacturing jobs throughout the 1970s led to increasing urban unemployment, whilst the middle classes and service sector jobs fled the city for the suburbs and the countryside. Even China was not immune from the attack on the city. From 1966 to 1976 the Cultural Revolution, brainchild of China's 'Great Helmsman' Chairman Mao Zedong, sought to purge the enemies of socialism and reassert control through mass murder and emptying the cities of revisionists. Cities helped maintain what Mao termed the 'four olds' – old ideas, old customs, old habits and old culture.

The city was under attack across the world in the 1970s, but it was in New York where it was to reach a low water mark. In October 1975 New York couldn't meet its debt repayment requirements of US$450 million. Banks refused to extend the loans and the federal government and US President Gerald Ford declined to bail the city out. Large areas of the city had become no-go areas overrun by crime and violence, where rubbish remained uncollected. The *Daily News* pithily summed up the situation in its famous headline on 30 October 1975: 'Ford to city: Drop dead'. Eventually the city's financial crisis was averted, but New York's position was seen as typical of many cities at the time, as places where poverty and social need were concentrated and unrest and violence were common. The attitude within governments echoed the 'city of the dreadful night' narrative: cities had had their day.

The 'city of bright lights'

And then the story changed. The 'city of the dreadful night' increasingly felt out of step with reality. If the 1970s were the low point, we are, in the 2020s, living in what some see as the city's heyday. The story of the city is now one of celebration, as humankind's greatest achievement. Far from being places of darkness, some claim that cities make us happy and are good for us.[10] If the story of the 19th- and 20th-century city was one of desperation and destitution, then the story of the 21st-century city is one of opportunity and excitement. This dramatic reversal reflects the renaissance in some of our major cities, places that are booming, vibrant and trendy. From being 'cities of the dreadful night', Paris, New York, Hong Kong and London are now cities that never sleep, and some say that we are now living in a 'golden age' of cities.[11] Figures are enthusiastically recycled as part of the optimists' canon to reinforce and persuade the unconverted: by 2008 more people lived in cities than rural areas for the first time in human history. By 2014 that proportion had risen to 54 per cent, and by 2050, the United Nations (UN) projects it to increase to 66 per cent. But the new story of the city points to bigger changes to come. Most of the developed world is already highly urbanised – 82 per cent of the US population live in cities, for example. There are also seismic changes underway in developing countries – Africa and Asia are home to nearly 90 per cent of the world's non-urban population, and India has the largest rural population (857 million), followed by China (635 million). By 2050, India is projected to add 404 million urban dwellers, China 292 million and Nigeria 212 million. And this growth won't be evenly spread.

In 1990 there were just 10 'megacities', those places with populations of over 10 million. In 2020 the world had 33 megacities, and by 2030, 43 are projected, mostly in developing countries. Some forecasts have Lagos in Nigeria as the world's largest city by 2100, a 100 million-person megalopolis stretching hundreds of kilometres. Optimism morphs into an almost evangelical frenzy as ever more staggering and incomprehensible numbers are rolled out.

Part of the new story of the city includes an explanation of this turnaround in the fortunes of the city, one that emphasises a particular free market, entrepreneurial attitude. Cities are now magnets for those hoping to improve their lives and those willing to better themselves through hard work and energy. Successful cities are driven by migration linked to economic growth. As Edward Glaeser puts it in his book *Triumph of the City*:

> There is a near perfect correlation between urbanisation and prosperity across nations. On average, as the share of a country's population that is urban rises by 10 per cent, the country's per capita output increases by 30 per cent. Per capita incomes are almost four times higher in those countries where a majority of people live in cities than in those countries where a majority of people live in rural areas.[12]

Cities contribute between 70 and 80 per cent of global gross domestic product (GDP). Cities bring people and ideas together, and this proximity saves time and reduces costs, making cities more innovative, vibrant, productive and wealthy. This celebration of the economic success of cities inevitably leads to views on what the flourishing, vibrant city should do to sustain this growth. Such ideas almost always involve proposals to lift what are portrayed as breaks on growth and freedom, specifically the 'heavy hand' of regulation. The problems of cities – traffic congestion, air pollution, unaffordable housing and overstretched public services – are portrayed as issues of success that can be fixed by more success. Cities are too complex to be planned and regulated, the story goes, and their evolution should be left to the invisible hand of the market. This optimistic story is peddled by a cadre of academics, journalists, think tanks and governments that see the city through a narrow lens, one that focuses on the advantages of globalisation and the so-called 'flat white' economy.

The urban reality

The 'city of the dreadful night' and the 'city of bright lights' provide very different stories, but both sold us a false impression of urban living. Despite the urban optimists' story that the 21st century is the century of the city, or that we are now an urban species, clearly all is not well. There is an inconvenient truth about the darker side of urban living that dims the 'city of bright lights' story. Poverty and inequality in cities haven't gone away but have been eclipsed, ignored and wished away as consequences of growth. As the population urbanises, so does poverty and inequality. My own city of Cambridge is the fastest growing city in the UK, averaging over 7 per cent growth per annum. It is also one of the UK's most unequal cities, with a difference in life expectancy of almost 10 years between the 'haves' and the 'have-nots'. And this inequality exists in a city of just over 100,000 people. In other cities the differences are even greater: Baltimore in the US has a difference in life expectancy of 20 years, and in parts of London, it is 16 years. In the European Union (EU) an average of 10 per cent of urban residents experience severe deprivation, a proportion that rises to 26 per cent in Bulgaria and 22 per cent in Romania. Despite being home to over half the world's population, cities are also home to some of our greatest challenges, from inequality and poverty to pollution and crime.

The celebration of the city also overlooks the fact that even in the superstar cities success is confined to a small minority. One particular cause of concern in alpha cities such as New York, London and San Francisco is gentrification, or the replacement of long-established communities by wealthier residents and businesses. When Google announced it wished to establish a new campus in a former electricity sub-station building in Berlin, it led to huge local protests and resistance. A website was created and signs sprang up in the Tech Giant's familiar typeface with a clear message: 'Fuck off Google'.[13] The concerns were around the impact of the company and its highly paid workers on the existing community, a part of the city that was already sensing the impact of rent rises and the slow displacement of residents by those who could afford to pay more. Shops and cafes were also feeling the effects as their traditional customers moved on and high-end cafes and bars sprang up, catering for the influx of new, wealthier residents. This kind of colonisation of a community isn't an accident or some natural outcome of the market. Berlin, along with many other cities around the world, has been keen to promote the digital economy, wishing to attract the kind of global companies and creative economy that its residents were now actively resisting.

Despite concerns, there are many places where gentrification isn't the most pressing issue. For every San Francisco, Berlin or New York there is a Baltimore, Sunderland or Leipzig, scrambling for investment and growth and facing severe social and economic problems. These are our cities on the edge. And it's not just in the developed world where the notion of the successful city rings hollow for many. Over 1 billion of the world's population live in urban poverty, around 1 in 3 of all urban dwellers. That figure rose to 1.5 billion by 2020 and is set to rise to 2 billion by 2030. Every day 100,000 people move into urban slums, about one every second. Many cities are struggling to cope with such change, particularly with regards to infrastructure such as water, power and housing. For these millions of new urban dwellers the 'city of bright lights' holds little prospect of a better life. The urban optimists have been found out, exposed as being too narrowly focused and partial in their view of the world, peddling a neoliberal, market-led agenda, a view that is at odds with the realities of millions of city dwellers.

A much-discussed consequence of the global pandemic of 2020 has been whether cities have lost their allure and functionality. The highest death rates from COVID-19 have been in cities. Those who could afford to and were able to leave did so. Demand for locations and properties outside cities soared as commentators speculated if the era of the city centre office was over with many now working from home.

Whilst pessimists and optimists have never been the only stories in town, they are important because they drive public attitudes and government policy – theirs are the stories that are more compelling, more convincing and more popular than the alternatives. What connected both dominant stories of the city was a common attitude towards the poor and disadvantaged. The 'city of the dreadful night' abandons the city as well as those who couldn't leave. The 'city of bright lights' hawks a different approach, one that celebrates success, growth and deregulation, and in doing so paints a partial and misleading view. Both stories relinquish responsibility for the whole city, particularly those at the bottom. The result is that our cities have been and remain deeply divided, riven by social and economic inequality. Urban policy has been captured and influenced by a succession of stories that privilege the few and ignore the plight of the many. We have recently seen the democratic consequences of this approach with the rise of populist politics, witnessed in the referendum that led to the UK voting to leave the EU, the election of Donald Trump in the US and the election of far-right politicians across Europe.

In science, theories tend to endure until a better one comes along, one that makes more sense of the evidence. And so it is with the stories of the city. There is a new story of the city emerging. This story is one of digital technology and how the city of the future can succeed and thrive by becoming 'smart'. Like its predecessors, a range of powerful interests that sees an opportunity to sell goods and services is driving the 'smart city' story. Like its predecessors, government and politicians are shaping policy in line with the 'smart city' story and facilitating the rollout of digital technology in the city, promising a positive future. But there are important differences in the current story of the city. Unlike its predecessors, the 'smart city' story is not just an attempt to 'frame' the city and urban living. Instead, it is an attempt to fundamentally change the very nature of the city and society, from its economy to its politics, and by doing so it is creating uncertainty, social polarisation and disruption. The impacts are all around for us to see, from the loss of affordable housing through Airbnb to the closure of shops and offices as retailing moves online, facilitated by out-of-town giant Amazon 'fulfilment centres'.

Less obvious but of equal import are the impacts on how we manage our cities and think about the future. We're being sold the idea that digital technology – the smart city – can solve the challenges that we face, from traffic congestion to crime. In some areas this is absolutely the case. The use of real-time data can help manage traffic controls at certain times of the day to avoid pollution and congestion. Visualisation of designs can help explore how development proposals will impact on different communities, whilst the creation of digital twins of cities can model the effects of climate change. But for all of the upsides there are less than positive consequences too. The loss of local news coverage as Google, Facebook and Twitter undermine the revenue streams of traditional media sources means there is less accountability and information locally. Handing over decisions on how to manage traffic in our cities to keep it flowing avoids the more fundamental question of whether we should be investing more in public transport. Encouraging the gig economy benefits consumers whilst up to a third of jobs in some cities will disappear through AI (artificial intelligence) and machine learning. The story of the 'smart city' is a selective one.

The city survived previous stories, but this time it's different. Not only does digital technology and the 'smart city' story threaten the future of our cities, but in doing so, it also threatens the future of the planet and humankind. From climate change to the pollution of our oceans, from soil erosion to decreasing biodiversity, cities can bring people together to figure out how we can co-exist without destroying the planet. Cities can be incubators of democracy and tolerance, places where diversity and proximity require us to work together, putting aside disagreements and focusing on our common interests.

Time for reflection

There is a momentum and eagerness towards a smart future for our cities. An alliance of interests, from Big Tech to government, is pushing and facilitating digital solutions that promise better and cheaper public services whilst allowing us to approach urban living much as we do online shopping – pointing and clicking, behaving like consumers in a marketplace of choice. A smart future promises that we don't need to engage with messy and time-consuming processes such as voting or actually talking with and listening to the views of others. What's not to like?

The problem with this digital future is that it ignores the simple fact that successful cities don't just 'happen': they are managed and planned for all of their inhabitants, not just the powerful and wealthy. Successful cities are inclusive, balancing long-term investment and management with room for innovation and change. The digital revolution is atomising our cities, hollowing out their economic base, fragmenting their politics, focusing our attention on certain, technology-related issues, and ignoring those that do not easily fit the digital framework. But the other problem with this view is that digital technology doesn't just present a challenge to cities; it potentially represents an existential threat to them. And because cities are vital to how we tackle the pressing issues that face us as a species, the digital threat isn't just to cities but also to the future of the planet.

Why does any of this matter? Digital technology is disruptive, but so was steam and water in the 19th century and steel and the internal combustion engine in the 20th. Cities have always come with poverty and wealth inequality accompanied by precarious work. If cities are being undermined by digital technology, maybe this isn't all bad? After all, cities didn't exist for 97 per cent of human existence, so perhaps we don't actually need them to survive as a species.

Yet the future of our cities is important – not just to their inhabitants, but to humankind too. Climate change is the pressing issue facing the world, and cities are the key to addressing it. Cities emit 75 per cent of all carbon dioxide in the energy they use, whilst large metropolitan urban areas like London import 80 per cent of their food, from all corners of the planet. Cities are also feeling the brunt of climate change. In Europe alone, 70 per cent of cities are vulnerable to rising sea levels in the next 100 years. But cities are also our best hope of tackling climate change, shifting behaviours in consumption and production.

Grey is the new green. If we lose the city, then we are losing our best shot at saving the planet. At a time when some national governments are turning their backs on the global need to address the climate emergency, many cities are stepping up their commitments and their efforts. High voter turnout in cities and support for progressive policies including actions to help tackle climate change highlight that city residents feel that cities are arenas in which people work towards common goals. None of this should be a surprise. Cities require us to think communally, to face up to the collective nature of communal living rather than turn our backs on it, forcing us to face common challenges. Confronting our collective problems and creating an inclusive city is critical, because the unequal city has no long-term future. Richard Florida quotes New York Mayor Bill de Blasio: 'History has taught us that no economy – and no city – can thrive in the long term under such circumstances.'[14] Could our cities adapt and absorb these challenges as they have in the past? This time it's different. What cities are experiencing at the moment is an alignment of digital technology-driven challenges, linked to the rise of cloud computing and AI, that provide new and potentially existential risks, particularly for those places and people that are not well positioned to adapt.

Taking back control: a new story of the city

So how do we find another way, a path that avoids increasing segregation within cities and between them, one that uses the many benefits of digital technology to actually support cities and society? A new story for the city requires a vision that puts the needs of people at the centre. This story isn't one that can be taken 'off the shelf', like the smart city, but must be owned and developed by all of the city. For many places, however, successful and failing cities alike, it will involve an urban renaissance, a commitment to the city not simply as a place where we live and work, but also as a means to make everyone's future better. And the first step towards an urban renaissance is to acknowledge that we have a problem and to accept that not everything digital and smart is beneficial. This requires us to look beyond the immediate benefits of digital technology and our uber-connected world and to see the necessity to match the actual and potential benefits of smart with the needs of the city and all of its people. The second step is to level the playing field and make it a fair fight. Aligned with the rush to smart is an alliance of powerful interests, some of which are the most valuable companies on the planet. These interests won't step back without a fight. In some cases there will also need to be a rebalance to allow alternatives to emerge, such as the much-discussed 'Amazon tax' that would help shift the unfair competitive advantage of online and out-of-town retailing.[15]

Once we have the will to take back control, there are a number of steps we need to take. The first is to revisit the focus of regulation and city planning. The physical spaces and buildings in our cities were where things happened. Controlling them controlled and shaped activity and growth. Now things happen in a virtual world, physically disconnected from the places in which we live. There is no physical footprint, only physical consequences. The levers of control haven't caught up with technology. The second is to rethink the processes of city planning and management. The linear, ponderous approach to managing change has been disrupted and overtaken not only by the speed of change in the digital world but also by its networked, non-linear approach. Planning our cities needs an approach that works with digital technology, using live data and flexible, fleet-of-foot mechanisms. Finally, we need to rethink the nature of space itself. The traditional, territorial, physically bounded focus of cause and effect in cities is redundant when London has more in common with New York and Singapore than other cities in the UK, and looks to global labour markets and finance to support its growth. Likewise, controlling digitally led change requires a focus on the individual and the choices we all make as users. Cities need to look to both the individual and the global as the future spaces of influence.

This isn't an argument for control and dirigiste intervention: cities need a complex mix of planned and unplanned, order and chaos in order to successfully adapt. They need long-term thinking and the room to evolve, to experiment and to fail. They also need space for the serendipitous and the unforeseen, the risky and the innovative. The 19th-century city wasn't just the 'city of the dreadful night'; it was also the 'city of rapid technological change'. The 'city of bright lights' also thrived on managed chaos and complexity, melding the public and the private, managing change and allowing for the new. This book isn't an argument against Big Tech and digital technology in our cities; there have obviously been huge benefits to individuals and society from digital technology, not least during the global pandemic in 2020. Instead, this book is about making sure that the story of the city works for everyone, a story that saves the city for the sake of the planet, and one that uses the best minds of our generation to think about a better future, rather than finding new ways to keep us looking at our screens.

How can we plan and look to the future? This is the digital age and we can all tell our own stories about the 'smart city', using the very technology that threatens to undermine the city to save it. The digital age is well suited for this: it's non-linear, allowing us to jump back and forth and access huge amounts of information; it's deeply participatory and interactive, opening up communication between individuals and a mass audience, bypassing the traditional gatekeepers of the media; and it can include all media – written, oral, visual and audio. This book is one of those alternative stories, an attempt to find meaning and to communicate it. It's another story.

2

The 'smart city' story

In many respects the smart city is already with us: phones, laptops, watches, cars, remote sensors and other devices interact, generating, analysing and communicating data, allowing cities to monitor, control and make decisions in real time. From managing traffic signals and road charging in order to reduce congestion and pollution to monitoring and predicting resource usage, allowing more efficient use of energy, the smart city is already shaping our lives. At a personal level we are encouraged to use our phones to engage with government and other service providers. So-called 311 apps[1] in the US allow residents to let city governments know about a wide range of issues through their smartphones, texting photos of broken street lights and potholes and receiving an instant response. Citizens have become the eyes and ears of their cities.

More widely, city authorities are using digital technology to enhance consultation, making data and information openly available, publishing proposals, inviting individuals and communities to engage, and even facilitating the co-design of services and infrastructure through Building Information Modelling (BIM) and City Information Modelling (CIM). Some have even gone as far as to create 'digital twins' that allow the modelling of different scenarios and possibilities including the possible impacts of climate change on a city and what actions would help mitigate the consequences.

So far, so worthy and sensible. Yet the 'smart city' story is nowhere near its conclusion. The German engineering giant Siemens confidently predicts that:

> Several decades from now cities will have countless autonomous, intelligently functioning IT systems that will have perfect knowledge of users' habits and everyday consumption, and provide optimum service.[2]

For IBM, which registered the phrase 'smarter cities' as a trademark in 2009, there are mysterious and powerful forces at work, forces that could be harnessed to help cities:

> The world is moving to cities, fast and for the long term. In a cognitive era, cities themselves are moving: evolving, ever-changing, not fixed on a marked destination. We are at an important point in that evolution, as new forces emerge and combine to create new ways for cities to work.[3]

Whilst the smart city has attracted a wide and eager audience, influencing our cities from Bristol to Barcelona, we are only at the first stages of what is envisaged. There are early signs of what is to come: in Lyon there are autonomous buses, Leeds is trialling sensors to detect when roads need repairing, and London is using digital assistants to help residents find information. These changes have gone beyond supplementing and supporting public services to begin to replace people with digital technology and solutions. And this substitution is attractive for those involved.

For a public sector facing cuts and deficits, the prospect of providing services at lower costs is compelling. For the private sector there is an equally powerful motivation. IBM's stock price rose by 50 per cent within 12 months of the launch of its Smarter Planet initiative in 2012.[4] Other tech companies have followed IBM's lead, persuading some governments to build new, exemplar, smart cities such as Masdar City in the United Arab Emirates (UAE), Songdo in South Korea or PlanIT Valley in Portugal. These cities are held up as places where living is 'optimised' through the embedding of digital technology, minimising the use of natural resources and maximising personal connectivity. During the global pandemic of 2020 elements of the smart city and digital technology received a significant boost as home working and schooling along with online ordering and home deliveries of food and goods became the norm. For some, digital will help cities adapt to the new, post-COVID-19 realities of more remote working, fewer shops, more open space and the need to allocate space and visits to museums, bars, cafes, and so on through online booking. These shifts are being rolled into the smart city narrative as a new chapter – digital can keep you safe!

There is no one story of the 'smart city'. Instead, there are many tales that weave and suture various elements, shifting emphasis and taking advantage of deliberate ambiguity to adapt to circumstances and opportunities in different places. Take IBM's analysis of cities in the digital age, a classic example of saying everything and nothing at the same time, quoted on the previous page.[5]

Despite the differences in the range of stories and the take-up in different places there are common themes in the 'smart city' story. The basis for most stories is that cities are facing unprecedented and existential threats, from rising populations to traffic congestion, an ageing infrastructure to shrinking tax revenues. Traditional solutions won't do, and new approaches are needed. Unsurprisingly, the ways forward are centred around the kind of goods and services that Big Tech can provide, but the benefits of smart solutions are always just over the horizon, in the near future: there is a profusion of 'can' and 'will' in 'smart city' stories. At the same time there is more confidence that the city is knowable, predictable and measurable, that there is an opportunity for a seamless connection of different kinds of data, allowing the city to be 'optimised'. Such positive-sounding ambiguity allows a wide audience composed of different groups to read into these stories what they wish: city councils read cheaper and better services, businesses read opportunities to reduce energy costs, residents read more effective social programmes and public safety.

Smart cities are not the only stories in town. They are part of a constant babble of narratives around contemporary cities that seek to capture the future, usually in the interests of certain groups over others – sustainable cities, resilient cities, liveable cities and smart cities, among others, are all being peddled as stories by different interests and groups. City stories are important because they determine how we frame issues like congestion and homelessness, highlighting possible solutions and what resources and research should be focused on. The point about 'smart city' stories is that their solutions are singular – there is only one way forward, and that is around digital technology. Yet it's a story where nobody knows the ending, not least those championing it. All we know is that there is and will continue to be disruption, and disruption is a good thing, according to those in Silicon Valley, an industry whose motto is 'move fast and break things'.[6] This isn't how we should plan and manage our cities – they are far too important to the future of humankind to be left to the whims of Big Tech. There is another story of the city that is being overwritten by smart. This is the story of wicked and sometimes intractable problems. What does the 'smart city' story have to say about homelessness and housing affordability? What solutions does Big Tech suggest for dealing with the ageing population, childhood obesity, or the impacts on our health and social services?

The 'smart city' story displaces and distracts from these issues. The real challenges of our cities that smart should be focusing on are covered in Chapter 6. In this chapter I focus on two other points. First, that the 'smart city' story is evolving and by no means fixed – we can write the ending ourselves, particularly if we recognise where some would prefer it to end and decide that this is not the direction we want our cities to move in. Second, that smart is psychologically comforting and politically compelling: it glosses over the difficult-to-address issues with vague and near-future promises. It persuades us that we can do something to address difficult and complex issues at little to no cost – we can carry on as before and the future will take care of the difficult decisions for us. What's not to like?

The 'smart city' story

Like its predecessors – the 'city of the dreadful night' and the 'city of bright lights' – the 'smart city' story has a strong lineage in fiction. Around the time D.H. Lawrence was berating the city, an equally well-known contemporary, E.M. Forster, was imagining a future, smart city, one where the worship of technology would lead to the collapse of society. Better known for his explorations of class, hypocrisy and love in Edwardian England, Forster also penned a prescient short story in 1909 called 'The Machine Stops'. Set in a hyper-connected future, where all human needs are provided for by 'The Machine', Forster depicts a world where people are forced to live underground because of some catastrophic but unspecified past event. In this subterranean existence people live alone, shunning personal contact and communicating via electronic devices. Anything that is needed is provided via these tools. When people need to move they summon an autonomous vehicle.

Those who question The Machine and the religion of Technopoly – Machine worship – are banished and forced to live above ground. One of the two characters in the story, Kuno, begins to doubt the omnipotence of The Machine and visits the surface, a trip that exposes the myth that The Machine is necessary for human existence. Above-ground society exists without The Machine, and the orthodoxy that there is no alternative to underground living is exposed. As more people question the necessity, The Machine itself begins to collapse, accompanied by a realisation that humanity and nature have been sacrificed to technology.

The current 'smart city' narrative seems to have ignored the warnings and instead used Forster's portrayal as a playbook, confidently projecting an upbeat view of the role of technology in making our lives better. As one leading advocate of smart cities puts it:

> Today's smart city is an engineer's or computer scientist's dream come true. Every piece of information is instantly revealed, and the urban machine can be controlled and optimised.[7]

This optimism has been a common theme of the 'smart city' story, even in the embryonic early years. The term 'smart city' emerged in the mid-1990s at a time of huge excitement around the potential and impact of digital technology, the

World Wide Web and the 'information superhighway', as it was termed back then. Tom Baldwin recounts the story of the 1996 US presidential campaign when a jeans-clad Bill Clinton helped install the cables to connect a local high school to the internet, announcing to the assembled journalists 'let the future begin'. In the UK at the same time, Tony Blair was preparing for the forthcoming general election, portraying himself as a moderniser, and rebranding Labour as 'New Labour'. The internet and its stardust were liberally sprinkled across Blair's speeches to help depict a bright future linked to voting for the youthful leader. Cities around the world sought to cash in on this early enthusiasm, aligning themselves with the excitement of the new and the image of a positive sounding, though vague, future state, where government services would be more accessible and open. Much of this signposting was overkill, a rush to self-brand as 'smart' so as not to be left behind (who would want to be a 'dumb' city?).

In reality, the first act of the 'smart city' story largely involved the introduction of online information and limited online services. Yet around the same time a small number of new, smart cities were announced, one near Adelaide in Australia and Cyberjaya and Putrajaya in Malaysia. The vision for these new cities was more ambitious, going beyond the provision of e-services to thinking about how the digital city should be shaped and run. Despite the ambitious branding, in part driven by the need to distinguish and market these new places, little in the actual developments has actually emerged to justify the label.

This first act in the 'smart city' story set the scene for what was to come. External branding and the emergence of a 'smart city' story really took off when the opportunities for business to sell products and services became clear from around 2008 onwards, aligning business interests with the rollout of digital technology in cities, a move that was led by IBM. Established in 1911 as the snappily named 'Computing-Tabulating-Recording Company', it changed its name in 1924 to International Business Machines (IBM). The company's heyday of the 1960s and 1970s, when it supported NASA in the moon landings, was far behind it by the 1990s and 2000s, when the company was making annual losses running into billions of dollars.

In November 2008 IBM launched its Smarter Planet campaign after analysis highlighted the potentially large market in urban technology. According to then CEO Samuel Palmisano, cities needed to become smarter in order to achieve wider objectives of sustainability and economic growth, pitching digital technology as a means to deliver challenges that were top of the political and popular agenda. IBM followed this by registering the term 'Smarter Cities' as a trademark in 2011. Other large tech and engineering companies followed suit, with the likes of Siemens and Cisco also developing urban-focused products and services accompanied by similar narratives and stories linking the future success of cities to digital technology. The importance of this new market is clear to companies such as IBM, as its Smarter Cities products and services represent around a quarter of its income globally.

In order to further embed and encourage as well as develop the smart city as a marketplace, a large number of indices sprang up around the world ranking cities on the basis of buy-in to the idea. Huawei sponsors the UK Smart Cities Index, an annual ranking of how cities are using digital technology to address urban problems. The ranking is stratified into 'leaders', 'contenders', 'challengers' and 'followers', the implicit and unquestioned assumption being that all cities should aspire to be 'leaders' and that there is shame in being classified as a 'follower'. Indices and reports on smart city progress also include advice and information on what is needed to move up the rankings, encouraging cities to compete to be 'the smartest' and achieve the promised impacts of investing in digital technology. What these indices do not do is measure impacts and outputs: to what extent has 'smart city' status and investment actually improved people's lives or met some of its claims? Instead, recognition is given for initiatives regardless of what they achieve and regardless of whether digital is the most appropriate means to achieve policy objectives.

In the UK, cities such as Bristol and London have been keen to draw attention to their digital credentials. Bristol promotes itself with the tagline 'Bristol is Open', emphasising the attractiveness to business that underpins many smart city initiatives. Yet the focus on digital has also been broadened to include others in the city. In language echoing the vague, future promises of the 'smart city' narratives of Big Tech, the City of Bristol claims that:

> It is important that smart city strategies don't lose sight of the local issues and work collaboratively to break down silos. This will lead to smarter, more effective ways to provide city wide services, make better use of the funding and allow cities to support all citizens – from those living on or near the poverty line to those who are more fortunate.[8]

These city-led attempts to become 'smart' have proved to be less effective on the ground than the hype that accompanies them. Many smart cities justify their approach and investment by identifying a range of common issues that require non-traditional solutions, typically the need to accommodate growing populations and tackle climate change, the necessity to use resources such as water and energy more efficiently, and the requirement to reduce traffic congestion and better integrate public transport. Yet there is little specific or concrete information on how digital technology will actually help address these pressing issues. It will happen somehow at some point in the future, if we believe it will. The smart city is deferring assessments of outcomes and outputs, preferring instead to link investment in digital to some vague, better future.

Another characteristic of the smart city push is the promise of pain-free shifts to achieve such goals. In Vienna, the driver for its smart city initiative is sustainable development. As a species we are living beyond our means, using up the earth's resources at an unsustainable level, changing the earth's climate. Cities are both the cause and the victim of this:

> Cities, like Vienna, are particularly affected by this development. People live in close proximity. Residential, work and leisure uses share close quarters. Energy consumption and the emission of damaging greenhouse gases like carbon dioxide are concentrated in cities. Urban spaces suffer the greater

consequences of global warming and resource scarcity
that will seriously affect people's future life.[9]

The answer is to use digital technology to make resource use
more efficient. The Smart City Wien Framework Strategy[10] sets
out how the city will maintain living standards whilst reducing
resource use. Vienna, like other cities around the world, is
wanting to have its cake and eat it, using digital technology
to provide pain-free solutions to bypass difficult and contested
choices around changing lifestyles: we can save the planet by
being more digital, you won't feel a thing and it will save you
money, the smart city enthusiasts are saying. Smart is presented
as the panacea for our addiction to carbon-intensive lifestyles
and resource consumption, a way of allowing us to carry on
and avoid the cliff edge of climate catastrophe. This use of
smart and digital technology to defer and displace difficult issues
and decisions is not the only way in which it is being used
in cities. There is a strong drive in some places to distinguish
and differentiate new developments through their connectivity,
places like Songdo in South Korea.

Songdo International Business District (to give it its full name)
is a new, 600-hectare development 30 kilometres south of Seoul.
The city began life in the mid-2000s, funded and designed by
US developer Gale International with part ownership from two
other real estate investment companies. The design of Songdo
had two main components. First, it sought to assemble elements
of other iconic cities from around the globe, including Venetian
canals, New York's Central Park and Sydney's waterfront.
Second, Songdo was presented as being not just *a* smart city
but also *the world's leading* smart city, designed as a place where
digital technology would connect and underpin all the needs of
its residents. In order to underline this distinction, Songdo was
marketed as the 'ubiquitous city', emphasising the immersion
of buildings, services and residents in a digital world of sensors
reporting in real time on everything from public transport
availability to energy use. In Songdo services are prefixed with a
'U': 'U-health', 'U-traffic', 'U-governance', etc. The 'U' stands
for ubiquitous.

With a pick and mix selection of the world's iconic landmarks and ubiquitous digital connectivity, the backers of Songdo thought they couldn't fail to succeed. But the city has not taken off, failing to attract people and businesses, and much of the technology is unused. One commentator has even remarked on its Chernobyl-like emptiness.[11] The reason seems to be that it just isn't an attractive place to live, regardless of the digital connectivity. The assumption that digital connectivity is the 'killer app' that will drive real estate sales whilst giving regions and nations an economic boost was a common one and not confined to Korea – other countries around the world, from Portugal to the UAE, followed a similar path. It was an assumption that blinded developers, architects and planners to the importance of good place-making in the success of cities. Smart became an aspirational 'must have' for cities around the globe, yet this second chapter in the story of smart was not all real estate-led. Some cities took a different approach to smart, places like Taipei that used digital technology to help manage traffic congestion with flexible road charging and improved public transport. Or places like Singapore that developed health services and diagnostics online, or Rio that used real-time data from a network of CCTV cameras to monitor for crime along with environmental threats such as flash flooding. For these places, smart helped address specific issues rather than being the automatic solution to all the challenges cities face.

These first two chapters of the 'smart city' story were merely preludes to the massive onslaught that digital technology has wrought on cities since the early 2010s. There are two distinct developments in this era of smart, however. The first is that the centre of gravity in digital investment and market opportunity shifted from the public to the individual and corporate. Cities and governments have continued to promote the smart city and the benefits of digital technology, but this has become almost an irrelevant backdrop to the bottom-up spread of smartphones, the creation and sharing of massive amounts of personal data, the growth of online retailing and services, and the availability of cloud computing that helps facilitate these developments.[12] The ubiquitous digital city is here, but its mobile ubiquity is focused on the personal and not the public, and driven by corporations, not city councils.

This leads to the second major difference in this era of the 'smart city' story. Previously, digital technology was supposed to support growth and plans for change, making cities better places. The corporate-personal smart city is less controlled and controllable. There are now multiple players driving the rollout of digital technology, seeking to disrupt and replace established business models in experimental ways that lack integration and direction. Despite the advantages and upsides to much of this technological change at the personal level, this chapter of the smart city is actually making the problems of our cities such as housing affordability and insecure employment worse, as I argue later, in Chapter 3.

Having paved the way and helped persuade us that this is how we would make things better, through quicker, cheaper and more effective services, our cities have lost control of smart. The impact of smart city initiatives and digital technology may be mixed, but there is one effect that has been critical: the 'smart city' story has created an atmosphere and acceptance that the digital city equates to the 'good city', and that smarter cities are successful cities. This positive image has opened the door for the flood that has followed, creating a conducive atmosphere to technological-led solutions and allowing the likes of Google, Amazon, Uber, Airbnb, and so on to piggyback on the digital zeitgeist as well as the physical infrastructure provided by government. This is the era of mobile ubiquity, an age when the limitations of wired connection and physical spaces have given way to ever-present, wireless connectivity.

One consequence of this ubiquity is some devaluing of the moniker of smart city – if smart cities are now everywhere, then what are the advantages in promoting and distinguishing a place as 'smart'? This isn't a point that has been lost on some, and the term 'smart city' has been supplemented and even supplanted by other labels such as 'intelligent city', a term that maintains the positivity and vague promise of a better future. There is also the possibility that we are now entering what some term the 'post-smart city' era[13] as cities begin to look for new themes and mobilising devices to distinguish themselves and attract investment and business, be it the resilient city, sustainable city or whatever. This doesn't mean that smart will go away, but that cities are projecting a range of images and stories to different audiences and interests.

Yet the implicit suggestion of smart city branding is that it is the cities themselves that are in the driving seat, investing and developing in digital technology. This might have been the case, but cities have now lost control of the story. From being the protagonists, cities are now simply the backdrop to the story. So before moving on to speculate about the next chapter in the 'smart city' story, we should pause to reflect on why cities are no longer the authors of their own destiny.

What's driving the corporate-individual smart city?

The reason why we have seen the shift from public, city-led smart to the corporate-individual digital city is simple: it's people. Cities are where the majority of us live. They are the planet's largest physical marketplaces, concentrations of people who need goods and services. Personal digital technology mainly, but not exclusively, in the form of smartphones provides new, more efficient and more effective ways of gathering data on us – what we want, when we want it and where – and then using this data to persuade us to buy more stuff. The public smart city may project a rosy image of autonomous vehicles, a vision of making cities run more efficiently and more sustainably, reducing crime and improving health, but smart cities are now actually about collecting data to better entice us to hand over money, be it Google or Facebook targeting us with adverts, Amazon selling us anything it can, or Uber and Airbnb moving us around or providing places to stay. There is a synergy between the two, however: more efficient public transport, flexible labour markets or other outcomes that help with information asymmetry help make cities more efficient and profitable marketplaces.

The stakes are incredibly high. Apple and Google became £1 trillion+ companies in mid-2018, with both worth around £2 trillion in 2020. Three of the richest people on the planet are Big Tech leaders, and five of the world's biggest companies are those involved in digital technology and data. There have been big companies before and, adjusted for inflation, some companies in the past were larger, but what marks out the current crop of Tech Giants is that they are so dominant in their specific sectors and employ far fewer people – their huge wealth is spread much more thinly.

Can't we have both? Isn't it possible for the public smart city to secure the advantages of digital technology alongside the rollout of the corporate-individual smart city? Surely these two symbiotic outcomes are not mutually exclusive? It's worth bearing in mind a couple of points when considering these questions. First, cities have lost the initiative and ceded control as the balance between public and corporate-individual has shifted. An upshot is that the public good has been redefined to supporting the development of the corporate-individual smart city and attracting investment and jobs. When Amazon decided to build a new headquarters it announced a competition inviting cities from across North America to bid and include the kind of incentives that might help persuade the company to go to one city over another. Cities offered huge tax breaks, incentives that would be paid for by residents who would also have to cope with increased house prices and rents when the company and its employees relocated there. Corporate-friendly policies such as tax breaks are overshadowing public policy and priorities as cities are involved in a race to the bottom of tax incentives and giveaways to attract investment. This isn't an equal partnership by any means.

Second, this conflation of the two streams of the smart city means that many issues and challenges that cities should be addressing are being overlooked or sidelined. Many, if not most, of the issues that cities face are intractable. Some would go as far to label them 'wicked problems'. Yet there is a gap between these issues and the solutions of digital technology. Take Bristol, widely held to be the UK's leading smart city and an icon of how government and Big Data are working hand in hand for a digital future. Bristol is Open is a joint venture between the city, the University of Bristol, Nokia and NEC, among others, with the aim of creating an environment for innovation and entrepreneurship, 'hacking the city', as they put it. So far upwards of 200 datasets covering everything from pollution and energy use to health and traffic have been made available online, much of it gathered in real time from 1,500 radio-linked lampposts, transmitted through hundreds of kilometres of new fibre optic cables and broadcast from public Wi-Fi spots. Bristol is Open sets out its worldview thus:

> The way cities work is changing. Using digital technologies, we are creating an open programmable city that gives citizens more ways to participate-in and contribute-to the way their city works.[14]

The ambitions are clear: 'We are going to drive innovation', says Professor Dimitra Simeonidou, project lead and chief technology officer at Bristol is Open. 'We're creating an environment where in a year or two, not five, the whole world will look at Bristol for the future of smart cities.'[15]

Yet Bristol tops another league table too, one that it is less proud of. Average opioid prescriptions per head in the city are by far the highest in the whole of southern England, around twice as high as the average elsewhere.[16] The incidence of opioid prescriptions reflects other socioeconomic indicators, particularly poverty. Bristol continues to be included within some of the most deprived areas in England: in 2015, 16 per cent of Bristol residents, or 69,000 people, were living in the top deprived areas in England. This figure includes 17,800 children and 10,500 older people.[17]

The problems that cities face are complex. Government and city authorities are facing the perfect storm of 'wicked problems' – limited resources and insubstantial levers alongside a distracted electorate and diminishing attention spans used to 'one-click' solutions. It's no surprise that governments – local and national – are focusing on 'easy wins' in line with public demand. In part, the smart city drive is happening because it appeals to leaders – they, too, can be seen to be doing 'something', maybe not what the city needs, but 'something' nevertheless. The 'smart city' story is one that we want to hear.

The smart city and digital technology-driven solutions have little to say about such complex social and economic issues. But is this a problem? Well, the smart city promises 'something' too, a series of solutions that tackle a narrow but less complex set of issues. Yet the 'smart city' narrative focuses attention on some issues and not others. Problems are defined by whether they fit the digital technology 'frame'. Opioid addiction isn't the only complex problem that cities face: housing affordability, obesity, an ageing population and economic disparities are all part of the problems of cities, successful and otherwise, but what has become increasingly clear is that the emerging corporate-individual smart city is making matters worse, not better, as I argue further on in this book.

This isn't to say that there are not advantages and benefits to us as individuals and as a society as a whole in the current rollout and trajectory of the smart city. Yet some have wasted no time in linking smart cities to the coronavirus pandemic, highlighting the ways in which digital technology has helped to curb the contagion and how it could play a major role in curbing future outbreaks.[18] According to some, the only thing stopping the smart city saving us from COVID-19 and other pandemics is our sensitivity to personal data issues around track and trace. If only we would be happy to share more personal data – with appropriate safeguards – then we could be safe in the city. Others are claiming that the empty streets, and reduced carbon consumption and pollution in our cities that have come as a result of the pandemic show us what life would be like in a truly smart city[19] – social distancing is aided by people using their smartphones and sharing data. Again, this could be the future, if only we invested fully in 'smart' and overcame the reluctance some communities have to immersing themselves in digital solutions.

There has also been a subtle shift in focus from the advocates of smart, as workplaces in city centres have been eschewed in favour of homes as workplaces in the suburbs and peripheral towns with talk of the need to invest more in greater digital bandwidth outside the city. How cities and digital technology respond to the COVID-19 crisis is yet to be seen, although it is likely to impact different places and communities variably. Existing inequalities within cities have already been widened by the pandemic, particularly in the impact of job losses on those who cannot simply work from home, whilst there have also been differential impacts based on race and age.[20]

So, what is the next chapter in the 'smart city' story?

The 'smart city' story is emerging and evolving, bringing with it upsides and downsides. Are there any indications as to where the story is heading? What's the next chapter likely to be? There are plenty of fervent and excited predictions from a range of sources that paint a bright and Panglossian digital future, although COVID-19 is certain to play a role in how digital rolls out in our cities. There is no doubt that the future of cities will be driven in large part by digital technology, particularly given the intention of Big Tech to build on the momentum towards smart.

If the Big Tech anarchists were under the political radar in the past, they are far less so now as the industry is becoming increasingly political and politicised, as I discuss in Chapter 4. The consequences of their disruptive ethos, from AI to the gig economy, housing affordability to taxation, healthcare to financial services, are now in the mainstream political debate. When and if the likes of Apple and Facebook launch their global digital currency it will be too late to put the genie back in the bottle – Big Tech now has the political and economic power of nation states.

More likely, in my view, is a corporate takeover of our cities, not only in terms of services, but also in terms of what the French philosopher Michel Foucault called 'bio-politics'.[21] Foucault advanced the idea that traditional approaches to controlling the individual and society, such as state-sanctioned force and incarceration that characterised society in the Middle Ages, have been replaced under liberalism by new forms of compliance and control. In modern societies our activities, what counts as knowledge and truth and the scope of what we expect from our lives, are internalised: we control and govern our own behaviour and actions. The norms that we internalise come from powerful interests and government. The focus of politics and what is considered acceptable behaviour in our cities is increasingly determined by the 'smart city' story. And as we saw in the last chapter, it is a story that has had the sharp edges removed and replaced by rounded corners, infantilising options and choices. Politics and choice haven't disappeared under digital technology; they've merely been shifted to new arenas and been led by new actors. Cities and governments are aligning the solutions of digital technology with the problems of cities, putting the answers before the questions. If this is the trajectory of the 'smart city' story, we face a simplified future, one where the difficult choices are not only made for us, but we don't even see the alternatives. The disruption and challenges that digital technology brings are simply the cost of the advantages of our connectivity. Yet there are some cities that are not buying into this stultifying and homogenising, omni-directional future. There are some that are waking up to the challenges that digital technology brings in its wake. There are alternatives to the 'smart city' narrative, if we look more closely.

3

What happens when 'smart' comes to town

In 1984 Steven Levy's *Hackers* was published,[1] the same year that Apple launched the Macintosh. In his acclaimed book Levy charted the rise of what he termed 'digital explorers', the band of early techies who went on to found and run some of the biggest companies on the planet. But back then, the notion of money and success took a back seat to a culture, an *esprit de corps* attitude founded on taking an aesthetic and personal pleasure from the beauty of computer code and electronics, of making something better, pushing back against centralised systems and products. This was 'hacking'. One thing was certain – hacking wasn't about the money. It was about the lone person in the bedroom improving code to make programs run quicker or more elegantly; it was about the camaraderie of a bunch of like-minded friends getting together to design and build cheap computers for the masses.

This hacker attitude is now Silicon Valley folklore – indeed, Facebook's address is 1 Hacker Way. Whatever the history, the hacker myth now serves a useful function for Big Tech in self-deception and public reassurance, in helping persuade us that some of the biggest companies on the planet aren't the threat that they currently appear to be. How can Facebook be helping bring down democracy when it's just a company that wants to bring people together? Amazon can't be intent on being the world's biggest retailer and provider of digital services – it just allows people to buy cheap stuff. The hacker myth gives Big Tech the benefit of the doubt. Apple's own hacking myth has been built around the two Steves, Jobs and Wozniak, designing and building the first Apple computer in 1976 in their garage, selling their VW campervan to help fund themselves and their dream. Urban legend has it that the Apple logo represents the bite taken by the founder of the modern computer, Alan Turing, who committed suicide by eating a poisoned apple when he was persecuted and prosecuted for being homosexual. The cynical might suggest that adopting this logo plays well with Apple's liberal, creative image.

Google's foundational story echoes many of these tropes with then students Larry Page and Sergey Brin trying to crack an interesting mathematical challenge, working in Page's front room. According to their backstory they begged and borrowed spare computer parts and took up to half of Stanford's network bandwidth to hack a better way to index and search for information on the web. Of course, this humble story ends with what would become the world's most valuable company. Airbnb's myth is around its founders Brian Chesky and Joe Gebbia who, back in the mid-2000s, couldn't afford the rent on their apartment in San Francisco. To raise extra money, they converted their loft and rented it out in 2007, developing a website with pictures of the space with three air mattresses, and included breakfast in the price of US$80 a night. Hacking the established system of hotels for cheap overnight stays was a success, and according to the myth it was their regular guests who encouraged them to roll the idea out to other cities. As Gebbia puts it, 'People told us what they wanted, so we set off to create it for them. Ultimately while solving our own problem, we were solving someone else's problem too.'[2]

Yet despite the hacker image of openness, beauty, intellectual curiosity and improving lives, we are now dominated to an extent never seen before by a small number of Tech Giants including Google, Facebook and Amazon, their subsidiaries such as Instagram and YouTube, and others such as Uber, Airbnb, Twitter and Spotify. These companies all operate as monopolies or close to monopolies in their fields of search engines, video streaming, online retailing, social networking, music streaming, and so on. But it wasn't meant to be this way. The internet and digital technology were supposed to set us free. Monopolies, in the 20th-century sense, were widely predicted to be a thing of the past, replaced by a diffusion of creativity and power underpinned by the so-called 'sharing economy'. According to the early promises, Big Tech should never have happened. We were told that the internet would herald an era of open competition that would benefit consumers and the economy. The hacker culture would disperse knowledge and information, provide choice and competition, and make the world a better place.

But rather than dispersal and competition we have concentration and monopoly. Many tech companies run at a loss, undercutting competitors or established players until there is no competition. In the first quarter of 2019 Uber lost more than US\$1 billion, despite having 93 million regularly active customers, a revenue of US\$3.16 billion and annualised gross bookings of US\$59 billion. In 2018, 5.2 billion people rode in an Uber, although each trip lost the company an average of 58 cents. Like other platform economy companies, Uber and its investors are gambling, losing billions of dollars to see off the competition, in this case Lyft, another ride share company. Instead of competition we have dominance and restricted options. Companies such as Google and Facebook have the resources to buy up their competitors, releasing them from the need to innovate, invest in R&D or, indeed, hack. Since 2001, Google and its parent company, Alphabet, have bought over 200 companies, including YouTube, Android and FitBit, according to research firm CB Insights.[3] These so-called 'kill the crib' strategies deny the development of alternative sources of innovation and competition.

Despite the dominance, market worth and profits, Big Tech still likes to portray itself in a folksy way, founded on its hacker culture. It is this 'on the side of the people' image that is also used to sell digital technology to our cities, providing a compelling narrative with familiar themes and images of challenging established power, releasing entrepreneurialism, providing freedom and choice, and supporting communities. The 'smart city' story is bound up with the hacker myth. In the views of smart city advocates, usually large, multinational companies or government, we can reprogram the city, create new code to make it work better, helping it become greener, more efficient and cheaper to run. Civic hackers will use data from the Internet of Things to make real-time changes and optimisation. In the words of two leading urban digital evangelists, we should 'hack the city!'.[4]

Game of homes: from the hacker myth to reality in our cities

During 2020 cities around the world experienced massive disruption including seismic economic impacts as shops and services closed owing to the impact of COVID-19. The UK's economy contracted by 2.2 per cent in the first three months of the pandemic, with the closure of bars, restaurants and shops hitting urban economies hard. Other leading economies suffered similar impacts. The long-term consequences on cities are difficult to predict, particularly with successive waves of infections and restrictions.

The pandemic has initiated some potentially far-reaching impacts on and changes for cities, including the need for space, as many companies reflect on the experience of home working and whether it makes sense to continue to rent or own expensive office space in cities. Public transport usage was also significantly hit as people no longer needed to travel and then, when they had to, decided it was safer to drive. On the other hand, companies such as Amazon and other online providers saw demand surge, accelerating the shifts away from bricks and mortar retail, mostly located in city centres. The ongoing uncertainty over the future of cities is distracting us from some of the impacts of digital technology. In fact, we've generally been grateful for the ways in which online has enabled some level of continuity as many were able to work and shop from home. Yet the underlying impacts of smart on the city have not disappeared. In some respects they have been accelerated as online retailing has expanded and the surge in staycations further fuelled property rental platforms.

Prior to the coronavirus pandemic many cities around the world were experiencing the 'Airbnb effect' as residents rented out space to feed the growing demand for short-stay visitors.[5] The situation reached crisis point when 10 cities asked the European Commission for help in tackling the growth of short-term home rental services, claiming that they were struggling to provide affordable homes. The reason? Many homes in these cities were being made available through Airbnb for visitors instead of being available for locals. In a joint statement, the 10 cities claimed that they and their housing stock had been subject to an 'explosive' shift from homes for locals to places for tourists to rent: 'Homes are needed for residents to live and work in our cities', they claimed, 'without them we will become more and more considered as a market for renting out to tourists.'[6] The Deputy Mayor of Paris in charge of housing, Ian Brossat, clearly set out the challenge that cities face: 'In the four central *arrondissements* of Paris, a quarter of all properties are now no longer homes, but purely short-term rentals for tourists.'[7]

The threat to these and other cities is not simply from the loss of homes to Airbnb, but also from the loss of control and the ability to do much, if anything, to counter the impacts of the digital economy. If left unaddressed there is a danger that cities will no longer be able to collectively and openly plan their futures:

> We think that cities are best placed to understand their residents' needs. They have always been allowed to organize local activities through urban planning or housing measures.[8]

The original hack of the home-sharing economy was to offer spare rooms, providing an income to homeowners and an alternative to hotels. These early, worthy desires have been eclipsed as Airbnb and other sharing platforms increasingly offer whole properties for rent, often throughout the year. Flats and houses that would have been rented to locals are now used for a succession of short-term visitors whilst investors have now begun to purchase properties to offer on Airbnb, effectively removing them from the local housing stock. In popular city destinations such as Amsterdam, Berlin and Edinburgh, the impacts on locals have been rising rents and worsening housing affordability, particularly for the young. The impact on housing affordability is not confined to the major cities, however. Airbnb's site lists more than 6 million rooms, flats and houses in over 80,000 locations across the globe. Every night in 2018 around 2 million people stayed in an Airbnb rented property, and by late 2020 the company's market worth was over US$100 billion.

Janet Sanz is a Barcelona councillor who heads the council's housing portfolio. For her the problem of worsening housing affordability is fundamental to the future of the city, where there are 16,000 properties available on Airbnb. 'Our attitude is zero tolerance', she said. 'We will do everything we can to guarantee the right to housing in the city. What these people have to understand is that Barcelona exists for its people. The priority is it's a place to live.'[9] And she has significant support. As one handwritten sign in Barcelona proclaims: *Barcelona no està en venda* (Barcelona is not for sale).

The reduction of properties in the rental market is having profound effects on individuals, communities and neighbourhoods. Take one case:

> It all started in early September. Our landlord informed us and the two other tenants that he was selling the building. Surely this wouldn't affect us much because our building wasn't near anything important and had full, long-term occupancy. We were wrong.… After some basic Google searches we discovered that our new landlord owned 17 buildings in town. All of those buildings were dedicated Airbnbs. We are the last to leave this building, as well as this block. There used to be multiple apartment buildings up and down the street, but all that's left is a Thai restaurant and an advertising agency. Every residential building is owned by the same man and each unit is rented out as an Airbnb. No one actually lives here any more.[10]

The advice from this victim? 'If you visit a new place, don't rent from "Superhosts". Nearly all of them are big time landlords who use Airbnb to destroy communities and drive up rent. Rent your spare room – that's fine. Don't buy property just to evict the current residents and convert to short-term rentals.'

Having disrupted the market and cities Airbnb is now joining forces with hotels chains and property developers, moves that will see new homes developed and exclusively offered for short-term stays rather than for rent and purchase in the local market. And Airbnb isn't the only digital economy giant to expand its services. Uber is moving into food delivery with Uber Eats, and growing its operations to include freight, moves that accelerated with the COVID-19 shift to online. When the likes of Uber and Airbnb emerged into the marketplace it was easier to believe the hype that the platform economy would disrupt and displace existing players, unleashing a latent entrepreneurial spirit, empowering individuals and benefiting the economy and consumers. The disruption of the economy and our cities is well underway, although not in ways that the hacker myth would like us to believe.

As the 10 EU cities that were calling for action to curb the impacts of Airbnb and other room-sharing economy services are finding the impacts severe, there is little in the current armoury of controls and levers to curb it. Platform economy businesses such as Airbnb, Uber, Task Rabbit and Deliveroo do not employ workers but act as an intermediary between customers and providers. Those who provide the service are not employed but classified as 'independent contractors', taking advantage of the flexibility that this arrangement offers. In 2019 the UK's Trades Union Congress (TUC) estimated that 1 in 10 of the workforce were now employed in the platform economy. That's around 4.7 million workers, a figure that doubled between 2016 and 2019. The companies behind the platform economy talk of individuals becoming entrepreneurs, working when they like, whilst critics point to the precarious nature of zero-hour contracts, the lack of social benefits from part-time work and the impacts on taxation.

The initial attraction of flexibility for workers is fast disappearing. Contractors are increasingly required to work longer hours for less money as intermediaries take a larger percentage of the fee for connecting the service provider with the consumer. As one Uber driver put it, 'I had to force myself to stop the car in the middle of nowhere sometimes, get fresh air, get Red Bull, just something'.[11] Those working as independent contractors are also struggling with the effects of isolation, hired by an app and lacking any social interaction: 'It's very, very lonely – it's just you inside your box, driving with London traffic, with all this stress. The long-term effect, honestly: it's like a bomb waiting to explode.'[12] According to the same driver, tiredness is behind many accidents involving Uber drivers, and there's little the company does to prevent drivers working long hours. Uber's investment in the development of autonomous vehicles, alongside Amazon's development of drone delivery, will ultimately do away with drivers entirely.

The big players in the platform economy are becoming the kind of Establishment that they initially set out to disrupt. During the coronavirus pandemic the number of delivery contractors mushroomed as individuals stayed home and met their needs through online ordering. There were calls for better protection for delivery workers who were putting their own health at risk in order to help keep people supplied with food and goods. Despite calls for better protection, many still received no sick pay because of their self-employed status.

The platform economy is not the only way in which our smart cities are undergoing radical transformation. A common sight over the past few years has been the growing number of empty shops and buildings across struggling and booming cities alike – 2018 saw the failure and closure of some retail mainstays and the announcement of hundreds of store closures by others. In all, 30,000 high street retail jobs were lost in 2018 in the UK, a number dwarfed by the loss of retail jobs due to COVID-19 when up to 10,000 per week were being lost. During 2020 those numbers rose significantly as many economies moved online during the pandemic. In the UK big high street names such as Marks & Spencer and John Lewis announced store closures. One reason for the loss due to digital is that business taxation is proportionately much higher for high street retailers whilst online retailers such as Amazon run their operations from giant out-of-town warehouses and pay much lower business property tax. Rents, land values and staff costs are also proportionately lower, allowing online retailers to undercut high street competition, forcing them to move online or to fold. The former CEO of Tesco, Dave Lewis, has pushed for an 'Amazon tax' of 2 per cent for all goods sold online in order to help level the playing field between online and traditional high street retailers.[13]

The influence of the digital economy on retailing is being charted by the Bespoke Investment Group that has been tracking an index of 54 retail stocks that they call the 'Death by Amazon' Index.[14] In 2017 the index fell more than 20 per cent on an equal weighted basis, losing US$70 billion in its value, whilst Amazon gained US$120 billion, according to Bespoke. Owing to the massive shift online in 2020 due to the pandemic, the gap has widened even further:

> Amazon is now up over 1700% since inception of our Death By Amazon indices, while our equally-weighted Death By Amazon index has lagged the S&P 1500 by 70 percentage points over that period.[15]

Like Airbnb, Amazon is not content with its current market domination and opened 10 shops in the UK in 2019, selling everything from food to consumer electronics. This shift into the high street, dubbed a 'clicks and mortar' expansion, follows its fashion store in London and mirrors the move of other online retailers as eBay opens a store in Wolverhampton and Amazon Go rolls out its grocery stores in the US and Canada. Amazon is also expanding into a wider range of markets, including television, the manufacture of consumer electronics, a music-sharing platform, labour brokerage, book publishing, small loans and healthcare. Expansions will further impact on cities as the company uses its massive data advantage harvested from its online dominance to know what you want and don't want, where you live, what you watch and what you listen to.

Digital technology is also beginning to disrupt other areas of the city economy. The OECD estimate that 9 per cent of urban jobs are at high risk of automation, and another 25 per cent will likely experience a major retooling because of automation. Yet this broad figure masks disparities between places and the impact on specific areas of the workforce.[16] Analysis by the Centre for Cities in the UK highlights that one in five jobs in cities is likely to be affected by a combination of continued, deepening globalisation and automation and technological change.[17] That's 3.6 million jobs in the UK alone. Some estimates put this figure much higher. Analysis by Oxford Economics on the increase in the automation of jobs paints a similarly bleak picture, despite the techno-optimists' view that technological change creates more jobs than it destroys.[18] Like the OECD, the research claims that the impacts will not be evenly spread. Whilst an additional robot displaces 1.6 jobs on average, in lower-income regions this figure is 2.2 jobs, and in more affluent areas, 1.3. As the report states:

> The negative effects of robotisation are dis-proportionately felt in the lower-income regions of the globe's major economies – on average, a new robot displaces nearly twice as many jobs in lower-income regions compared with higher-income regions of the same country. At a time of worldwide concern about growing levels of economic inequality and political polarisation, this finding has important social and political implications.[19]

Whatever the number, the impact will not be evenly spread, and cities outside the relatively affluent South East of England will be hit hardest. In some cities the number of jobs at risk is closer to 30 per cent, whilst in others it is nearer 15 per cent. The categories of jobs at risk also have an impact on cities. Just over half of all jobs under threat in cities are in five categories – sales assistants, administration, customer services, finance, and storage. These categories are not equally shared across cities, and it is those cities that have attracted lower-skilled jobs and are generally weaker-performing that are most at risk. The cities that will be least affected are those that are already the most successful.

Colonising, dividing and cleansing: how Big Tech is shaping our futures

Alongside the undoubted benefits, digital technology is creating deep divisions within and between our cities. Besides fuelling the platform economy, undermining large parts of the service economy and facilitating a reduction in the availability of homes through Airbnb, digital technology is also having other impacts in some cities. For example, the increasing numbers of highly paid tech workers in places like Silicon Valley is exacerbating the wealth differences by pricing locals out of homes. Abigail De Kosnik, Associate Professor at the University of California, Berkeley, claims that the protests that emerged in 2013 against the buses Google put on to ferry its workers from the San Francisco Bay Area to Silicon Valley reflect deeper concerns and opposition to the gentrification of the city by Big Tech generally. The influx into the city of tech workers employed by Apple, Google, Facebook and others has displaced residents already affected by economic disruption and precariousness, exacerbating the problem of affordable housing and creating wealthy enclaves, akin to gated communities. According to one resident:

> The buses roll up to San Francisco's bus stops in the morning and evening, but they are unmarked, or nearly so, and not for the public. Most of them are gleaming white, with dark-tinted windows, like limousines, and some days I think of them as the spaceships on which our alien overlords have landed to rule over us. Sometimes the Google Bus just seems like one face of Janus-headed capitalism, in that they contain the people too valuable even to use public transport or drive themselves.[20]

San Francisco was the beatnik city, a refuge for those who wanted to side-step the American Dream of accumulation and consumption, a safe haven of liberal, progressive politics. Now it's the city of unbridled capitalism, where family homes average US$2 million and monthly rents for one-bed apartments are US$4,000. Big Tech companies – Google, Apple, Uber, Airbnb, Slack, Lyft, Twitter, to name a few – and their workers have led to deepening social and economic divisions within the city. The San Francisco Bay Area has more billionaires than any other city on earth, and the number is growing. According to Julie Levak–Madding, this amounts to 'hyper gentrification', a process that is having profound effects on the social make-up of a city,[21] including the lowest percentage of children of any major US city and a declining African-American population, currently standing at 5.5 per cent, half the proportion from the middle of the last century. The former vibrant artist community is also fast disappearing as rents rise, pushing out critical public workers such as teachers, who are unable to afford the housing. The city is becoming homogeneous, devoid of shops that sell everyday goods. According to Rebecca Solnit, a long-time resident and commentator on the city, 'Our rich are richer. Our homeless are more desperate. Our hipsters are more pretentious.' The upshot is that 'San Francisco is now a cruel place and a divided one'.[22]

In other leading tech cities, rents, evictions and homelessness have similarly gone up as the wealthy tech-elites have moved in, dividing cities and creating resentment. One outcome has been widespread protests that have included smashing bus windows and slashing tyres. Elsewhere, police in Chandler, Arizona recorded over 20 incidents of residents attacking autonomous vehicles being tested by a subsidiary of Google. The motivation? Fears over job losses and road safety.

Gentrification isn't just about an influx of wealthier residents displacing existing residents. East Palo Alto, the city in northern California now synonymous with Silicon Valley, was a diverse, multi-ethnic place in the 1960s, home to Hispanics, blacks and others. The new influx of tech workers is introducing uniformity.[23]

It is fear of what happened in San Francisco that has driven grassroots community resistance to Google in Berlin. In the up and coming fashionable district of Kreuzberg, activists have organised themselves to oppose a Google Campus being set up in a former electricity sub-station. Concerns over *Gentrifizierung*, as it's known in Germany, are motivating some, although there are also concerns about the impacts of Big Tech. As the activist behind the website fuckoffgoogle.de, Sergey Schmidt, puts it: 'As much as I do believe it's critical for the future of Kreuzberg, for the neighbourhood, it's much broader than that. I care about Google not just as a terrible neighbour, but as a terrible entity to have in the world.'[24] In the face of organised and sustained opposition, Google has withdrawn the proposal for a campus.

There is little doubt that Kreuzberg may have won this particular skirmish, but with the support of local politicians it is only a matter of time before Google and others get the foothold they are looking for in Germany's capital.

As might be expected, digital technology is hitting cities in different ways. In some places like San Francisco, Berlin and London, it is widening divisions, driving up costs and pricing many out, leading to 'same places', devoid of diversity and difference. Other, struggling places are being further hollowed out through the loss of jobs and the impacts on communities when shops and facilities close and move online. What are cities and governments doing to curb the impacts? At the moment many can't make their minds up. There is a struggle between different levels (local, regional, national) and even different parts of the same government. This is a city schizophrenia with parts of government wanting to simultaneously regulate and mitigate the impacts whilst encouraging and facilitating Big Tech and the 'smart city' rollout.

The main driver of this dual-think is that cities around the globe are competing for digital jobs by relaxing regulation and incentivising companies to set up or relocate. In New York the decision by local and state politicians to provide up to US$2.8 billion in subsidy and tax breaks to Amazon in return for locating the company's next 'hub' there proved to be controversial, to say the least, particularly given the extent of homelessness in the city. Good Jobs First, a watchdog group that analyses the sweeteners paid to Big Tech companies, calculated that US$9.3 billion had been promised by state and local governments across the US to lure some of the richest and most profitable companies on the planet.[25] There are two main reasons for this largesse. The first is that bringing jobs, particularly tech jobs, to the city helps local and state politicians with re-election. The 'smart city' strategy provides a 'politically feasible trajectory' and a 'plausible political fix' for communities looking to reverse economic decline in the face of global competition and limited resources.[26] Yet these subsidies favour the larger companies over the small – one would look in vain to find similar support for a small, local firm wishing to expand. As one critical commentator put it:

> If you can bring a lot of jobs to a community, it looks really good…. So program administrators will offer subsidies to Amazon to bring a distribution center and 600 jobs to town, but not to a local stationer who might add two or three jobs in a storefront.[27]

The second reason is that Big Tech is sexy. The 'smart city' story not only sells the idea that the digital economy is the future, but that it also helps solve many of the challenges facing cities, more effectively and for less money. Yet the competition to attract tech jobs is distorting the economies of cities to favour one sector, and the larger firms within that sector. Cities are in danger of losing their economic resilience and overlooking the fact that it is digital technology that is helping disrupt and destroy jobs alongside creating new ones. The previous rounds of economic restructuring, from manufacturing to service, for example, took place over a longer period, although they have left their mark on some cities and regions, many of which have failed to recover. The digital challenge will add to these legacies.

Back to the future

In 1850 mill owner Titus Salt decided to abandon the overcrowded, polluted and insanitary conditions of Bradford in northern England and locate his factory on a greenfield site three miles away, on the banks of the River Aire. Alongside the new mill, Salt also built a self-contained new town called Saltaire, with homes, shops, churches, a library, a park, schools and a hospital. Salt's motives are far from clear but, according to his biographer, David James,[28] it was a mixture of social conscience, space to develop his factory, control over his workforce, the establishment of an industrial dynasty and a belief that he was doing God's work. What is less in doubt is that he abandoned Bradford, leaving it and its people, in their dire conditions, to their fate.

Fast forward to 2012, and Facebook founder Mark Zuckerberg announces that he intends to build Zee Town, an 80-hectare, US$200 billion development for his 6,600 employees and their families, close to their headquarters in Silicon Valley.

The initiative is part of Zuckerberg's desire to strengthen the corporate culture, develop greater loyalty and allegiance, and encourage his employees to focus on their work. Like its 19th-century forebears, Zee Town will be self-contained with schools, shops, hotels, and leisure and recreation facilities, and will be named after its founder. Paternalistic experiments in total living and a will for control over the lives of workers, Saltaire and Bournville, another factory town in England's Midlands built by the Cadbury family from 1879, had no pubs or bars whilst Port Sunlight, built by the Lever family in 1888, was underpinned by a requirement to attend church. The UK is not alone in these vanity projects: in the US there is Disney's town of Celebration, developed during the 1990s, and the privately owned and controlled Seaside in Florida built in the 1980s.

Apple has taken the other approach to corporate control. Apple Park in Cupertino is a 2.8 million square foot, US$5 billion circular building a mile in circumference and visible from space. The building, which opened in April 2017, houses 12,000 employees, in an already overcrowded, congested and expensive city of 60,000. As discussions between the city council and Apple began, there was reluctance on the part of the firm, with an annual turnover of close to US$300 billion, to make contributions to offset the impact of the development. Just 10 per cent of the workforce lives in Cupertino, and the site has 9,000 parking spaces, the vast majority in private cars. Local traffic congestion is one obvious consequence. An already over-heated local housing market has been further inflated, an increase in demand of around 284 per cent, according to one source.[29] Apple's answer? It paid US$5.85 million towards affordable housing in Cupertino. Traffic and affordable housing are not the only areas where Apple decided that it didn't want to help the community. Not wanting locals to have any access, the normal requirement of making public space available to the community was taken care of by Apply paying for a park to be built elsewhere.

Despite their seemingly different approaches, Apple and Facebook have a not dissimilar approach, with neither wanting to be part of the community in which their employees live and work. As Dan Winter put it:

Apple's new HQ is a retrograde, literally inward-looking building with contempt for the city where it lives and cities in general. People rightly credit Apple for defining the look and feel of the future; its computers and phones seem like science fiction. But by building a mega-headquarters straight out of the middle of the last century, Apple has exacerbated the already serious problems endemic to 21st-century suburbs like Cupertino – transportation, housing, and economics. Apple Park is an anachronism wrapped in glass, tucked into a neighborhood.[30]

Allison Arieff, Editorial Director for the San Francisco Bay Area Planning and Urban Research Association, puts the attitude of Apple towards the local community another way: 'They want to be innovative in everything, and they're not innovative in this thing…. If the intractable problems of the region are housing and congestion, they're giving the finger to all that.'[31] The local is not on the radar of international, global mega-companies like Apple and Facebook. But their impacts are very real for the cities and communities that they are turning their backs on, directly, in the case of Cupertino and Facebook's Menlo Park, and indirectly for the rest of us as we feel the consequences of the digital revolution. Big Tech is pulling away from the cities and the problems that it is creating, abandoning the public realm and shrugging off any commitment to being part of existing communities. What is as worrying in the move to build in ways that control work and home is the repudiation of a common future with the rest of society and ownership of the challenges that we face. Facebook may aim to bring the world together, but they see their own destiny in quite a different way. The concern is that we begin to see this attitude as normal and internalise it – Foucault's biopolitics, as discussed earlier. This attitude also reflects an ideological disposition that sees government as there to pick up the pieces, playing the role of nightwatchman, there in case of civil strife, to resolve disputes and provide basic public goods.

These impacts are not simply confined to one area or region: the impacts are spreading. In late 2018 Twitter signed a lease on Uptown Station, a 365,000 square foot office building in Oakland that will be the base for 2,000 of its employees. The city, which is a 12-mile drive from San Francisco, has been experiencing the ripple effects of the tech boom in its bigger neighbour for some time, as property prices and rents have risen and affordability has worsened. Locals fear that the decision by Twitter will inevitably makes matters worse. An affordable housing development by the city attracted 4,000 applicants for 28 homes, understandable as the city considers a six-figure salary as a low income. Even before the Twitter announcement there were more than 3,000 homeless people in the city and, like other areas that have caught the Big Tech contagion, the impacts are not even in terms of race and class. The proportion of African Americans living in the city has fallen from 50 per cent to 16 per cent since the late 1970s. Meanwhile, one of San Francisco-based Uber's co-founders paid US$72.5 million for a house in 2019.

There are some minor moves afoot in Silicon Valley, but much of it is too little, too late. Google announced that it will release land it owns in the Bay Area over a 10-year period for housing development that will accommodate up to 15,000 homes for a range of income levels. The company will also invest up to US$250 million to help subsidise housing development for lower-income households. Facebook has pledged US$500 million to support affordable housing in the San Francisco Bay Area, whilst Microsoft announced US$500 million in low-cost loans to build affordable housing in Seattle. Despite the increase of around 700,000 employees in the Bay Area between 2011 and 2019, the housing stock has not grown at anything like the rate needed to keep up. The built-up area of the region looks remarkably similar to how it appeared in the middle of the last century. Ironically, the very industry that one assumes could facilitate more flexible working that doesn't rely on everyone working in the same place seems to want to do the exact opposite, despite the economic and social costs. As a consequence of COVID-19 a number of firms, including Twitter, have announced home working as the new norm, although it remains to be seen whether this will be a permanent change.

Rather than contribute to sorting out the disruption and consequences, some see digital technology as a way to escape the upshots of digital technology on our cities. Writing in *The Guardian*, tech writer Douglas Rushkoff tells of being invited to an event to give a talk to super-wealthy investment bankers. Rather than wanting to know what was the next 'big thing', they quizzed him instead on how they should use digital technology to help mitigate the impacts of what they perceived to be inevitable societal breakdown:

> Taking their cue from Elon Musk colonizing Mars, Peter Thiel reversing the ageing process, or Sam Altman and Ray Kurzweil uploading their minds into supercomputers, they were preparing for a digital future that had a whole lot less to do with making the world a better place than it did with transcending the human condition altogether and insulating themselves from a very real and present danger of climate change, rising sea levels, mass migrations, global pandemics, nativist panic, and resource depletion. For them, the future of technology is really about just one thing: escape.[32]

Some cities are fighting back

Beyond the headline-grabbing resistance and fightback against the impact of Big Tech on our cities – restraining and restricting the spread of Airbnb (most major cities), curtailing the activities of Uber through licences (London), refusing to pay Amazon to locate its fulfilment centres in the area (New York) – opposition is underway in cities across the globe. The first step, according to Francesca Bria, Barcelona's Chief Technology and Digital Innovation Officer, is to disrupt and supplant the 'smart city' story:

> I think in the technological world it's very important to put forward a narrative that's different to the surveillance capitalism from Silicon Valley, and the dystopian Chinese model, with its Social Credit

System that uses citizen data to give them a rating that then gives them access to certain services.[33]

For Barcelona, this has meant reversing the pitch that data and digital technology can make the city run more efficiently, a proposition that locks in current trajectories and locks out change. Instead, the city uses digital technology to help identify and then deliver what citizens actually prioritise – affordable housing, energy transition, air quality and public space. Barcelona calls this 'technological sovereignty'. Taking on Big Tech and shaping it is easier if you're a place where it wants to be. It's less straightforward if you're a second or third order city, struggling to compete, and facing a multitude of complex challenges. In places like Sunderland, Leipzig or Baltimore, the issues are less around gentrification and housing affordability and more about empty, boarded-up shops, high unemployment, low wages and business closures. Some places, like Doncaster in northern England and Mulhouse in France, have successfully attracted people and jobs by focusing on what the online behemoths can't provide: an experience alongside shopping and leisure. Supporting and incentivising independent retailers provides an alternative and resilient model, one that is less susceptible to price-based competition. Some town centres are going back to the model of the ancient agora, serving as places where people go to meet. There is also a growing network of resistance and experiences as activists and cities use digital technology as a tool against itself, with activists in Berlin talking to those in Toronto. Yet despite this growing defiance, the economics are still against cities: the investment and jobs associated with a huge warehouse distribution centre or the promise of being able to deliver better services for less money are seductive, even if some of those challenges are actually driven by Big Tech. Except if you live in Schodack, New York. In June 2018 a local developer submitted a planning application for a 1 million square foot, US$100 million Amazon fulfilment centre (warehouse) along with the promise of 800 full-time mostly minimum wage jobs. Amazon has 75 of these across the US, and most have involved tax breaks from local and state authorities. In the case of the Schodack fulfilment centre, the subsidies were around US$13 million.[34] Reflecting on subsidising the world's richest man and the planet's most valuable company, the local newspaper, the *Times Union*, opined, 'Taxpayers' funds should help improve their communities, not fatten corporate profits'.[35]

The reaction from local people was interesting and revealing. The area was zoned for warehousing so it wasn't the principle that was the fount of reaction but a combination of factors, most notably the identity of the company, the kind of jobs that would be created in an area with very low unemployment levels, workers' conditions and the subsidies involved. But the planning system in the US, like many other countries, does not allow for consideration of the company behind the proposal, just the principles and impacts. Thus the local community found themselves having to fight the proposal on narrow, environmental grounds – increased traffic, air pollution, etc – rather than on the kind of community they wished to be. In other words, they didn't like the kind of company and its practices in their area. This was a reaction against growth for growth's sake. It's a fight they are likely to lose as they are forced to focus on narrower planning grounds rather than using the planning system to address wider concerns.

Across the Atlantic near the French city of Lyon, residents of a number of villages have taken to the streets to block plans for another Amazon warehouse. The *gilets jaunes*, or 'yellow vest movement', emerged at the end of 2018, initially protesting against proposed increases in fuel tax. Following widespread public support and backing from across the political spectrum, the protests spread to other issues and targets around economic justice, including picketing Amazon warehouses. The online retailer was singled out because it provided poor working conditions and pay whilst avoiding its fair share of tax, although pressure increased when Amazon fired 10 staff for online posts supporting the protests. As in the US it was the planning system that was used as a means to challenge proposals for the fulfilment centre near Lyon. Opponents advanced legitimate planning arguments around traffic impacts and air pollution whilst being more motivated by anger at working conditions, workers' rights, freedom of speech and taxation of online companies.

The digital colonisation of the city

The overall result of the tech shock on our cities is a complex mix of uncertainty, anxiety, precariousness, opportunity and growing inequality. Layer on top of this foundational, existential threat the impacts of COVID-19, and one begins to wonder about the future of the city. We just don't know what the long-term economic implications are for cities and what to do to manage these seismic changes and challenges. Economic challenges aside, there is a further dimension to the future of cities. Digital is not simply disrupting the city; it is also attempting a colonisation. In the view of the Deputy Mayor of Paris, Ian Brossat,[36] digital multinationals should not be allowed to become 'more powerful than cities, more powerful than states'. Yet the fight against this corporate encroachment is made more difficult by the alluring sell of the platform economy, not to mention the techniques that are used to draw us in, which I discuss in Chapter 5. Part of the seduction comes from the language and pitch that reinforce the myths that Silicon Valley is keen to perpetuate. Airbnb still talks of 'hosts', not landlords, 'hospitality', not business, even though the vast majority of its listings are whole flats and houses, not a spare room. We're also encouraged to think of such services as the sharing rather than the platform economy.

Some of the issues that are being laid at the door of Big Tech have been with our cities for some time – the residents of Kreuzberg may feel that they have avoided gentrification by Google, but the area has been undergoing change and will continue to do so. But this is more than a new wave of gentrification; it's a new wave of capitalism where business, in this case the digital economy, can see profit not just in cities as locations, but in the running of the city itself. And for many politicians this is attractive – digital technology is appealing because it avoids the messy, complex, time-consuming compromises of politics. If people can make choices, express opinions and do so efficiently and effectively, then what's the problem? As Maxwell Anderson, Executive Director of the New Cities Foundation, puts it, 'The idea that we elect people who fix things and we go back to our daily lives is being eroded.

Urban decision-making is going to rest on a much more active citizenry expressing preferences in real time through handheld devices.'[37] Digital technology is both the cause and the solution, undermining the politics and economics of our cities, the ways in which we manage and plan, and yet offering an attractive alternative to the disruption that it is causing.

Twenty-five years after the publication of *Hackers*, Steven Levy added an Afterword to reflect current hacker culture in Silicon Valley:

> A new generation of hackers has emerged, techies who don't see business as an enemy but the means through which their ideas and innovations can find the broadest audience. Take Facebook CEO Mark Zuckerberg.... Last year, he told the audience at an event for would-be Internet entrepreneurs that "We've got this whole ethos that we want to build a hacker culture".
>
> As was the case with Gates, Zuckerberg is often accused of turning his back on hacker ideals because he refused to allow other sites to access information that Facebook users contribute. But Zuckerberg says that the truth is just the opposite.... "I never had this thing where I wanted to have information that other people didn't," he says. "I just thought it should all be more available. The world was becoming more open and more access to information was really good. From everything I read, that's the very core part of the hacker culture. Like 'information wants to be free and all that'."[38]

In 2020 Facebook is the subject of a coordinated and widespread boycott by sponsors. Up to a third of its regular advertisers have withdrawn their adverts in protest at what they see as the lack of action to fight hate speech on the platform. Zuckerberg may want information, including hate speech, to be free, but profit is now dictating the hacker myth of Facebook and others. The simple fact is that Facebook, Twitter, Instagram and their ilk are powerful and influential, and that's why Adidas, Starbucks and others have pulled their support. Facebook may peddle the hacker myth, but the bottom line is the share price. The reality that digital media is powerful, can swing elections, and is all about the profit should be a warning to cities and those who run them.

4

Unholy alliance: how government, academics and Big Tech are colluding in the takeover of our cities

In 2017 Apple retail chief Angela Ahrendts announced that the Apple Store was no more. The company's ambitions for its bricks and mortar interface with the public was to now match its wider dream of global domination. 'We actually don't call them stores anymore', she said. 'We call them town squares, because they're gathering places for the 500 million people who visit us every year. Places where everyone's welcome, and where all of Apple comes together.'[1] At one level the idea behind this shift is quite simple – creating attractive places where people congregate will mean that they are more likely to spend money. But there is something else going on. Apple has form in setting itself up in erstwhile public spaces – old post offices, fire stations, libraries – colonising them and blurring the boundary between the commercial city and the public city.

Rebranding their stores as town squares is the next obvious step, one that more than hints at the reality of how close Big Tech is to the heart of our cities. It's just a short step from town squares to town halls, a distance that is getting closer as more and more of our city life is being seized by the digital advance. Why should we be worried by this? If Big Tech and City Hall can work together to improve our cities, then what's the issue?

Google, Facebook, Amazon, Apple and their like aren't interested in making cities better places; they're interested in data, revenue and share prices. Cities, to them, aren't homes and communities, workplaces and schools; they are merely hosts to large numbers of customers and consumers.

The new digital revolution seeks to gather our data and monetise it, shaping our attention and organising our lives, assembling information and guiding what we see and experience. Big Tech are gatekeepers to knowledge and information. But they are not neutral channels: they fashion what we see and when, what we buy and experience. They shape choices and markets, and because of their dominance in their respective fields there is little alternative – around 90 per cent of all internet searches are on Google, whilst Amazon represents around a third of all retail sales in the US, a proportion that increased significantly during the 2020 pandemic with the shift to online retailing. This level of dominance provides unparalleled control and influence by a handful of Tech Giants, three of which are in the top five most valuable companies in the world.

The impacts of digital technology and Big Tech on our cities are increasingly clear as jobs are lost, disrupted and replaced, democracy and collective action are undermined, and the issues we face, from homelessness to inequality, are made worse. The 'smart city' story provides a perfect vehicle for Big Tech to roll out their business plans, promising a better, more connected future, but helping undermine local shops and services, worsening housing affordability, fuelling the gig economy and zero-hour contracts, and distracting our attention from the things that matter to cities, including how we nurture and manage them for the sake of everyone who lives there.

Yet such impacts are not the only ways in which Google, Amazon, Uber, Airbnb, and so on are dominating and shaping our cities. Ask the residents of Seattle, a city that has been conquered by Amazon. The Tech Giant's 45,000 employees take up around a fifth of the city's office space, occupying more space than the next 40 largest employers combined. Jobs, local taxes and spending apart, the ramifications of this domination are being felt across the city, from traffic congestion and rising house prices and rents, to constant construction and the edging out of many communities, particularly poorer residents. Over the past 10 years rents have risen to three times more than the national average, and Seattle now has the third highest homeless population in the US. Seattle City Council member Lisa Herbold highlights the difficulties when faced with trying to shape the future city in the shadow of a behemoth like Amazon: 'A lot of people believe that all growth is inherently good and don't question what model of growth is good for cities that are already high-cost. There are other people who have a lot of concerns.'[2] One of those concerned residents is Jason Turner. 'I would say to Mr Bezos: "Look at the community you're in. Look at what you're doing to us. Just contribute to the longevity and culture that sustained this city for years". What is it that communities actually want? We just want to be able to stay in the community we established', says Turner.[3]

There has always been a close relationship between technology and change in our cities, for better or for worse. The Industrial Revolution in 19th-century England created and then transformed the city, generating wealth for a few and slums for the many. In the 1950s the US middle class climbed into their cars and drove out of the city for the suburbs, abandoning a generation to poverty and crime in places like Detroit. Technological advances in materials enabled skyscrapers to be erected, increasing building densities and changing the economics and environmental footprints of cities such as Chicago and New York.

The digital revolution is also transforming our cities, but through the collection and use of individuals' data, information that is then deployed and sold to better target us based on our posts, our 'likes', our purchases, our movements and the websites we visit. In 2017 a leaked report highlighted how Facebook had undertaken analysis in order to persuade advertisers that it could target teenagers in real time based on posts and photos that could determine when they felt 'stressed', 'defeated', 'overwhelmed', 'anxious', 'nervous', 'stupid', 'silly', 'useless' and a 'failure'. This unparalleled access to and use of personal data not only helps target advertising and news feeds, but also determines how we are understood by the police through the algorithms underpinning predictive policing; how much we can borrow and at what interest rate through our credit scores; how much we pay for goods and services through adaptive pricing; and how we access healthcare through data on our diets, exercise and general health. In short, data and digital technology determines our life chances.[4] The data revolution is disrupting our lives in ways that previous technology didn't.

But these are just early days for the smart city. Rather than inheriting an urban built form that was largely determined by previous revolutions from steam to the car, why not create something that reflects the digital age? Google is moving from the virtual to the physical world through its development arm, Sidewalk Labs, planning to redevelop large areas of our cities. Residents of Google's housing would be required to consent to their data being harvested when they access services, using their digital identities when they use public transport, when they pay for goods and even when they vote. This data will, in turn, be used to target them, influencing their choices and decisions through news feeds, advertising and social media.

It's hardly surprising that few have noticed, much less challenged, the creeping changes around us. In large part this is because what Silicon Valley offers seems costless. Big Tech deliberately hides behind what appear to be idealistic motives, providing services that are free to the user but are actually based on a hard-nosed business model that seeks to create monopolies across a wide range of markets. This pose amounts to what Franklin Foer[5] calls 'sham populism', or companies like Google and Facebook giving the impression they are making information and knowledge free to all whilst they capture and dominate a variety of traditional markets and economic models, from retail to news media. But it's not simply that we as individuals are complicit; our representatives are too. If we are struggling to see what's happening, then surely those responsible for our cities, our local and central governments, are aware? Well, they're part of the problem. In fact, there are five separate problems around Big Tech and cities. The first is what could be called 'dog eat dog capitalism': cities around the world are in competition to attract investment and jobs, and right now the main game in town is digital. Yet digital investment and jobs are truly footloose and in 'the cloud' – they can pick up and go anywhere where taxes are low and subsidies are high. The second problem is that Big Tech has become an effective lobbyer of government, increasing spending and influence in order to create a sector-favourable attitude. Third, large sums are spent by companies like Google on sponsoring 'independent' research in universities and research centres around the globe, research that coincidently maps onto subjects that digital companies wish to challenge, thereby providing a ready-made source of counter-material. Fourth, there is what I would call the 'smart city paradox': despite being fully aware of the disruptive and destructive nature of the digital economy, cities still buy into the 'smart city' narrative. Finally, even when governments and others such as the EU attempt to regulate and control the impacts and activities of the digital economy, companies like Amazon, Facebook and Google are too big to care – they can do more or less what they like.

The competition for jobs and investment

Although shiny and new, the challenges of digital technology to our cities are old wine in new bottles. What is behind the disruption and the populist, hacking myth of companies such as Apple and Google are good, old-fashioned concerns around selling products and services. It's all about control and power. Digital technology and smart cities are providing new ways for cities to address long-standing concerns, including controlling and monitoring the disadvantaged and the poor, protecting the better-off and the wealthy, selling products and services, and making cities run more efficiently and for less money. One can understand how the prospect of funding new, more effective and more cost-efficient ways to tackle these issues is attractive to politicians and governments of all political persuasions. As a result, cities have been active participants in the rollout of digital technology, bidding for government funds, participating in league tables of smart cities, marketing themselves as tech hubs and investing in infrastructure to facilitate it all. But it's not just the promise of new ways of tackling deep-seated issues that is appealing; there's an economic imperative too.

Globalisation has created a system that pits city against city in an international race for footloose capital and economic growth. In 2017 Amazon announced it was looking for a new location for its second HQ, imaginatively called HQ2. The company claimed it would create up to 50,000 jobs and pump billions into one lucky local economy. Amazon invited cities to bid against a set of criteria in order to secure its investment, including what the company called a 'business-friendly environment'. Amazon's announcement led to a frenzy of activity across the US, Canada and Mexico, resulting in 238 bids to host HQ2, reduced to 20 after shortlisting. The bids and the common interpretation of 'business-friendly environment' typically included billions of dollars in tax incentives paid for by the cities and their taxpayers. The city of Stonecrest near Atlanta proposed gifting 140 hectares of land and would allow a new city called Amazon to be built. The eagerness with which cities competed was described by some as the business equivalent of the *Hunger Games* death match. A 16,000-name online petition against the 'race to the bottom' of tax incentives and giveaways was signed by a wide range of academics and politicians criticising the use of Amazon's market power to extract incentives from local and state governments. Yet many places are desperate for jobs, even if the investment comes from a company that is helping destroy their economies and tax base. Amazon was playing one area off against another – a natural and rational strategy in a competitive, global world.

In the end Amazon plumped for New York after being offered huge incentives, rumoured to be in the region of US$3 billion, only to find that some local people and politicians weren't too keen on paying to host the behemoth. Opposition to Amazon came from State Senator Michael Gianaris, a Democrat representing Long Island City, the area that Amazon had chosen. As Gianaris put it: 'A community that was facing its own demolition was salvaged. And New York took a stand against the type of corporate subsidies that are increasing the wealth concentration in this country.'[6] Despite political support from the city and governor, there was enough resistance to what many regarded as the equivalent of a corporate Death Star to make it change direction and withdraw from the proposal.

The area in Long Island that Amazon and the city had settled on has a large homelessness issue, and New York Mayor Bill de Blasio knew when luring the company that the problem would be exacerbated by the influx of highly paid workers. Other areas of the city already subject to increasing numbers of homeless people displaced by such schemes would have experienced further growth in homelessness. The choices faced by city mayors like de Blasio are not easy ones. Cities have been captured by the sheer power and reach of the large corporations, competing against each other for buying into the idea that digital technology and smart cities are the future of growth and jobs. After Amazon's decision to pull out of New York, the city of Dallas didn't waste any time making another pitch, with a headline in *The Dallas Morning News*: 'Dear Amazon, New York doesn't want you; Dallas does'.[7]

The choices that cities face are not enviable ones. With limited resources and levers to effect change combined with deep and engrained issues including poverty, homelessness, congestion, creaking infrastructure and short electoral cycles, the lure of Big Tech and 'smart city' narratives and the promise of solutions is understandable. It's not as though cities and mayors are unconsciously making a pact with the digital devil; in many cases they're simply trying to stay afloat financially, maintaining services for the vulnerable against a backdrop of increased demand and decreasing resources. They're balancing the benefits against the costs of digital technology for their cities. And these choices are not being made any easier by the growing power and influence of Big Tech, which are increasingly developing links and allies within government and academia to project their case and head off opposition and criticism.

Government and Big Tech

Some have claimed that what we are facing is the emergence of corporation states, what Philip Howard calls *Pax Technica*,[8] or a new political order based on a deal or understanding between digital corporations and governments. This bargain has been led by Big Tech actively making alliances, recruiting allies and placing staff in governments around the globe. There has been a step change in activity to mobilise influence over the past few years with the Tech Giants. Some of the approaches to gain influence are mainstream – Apple, Amazon and Google all spent record amounts lobbying during the 2016 US presidential election and have upped spend to lobby the federal government on privacy, regulations, tax and immigration reform. In 2019 *The Observer* revealed that Facebook had directly lobbied politicians in all 28 EU countries to avoid data privacy legislation, linking the company's future investment decisions to the attitude of different states to regulation.[9] Amazon, Facebook, eBay, Airbnb, Dropbox, LinkedIn, Netflix, Google and others joined forces in 2012 to establish and fund the Internet Association, a representative body that lobbies the US Congress, the courts, foreign governments, federal and state agencies, and state and local governments on issues around regulation of digital technology. The Internet Association has lobbied on a wide range of issues including net neutrality, privacy, regulations restricting the platform economy operations such as Uber and Airbnb, the impact of digital services on small retailers, responsibility for harmful content and misinformation, and the labour conditions of some of its members. It spent US$55 million on lobbying in 2018, double the amount spent in 2016. According to Sheila Krumholz, Executive Director of the Center for Responsive Politics, 'They [Big Tech] are no longer upstarts dipping a toe in lobbying, they have both feet in'.[10]

Yet it is through the more covert attempts at influence that Big Tech has started to gain much more sway. The Tech Transparency Project has identified at least 80 moves from Google to EU governments over the past decade, and 258 instances of 'revolving door' appointments between Google and the US federal government, national political campaigns and Congress during President Barack Obama's time in office. These include moves from Google to government and vice versa, including Google hiring several people from the Federal Trade Commission, an agency that has conducted investigations into the company's conduct on privacy and antitrust grounds. As the Tech Transparency Project puts it, Google's hiring of key former government employees 'gives it valuable insight into the inner workings of government and politics. Having former Googlers steeped in its culture inside the government also gives the company a formidable conduit to influence policymaking on a variety of issues affecting its interests.'[11] In Europe, Google's hiring of government officials coincided with its bid to influence policy after a deal to settle the European Commission's antitrust investigation collapsed in 2014. Some politicians felt that Google's efforts to gain influence in this way was part of their business strategy to be close to government.

Both Facebook and Google have also been closely linked to political campaigns. According to an investigation by the Campaign for Accountability, major political campaigns such as the US presidential election receive free tools and services from Facebook and Google that enable them to gain insights and political allegiances. According to one Google employee, Ali Jae Henke, embedded with the 2016 Republican presidential campaign, 'we are so close [with the campaigns] that we are typically sitting in their offices or having daily calls'.[12] There were cases where the roles of embedded employees were less than clear:

> The process has also worked the other way as former Google employees have also exposed some of the firm's less well known tactics and secrets.
>
> Sometimes Google employees worked with campaigns at the same time as they lobbied for Google. Google's team lead for US politics, Rob Saliterman, said he sold ads to political campaigns while at the same time helping Google's lobbying arm influence elected officials on policies affecting the company.[13]

Google are not the only Big Tech company to undertake this role. From 2012 Facebook has also provided dedicated staff to work inside presidential campaigns, acting as consultants on branding, communications and overall strategy for the campaign, along with ad sales.

Does this all have any impact? The politicians think so. As Donald Trump said after his victory in the 2016 presidential campaign: 'The fact [is] that I have such power in terms of numbers with Facebook, Twitter, Instagram, etc. I think it helped me win all of these races where they're spending much more money than I spent.'[14] One Trump campaign insider was more succinct: 'Without Facebook, we wouldn't have won.' Support runs both ways, though. Eric Schmidt, former Executive Chair of Google, personally helped the Obama campaign in the 2012 presidential election, putting the company's data and analytics at the disposal of the campaign to significant effect.

The victories are not simply confined to the politicians. There is little doubt that such close and ongoing relations benefit Big Tech too, as I'll go on to discuss below. Read any political manifesto and you'll stumble over the same vague and positive-sounding predictions of the future. In the UK the Conservative Party Election Manifesto of 2017 set out the aim of delivering 'The world's most dynamic digital economy, giving digital businesses access to the investment, skills and talent they need to succeed'. This included commitments to transform public services, invest £750 million in digital infrastructure, prioritise visas for digital workers, and provide new training and qualifications in digital technology. As the manifesto put it: 'We will help provide the skills and digital infrastructure that creative companies need and will seek to build upon the favourable tax arrangements that have helped them.'[15]

This could be seen as common-sense support for a growing and important sector of the economy. But there's more to it. Digital technology gives politicians a free pass on pressing issues. Digital promises off-the-shelf solutions to many of the challenges and issues cities face, solutions that bypass politics, investment of scarce resources and tough choices. These solutions are attractive to city authorities because they tend to put the onus on the individual.

Stuck in traffic? There's an app for that that will tell you how to avoid congestion. Worried about air pollution caused by traffic congestion? Here's the data to tell you when it's best to go out. Rather take public transport to help reduce traffic congestion and air pollution? Try the Uber app: it's cheaper and quicker. As far as many politicians go, for every issue there is a market for a digital solution and one will pop up if you wait long enough. Hence why the Conservative Manifesto makes a vague promise for a digital solution to every issue, from economic growth to disability and health. All the digital economy asks in return is regulatory freedom, including the ability to employ people on zero-hour contracts.

Academia and Big Tech

Government is not the only ally and actor in this: some of academia has also been complicit. Google has sponsored research from academics to the tune of tens of millions of dollars, research that supports its position on various issues, particularly when under scrutiny from regulators and governments. The Tech Transparency Project identified 331 research papers that were published between 2005 and 2017 on matters of interest to Google, including antitrust, privacy, net neutrality and copyright. The number of these studies rose when the company needed support to combat scrutiny from regulators, particularly when the issue was around antitrust cases and the possibility of curtailing the ability of Google to use its search engine and mobile phone software to promote other products.

In the US, Google has largely supported research in existing institutions whereas in Europe support has been more aimed at creating new institutions. Google has funded the establishment of institutions within universities across Europe, institutions that have published hundreds of papers on issues that the European Commission has been investigating, including antitrust, privacy, copyright and the 'right to be forgotten'. Berlin now hosts the Alexander von Humboldt Institute for Internet and Society, launched after an €11 million donation from Google in 2011. The launch coincided with growing concern within Germany over Google's power, and the Institute has gone on to publish more than 240 papers and reports, some of which are published in a Google-funded journal. Other institutes have been established in France, the UK and Poland, whilst the company has endowed chairs at other prestigious universities. In the view of some, 'Google's European academic network helps the company exert a subtle and insidious form of influence on the region's policy makers, which often goes unnoticed by those who are being influenced'.[16]

This isn't the first time academics have provided supportive research for industries under scrutiny. Since the early 1950s the tobacco industry funded research and reports that supported its position, particularly on the harmful effects of smoking and passive smoking, an approach that has been mirrored by the oil industry in its efforts to challenge growing concerns over its role in climate change. The sponsorship of research and policy by these interests is often provided to sympathetic policy-makers and the media directly, a route made easier by the ability to disseminate directly through digital technology.

This aim and approach contrasts sharply with that of more mainstream academic research where there is a commitment to the advancement of knowledge through the force of better research and argument. Academic freedom and the Haldane principle in the UK, which states that decisions on what to research should be made by academics, and not politicians, is jealously guarded by researchers. Instead, much industry-funded research seeks a more targeted agenda focused on the issues that are of concern to the company, often with the aim of overwhelming debates and discussions with information and research, with the added credibility of 'independence' from academic institutions and individuals. This strategy of overwhelming any debate with information and views so as to obscure the argument is one recently followed by China. At the heart of the approach is the need for traditional media outlets – the print press, radio and TV – to create a debate on any issue, and this requires two or more views or opinions, automatically giving opinions on different sides of the argument equal weight regardless of the source of evidence. So sponsored research provides a ready alternative view, and one that puts a case that is difficult to dismiss as coming from those who will be affected. Instead, it comes from a 'trusted', 'independent' source, whether it is antitrust legislation, fines for data breaches or the right to privacy. But this is not the only role that the likes of Google, Twitter and Facebook play in shaping debate and discussion, including that which concerns them. The 'information overload' strategy plays to their advantage in the way that most of us source our information – through web search engines. Searches pull up a range of views regardless of the source and weight of evidence on any subject. This approach, in part, helps explain the situation where climate change sceptics are able to challenge the overwhelming weight of scientific research on an equal basis. It's little wonder that the public and some policy-makers are confused about the existence of climate change, never mind the role of Big Tech in shaping news and views.

Not only are the likes of Google, Facebook and others simultaneously shaping what counts as news and then providing opinions as news regardless of credibility, they are also undermining news in other ways. Big Tech provides the means through which many get their news and information, but it has also hollowed out and decimated traditional sources of news in the form of national and local newspapers and media. In the late 2000s many in the newspaper business began to feel the initial impacts of the ease with which advertisers could publicise their products and services online, often at little or no cost. Revenues from advertising began to decline. At this point the growth in digital avenues for news and advertising was seen by newspapers as an opportunity to reduce costs and increase readership through an online presence. What was not foreseen was the devastation that would be wrought by the likes of Google and Facebook as they targeted and individualised advertising through the combination of personal data and preferences, including internet search history, location, purchases, 'likes' and 'dislikes'. Their user database ran into the hundreds of millions, and patterns began to emerge in consumer behaviour that allowed service providers to predict with accuracy what individuals would watch next, what they might also like to buy following a particular internet search and what approach – layout, colours and placement – of adverts would be more likely to attract attention.

Google's advertising revenue rose from US$10 billion in 2006 to US$55 billion in 2013. Facebook experienced a similar growth in advertising revenue. The losers were newspapers, with revenue collapsing by half in the same period. The impacts on traditional news media have been severe. Staff numbers have dropped by a third in the US and the UK, with more expensive forms of journalism, overseas and investigative, being hardest hit. Newspapers have increasingly turned to repackaging existing stories whilst not having the resources to check facts. This 'churnalism' has been accompanied by an increasing centralisation of local news media through buyouts and takeovers, leading to journalists being based far from the community they serve. In the US, more than 500 newspapers have closed since 2010. In the UK the number is around 200. Not only have Google, Facebook and now Apple acquired the advertising revenue of local news, local news media have also increasingly become dependent on them as the Tech Giants provide small revenue streams for adverts clicked on local digital newspaper websites. The result is that newspapers have moved to include clickbait alongside recycled news, desperately trying to attract a fickle readership and encourage them to follow links that bring in minuscule revenues. So Google and Facebook have not only destroyed local media and news, but they are increasingly shaping that news too, either indirectly through encouraging remaining newspapers to prioritise scandal over local issues or by subtly changing algorithms to favour certain topics over others in searches and feeds.

As Nicholas Thompson and Fred Vogelstein put it in *Wired* magazine:

> Facebook hired few journalists and spent little time discussing the big questions that bedevil the media industry. What is fair? What is a fact? How do you signal the difference between news, analysis, satire, and opinion? Facebook has long seemed to think it has immunity from those debates because it is just a technology company – one that has built a "platform for all ideas."[17]

The symbiosis of Big Tech and government

Whilst the likes of Amazon and Google are unfurling themselves upon our cities, governments around the world have been simultaneously scratching their heads about what to do whilst embracing and facilitating the promises of digital technology, setting up initiatives and funding to support the rollout of smart cities. In 2012 the Chinese Ministry of Housing and Urban-Rural Development announced 90 'smart city' pilot projects, a target that increased to 193 by 2013. A government-run future cities competition in the UK supported 30 'smart city' proposals in 2012, awarding Glasgow £24 million to implement its plans. Since then 'smart' has become an aspirational label for many cities as they seek to catch up. A small number of new smart cities are being built around the world as exemplars with varying degrees of success, such as Songdo in South Korea and Neom in Saudi Arabia, with India pledging to build 100 new smart cities.

The digitisation of cities is seen both as a 'good thing' and as a threat by cities and governments. Yet the balance between the upsides and downsides is being shifted in favour of the smart city in three critical ways. First, lobbying and influencing through sponsoring research on subjects that are close to the interests of Big Tech is helping stave off criticism and create a conducive atmosphere for digital rollout. Second, the effects of globalisation in the form of the free flow of goods, people and services combined with decades of neoliberal, deregulatory, entrepreneurial public policy have created the perfect conditions for the digital economy to flourish. A deregulated workforce with little or no welfare safety net provides a large and compliant pool of labour who will take on precarious employment and long hours. Urban policy has also been encouraging competition between cities to attract global, footloose investment, persuading them to offer business–friendly contexts including being smart. Finally, political leaders and planners themselves are open to the prospects offered by digital, particularly as the need to compete with other cities is matched by the need to provide essential services against a backdrop where demand outpaces budgets. The pitch of effective and efficient approaches to service delivery from the smart city evangelists is pushing at an open door. And as governments cede control, the likes of Amazon, Google, et al increasingly act much like governments, running our services and transport, developing infrastructure, shaping the world physically, economically and socially, and doing so in alliance with actual governments. They even admit to it: 'In a lot of ways Facebook is more a government than a traditional company', said Mark Zuckerberg.[18]

None of these movements is uncontested. Hardly a week goes by without someone calling for Google, Amazon or Facebook to be 'broken up'. The fear of monopolies in Western societies runs deep. For generations we have been concerned that the concentration of economic and political power would undermine democracy and society. But Big Tech has changed the nature of the debate in three ways. First, a small number of companies, including Google, Facebook and Amazon, have come to dominate their respective marketplaces through destroying personal privacy. They track our data – what we order, what we 'like', where we are – building a portrait of us that gives them a significant market advantage. This makes it very difficult, if not impossible, for other companies to compete – they simply do not have access to the same level of information and insight, putting them at a distinct disadvantage. Second, the marketplace has expanded so that there are now so many more opportunities to hold a monopoly. In his book, Jamie Bartlett points out that many of our tech household names are difficult to pin down.[19] 'Standard Oil was an oil company', he states, 'what is Facebook? A media outlet? An online advertiser? A social media platform? An AI company?' Judging Big Tech by the standards of oil or steel monopolies misses the point that they want to monopolise everything, not just one area. Finally, as Bartlett goes on to argue, the new Big Tech monopolies tend to push prices down and provide excellent consumer products. Some products are seemingly given away for free in order to encourage users to provide data. There are consumer advantages to the domination of companies in the modern era, but there are significant implications too, particularly for cities.

In 2011 a group called Alliance for Main Street Fairness began lobbying for US states to crack down on Amazon's refusal to collect sales tax on online sales. The Alliance, representing traditional bricks and mortar retailers, pointed to how the lack of a tax, typically between 5 and 10 per cent of the sale price, amounted to unfair competition. Various states had sought to force Amazon to collect the tax but backed down in the face of the company's combative threats to close down fulfilment centres and sack staff. The revenues involved were crucial to the 45 states that had them, representing about a third of their tax income. Texas was one of the states to push Amazon to collect the sales tax, sending the company a bill for US$269 million for back taxes in the autumn of 2010. The company took immediate action, announcing it was closing its Texas warehouse and making its workers redundant. Negotiations led to Amazon confirming it would remain and expand its presence, but the tax bill was written off. This was a playbook move by Amazon, repeated in other states, from California to South Carolina. Charles McLure, a former Deputy Assistant US Treasury Secretary, commented that 'Amazon is aiding and abetting tax evasion'.[20] At a practical level the impacts ran deep. States and cities needed the tax to pay for essential public services. But there was another impact, too, on traditional bricks and mortar retailers, many of which were fatally undermined by the ability of Amazon to undercut prices by offering goods free of a sales tax. In the meantime Amazon has achieved market dominance and reinforced its position as the go-to site for online purchases whilst it also begins to move into the empty high street spaces it has created through new, physical locations in city centres, including groceries and fashion. In some cities there is such a desire to attract Amazon that deals are made to pay the company up to 85 per cent of the sales tax as an incentive, an offer that isn't available to other more traditional retailers. Traditional retailers have also moved online in the digital age but they have a lot of catching up to do: in 2020 it was announced that Amazon had paid just £293 million in UK tax on sales of £13.73 billion.[21]

Despite the changing nature of monopolies in the era of Big Tech there have been attempts to curtail their influence, yet Google and Facebook in particular have been successful in thwarting attempts to address market dominance, despite the evidence. They are simply too big, too footloose to be effectively subject to traditional regulatory levers. With Google expanding into property development and Amazon expanding into just about everything else, cities are being disrupted and transformed, unable to curb, shape or thwart the changes.

Challenging *Pax Technica*

With the effective collusion of Big Tech and government and the emasculation of local news media, where can the opposition come from? 2020 has not been the best of years for Facebook. In a letter to Mark Zuckerberg in June, more than 140 scientists currently or previously funded by the Chan Zuckerberg Initiative (CZI) or the Chan Zuckerberg Biohub, wrote a letter of concern.[22] The issue for them was the way in which Facebook had allowed incendiary statements and misinformation, particularly from President Trump, to be reported. As the letter sets out:

> Social media platforms, like Facebook, have emerged as primary ways of communicating information. While they have allowed dissemination of information across the globe, they also facilitate the spread of misinformation. The spread of news that is not vetted for factual accuracy leads to confusion and a mistrust of experts.[23]

According to the letter, Facebook needed to consider stricter policies on misinformation and incendiary language. The authors of the letter had been moved to write following Facebook's refusal to act on a post by Trump concerning nationwide protests following the death of George Floyd in May whilst being arrested by police in Minneapolis. Twitter had removed the Tweet 'When the looting starts, the shooting starts', although Facebook didn't follow this lead, with Zuckerberg wishing, instead, to explore options that were less 'binary' than leave-it-up or take-it-down.

Whilst pushback from scientists didn't achieve results, a more serious threat to Facebook emerged from a boycott by advertisers that grew to over 1,000 companies including Unilever, Coca-Cola and Starbucks. Again, the impetus for the Stop Hate for Profit boycott had been Facebook's failure to act over Trump's postings.

In its defence, Facebook claims it removes 89 per cent of hate content before it is reported. However, those behind the boycott say that any amount of hate speech is too much:

> Starbucks can't say 89% of its coffee doesn't have poison in it, Ford Motor Company cannot say 89% of its fleet has seatbelts that work and still sell them – most companies recall a product that is not at 99.9%.[24]

Facebook declined to make any concrete moves, only commenting that it was grateful to these groups and many others for their continued engagement, and adding that the company was committed to making the platform free of hate speech.

But advertisers and funded scientists are not the only ones who are pushing back against Big Tech: governments are starting to realise that digital technology comes with significant downsides too. The UK House of Commons established an investigation into disinformation, fake news and online privacy that reported in 2019.[25] In a wide-ranging and in-depth analysis, the report from the investigation recommended a range of measures including a new code of ethics for online platforms that made them liable for harmful and illegal content paid for by a 'tech tax'.

As the UK Parliament's Inquiry concluded, however:

> Among the countless innocuous postings of celebrations and holiday snaps, some malicious forces use Facebook to threaten and harass others, to publish revenge porn, to disseminate hate speech and propaganda of all kinds, and to influence elections and democratic processes – much of which Facebook, and other social media companies, are either unable or unwilling to prevent. We need to apply widely accepted democratic principles to ensure their application in the digital age.[26]

The attitude of those in the firing line was summed up by the repeated failure of Mark Zuckerberg to respond to requests to give evidence. Not taking the UK government seriously isn't the only way Big Tech is reacting to increased concern with its activities. The EU has levied some of its biggest fines on Big Tech, requiring Facebook to pay €110 million for misleading regulators on its purchase of WhatsApp, Google €2.4 billion for ignoring competition laws, and Amazon €250 million for accepting tax benefits, and it ordered Ireland to recover €13 billion in back taxes from Apple (although a legal challenge in mid-2020 reversed this decision). Yet for companies like Apple (net worth US$2 trillion and an annual turnover of US$280 billion), Google (net worth US$900 billion and an annual turnover of US$100 billion), Facebook (net worth US$527 billion and an annual turnover of US$70 billion) and Amazon (net worth US$1 trillion and an annual turnover of US$280 billion) in 2019/20, such sums are little more than an irritant.

A large part of the issue is that Silicon Valley transcends geography and nation state boundaries – it is truly global. Amazon has become its own regulator, deciding on prices, delivery and salaries, largely without reference to the rules and regulations of nation states, never mind cities. Its focus is its customers. There are offers to and engagement with cities because Amazon is still trying to create its monopoly of selling us goods and services. When it has that monopoly and can dominate the market, then governments become irrelevant – where else will we go? And as Amazon and others are moving into health, education, transport and groceries, that monopoly won't simply be about buying cheap stuff for next-day delivery online.

The digital takeover

Digital is taking over our cities, and despite the downsides, we're inviting them in. One argument could be that they're coming anyway, as we increasingly use our smartphones and online presence to live. Others could also claim that there has always been propaganda and political bias in the media, and the overall situation before digital is little different in this respect to what we have currently. Another argues that Big Tech is also hardly alone in its aversion to paying tax or lobbying to its benefit. In other words, what's really different?

What is changing under the digital economy is a matter of scale, reach and obfuscation. Scale in that the power of Facebook, Twitter, Google, and so on to influence politics comes not only through lobbying and research – although these are significant – but also through the way in which they can manipulate the news feeds to their benefit. After all, more than half of people get their news from social media.[27] In terms of reach, Big Tech is truly global, operating beyond national governments and at a scale that few can influence. Finally, digital operators are adept at obfuscation concerning what they are (is Facebook a social media company or an advertising platform, a currency operator or a vendor of personal data?). Further, where is the point of sale or revenue generation if the user is in the UK, the servers in Finland and the service being provided registered in Ireland?

These companies are becoming more like governments in their pervasiveness and lack of concern about regulation:

> In a democracy, we need to experience a plurality of voices and, critically, to have the skills, experience and knowledge to gauge the veracity of those voices. While the Internet has brought many freedoms across the world and an unprecedented ability to communicate, it also carries the insidious ability to distort, to mislead and to produce hatred and instability.[28]

It's difficult to see Facebook or others being undermined by a growing movement of criticism even if it begins to impact on their market capitalisation. Facebook's share price recovered before the boycott against hate speech had ended. The phrase 'too big to fail' is one that springs to mind to accompany 'too big to care'.

The implications of all of this for cities and city planning need to be borne in mind as Big Tech is encouraged to take over services and provide solutions. One clear consequence concerns the plurality of views and public involvement raised above. According to Susan Benesch of Harvard University, 'Facebook is governing human expression more than any government does or ever has. They have taken on the task of defining hate speech and other unacceptable speech, which is a quasi-sovereign power ... and we the public have no opportunity to contribute to the decision-making, as would be the case if the decisions were being made by a government.'[29]

Hate speech is one clear dimension. Other elements concern views on climate change, social welfare, scientific progress and even the role of democracy itself. Facebook and others are now acting as global censors, but there's more. The very notion of city planning emerged as part of a broader movement of Enlightenment thinking founded on rationality and progressive ideals. It involves the replacement of superstition and myth with open, rational and democratic processes. It is this foundation and its commitment to such universal values that is ultimately under threat. Yet Silicon Valley has its own internal values that are pushing out and replacing these. Part of the reason why there has been connivance between Big Tech and governments – national and local – is a broad alignment of interests. As Lucie Greene points out, Silicon Valley's underlying philosophy combines social liberalism – they are strong on issues such as LGBTQI rights and sustainability – and consumer-led market solutions. They appeal in different ways to both the political left and the political right.[30] This appeal is combined with a (now) implicit criticism of the ways in which cities are currently run and planned. Silicon Valley is about improving lives and making things better; governments and city governments are slow and unresponsive. Government is the problem and Big Tech is the solution. The overall impacts of this are starting to show: where do we look to solve our problems? It's no longer the state. Climate change is being tackled by Elon Musk, Amazon and Google are going to make health services more affordable and effective, Uber and Lyft will provide transport, whilst Udacity, set up by ex-Google executives, is moving into universities and education. Whilst Big Tech moves to take on the functions of government, it is also undermining what is left by taking away revenue streams – autonomous vehicles will not use public car parks and won't be fined for illegal street parking as they will be constantly on the move or back at the owner's home waiting to be summoned. New forms of revenue raising will need to be developed by local and central government in order to plug this gap.

What will be left to plan or, more accurately, what levers will remain to effect change? If government and the notion of the public good or community interest are hollowed out and replaced by corporate and individual interests, then what becomes of planning? If transport, education, health and other public services are run like Uber, Amazon or Airbnb, in monopolistic situations, then how can they be used to help support wider objectives? The state or government in all its various forms will be replaced by another monopolistic entity, only this one will be working to different ends.

5

Why we're the problem
(and the solution)

Throughout history cities have been subjected to challenges, disruptions and change. But cities are resilient or, in the preferred phrase of urban geographers, they're 'complex adaptive systems', able to recover and evolve. And there are plenty of examples of this resilience and evolution.

Along with many cities in the US, New York suffered from the fallout of the 1929 Wall Street Crash, boomed in the post-war era, was on the brink of bankruptcy during the 1970s following a collapse in oil prices and the impacts on the wider economy, and bounced back to become the world's leading financial centre in the 1980s. Yet, as I discuss in Chapter 9, there are tipping points beyond which the ability of cities to adapt is lost. Like the examples of cities that have bounced back there are many places that have been abandoned or are now merely empty shells, hosts to those who have little choice but to remain because of personal circumstances. The point is that there is nothing inevitable about urban resilience. Past abilities to evolve are not necessarily any indication of future adaptation.

Along with periodic economic or environmental disruptions, the latest challenge to the city is a familiar one in some respects. From an outbreak of bubonic plague in San Francisco in 1900 to the SARS epidemic in Hong Kong in 2003, cities have managed public health crises, often replanning and rebuilding as a result, as Paris did in the 19th century, in part to improve sanitation through new water and sewage provision and to provide open space or 'lungs for the city', as it was termed at the time. The coronavirus pandemic of 2020 is on a different scale. Rather than leading to replanning and rebuilding our cities it has changed them in different ways, reinforcing and accelerating elements of our online world, helping many access vital goods and services whilst self-isolating as people sought to work and school their children from home. What we can say is that the pandemic has overlaid and been closely, even inseparably, connected with the digital. However our cities respond, it will be difficult to disentangle the impacts and the extent to which digital was the cause of or the cure for how cities move forward from this particular challenge.

It's ironic that digital and online have been portrayed as our saviours in the time of a global pandemic when, up until relatively recently, they were driving disruption and threatening the future of the city. Yet the rollout and impacts of digital technology on our cities are not imposed on us. Instead, they require our active blessing and involvement. Nobody makes us shop at Amazon and choose to spend our money online rather than in local shops. We aren't forced to rent apartments on Airbnb, or to use Uber or Deliveroo. We could choose to buy local newspapers and vote for representatives who focus on the issues that affect our communities and cities, however complex and messy. And there is no compulsion to check our smartphones on average 150 times a day. Perhaps.

In the food industry there is a concept known as the 'bliss point', a goal of honing the proportions of salt, sugar and fat in processed food in order to make a product tasty, rewarding and irresistible. Over millennia we've evolved to crave these ingredients, and our brains release endorphins when we consume them, making us want more. Food companies spend billions on research to optimise this blend, fighting for what they call 'stomach share'. Yet, whilst we crave them, we no longer have the lifestyles that allow our bodies to process the abundance of fat, salt and sugar, leaving society to deal with the consequences of an obesity epidemic. The response of many food companies to accusations that we are being hooked on junk food is that they make healthy products too. We can make choices, and it's up to us to show willpower. But this misses the point. Our deep needs and reward mechanisms are being manipulated. Our strings are being pulled. The battle between food science and the individual is not a fair fight.

Big Tech's equivalent of 'stomach share' is the 'attention economy',[1] also called 'surveillance capitalism'[2] by some. Put basically, the likes of YouTube, Facebook, Google, and so on provide us with seemingly free services in exchange for our data, which they use to target us with adverts or sell to others to do so. Attention is also the aim of the plethora of platform economy providers that seek to make our lives easier or cheaper with next-day delivery, recommendations for what others bought or watched next, or quick and cheap alternatives to taxis or public transport. Again, our data – what we buy, where and when, what we watch, browse and read – helps them and their affiliates target us. In order to grab our attention and keep it, Big Tech use a variety of techniques and tricks that mirror those of the food industry.

The impacts of the attention economy on the individual have been well rehearsed. According to many, the upshot is that our attention is now firmly focused on virtual worlds, not our real worlds. We're looking inwards, focusing on the now. We find it hard to emote, to think outside the virtual, even to consider a future – everything we want is available at the click of a mouse. This all has implications for society, but the consequences for cities are also urgent and serious. Cities need our attention too, and we're turning our backs on them. Perhaps the most pressing and serious threat from the attention economy to cities is the notion of the collective, a notion that is fundamental to urban living.

According to James Williams,[3] digital technology and social media are distracting us and making it harder to keep in mind the various communities that we belong to and what we have in common with others who share the same spaces. If we lose this sense of community and citizenship of an actual place, then cities will become a collection of individuals, ceasing to function when they are needed most, unable to address common issues that need shared solutions. Democracy requires a common purpose, and the desire and capabilities for this in society are disappearing. More fundamentally, even if we wanted to be part of city politics, we have to face a torrent of information abundance, fake news and false facts. Again, this plays into the hands of the smart city optimists and advocates. The argument goes that we don't need to bother ourselves with politics and decisions. Politics isn't necessary any more because choices are being made for us – but only a certain kind of choice, one that is possible if it is reduced to numbers and data. Where to focus police resources, not what the purpose of policing might be; how to manage traffic flows, not whether we should reduce car access to our cities in order to improve air quality. This is about making cities more efficient, bypassing the difficult and messy issues and choices. And we're likely to lose more control. As Yasha Levine points out, Big Tech has turned our computers and smartphones into an industrial-scale, corporate data-harvesting exercise: 'Where we go, what we do, what we talk about, who we talk to, and who we see – everything is recorded and, at some point, leveraged for value.'[4] This isn't paranoia. Eric Schmidt, Google's former CEO, said in 2010:

> One of the things that eventually happens ... is that we don't need you to type at all. Because we know where you are. We know where you've been. We can more or less guess what you're thinking about.[5]

In this chapter I outline how we are being distracted in order to better understand what we, as individuals and society, are up against. It's important to grasp the challenge in the right way, the multiplicity of ways in which we are being distracted, and the consequences of this for cities and their future. Because what is clear is that responding to events like COVID-19 might be helped by our online worlds, but the collective, societal attitude is critical, how we respond and adapt as a community, and not simply as individuals.

Psych wars: getting us hooked on smart and the consequences

The food industry isn't the only sector to play on our addictive needs. In 1996 CBS aired an interview with Jeffrey Wigand, a former research scientist for Brown & Williamson, a subsidiary of British American Tobacco. Wigand claimed that the company had intentionally manipulated its tobacco blend with chemicals such as ammonia to increase the effect of nicotine in cigarette smoke, despite statements to the contrary from the company. In other words, Big Tobacco had been trying to get people hooked on smoking by making it more addictive, and had been doing so in the knowledge that there were serious health risks.

For digital technology there are a growing number of Wigands, those who have broken ranks and revealed how Big Tech has been using the same playbook as the tobacco and food industries. Individuals such as Tristan Harris, former product philosopher at Google, James Williams, former Google employee, and Roger McNamee, former advisor to Mark Zuckerberg and early Facebook investor, have all been whistle-blowers on how their industry uses various tools and data to grab and keep our attention.

On a daily level we don't give much thought to how social media and other digital platforms manipulate us – they are just 'there', providing us with information or linking us with friends, be it Facebook, Google, Instagram, Snapchat, Twitter, LinkedIn, or any of the other online services that appeal and make our lives easier, happier and more connected. Yet manipulated we are. James Williams and Tristan Harris have both lifted the lid on the ways in which product designers seek to grab our attention and manipulate us. Such tools, or, using the nomenclature beloved of Silicon Valley, 'hacks', as Harris calls them, are familiar to anyone who is a regular user of social media[6] or sites such as YouTube. These hacks include:

- **Controlling choices and shaping outputs:** According to Harris, product designers are adept at giving us the illusion of choice through the options and menus that we are presented with, which take us down predetermined paths that reflect the needs of the platform or product. Who or what determines the suggested news we are fed, the search results we read or the options we are given is carefully orchestrated and managed.

- **Playing on our psychological need for social approval though intermittent variable rewards:** A key aim of product designers is to attract the user to a site or app and then keep them there. Harris highlights that one way in which this is achieved is by drawing on the experience of gambling and slot machines. The aim is to create an addiction through our desire for a possible reward: a new notification, a 'like', being 'tagged', a retweet, etc, whilst inviting us to 'swipe left' to see what comes next. Sometimes we are 'rewarded' and other times not. The element of variable reward combined with approval that someone 'likes' what we've said or done is a winning combination to keep us hooked.

- **Fear of 'missing something':** Playing on our desire to be 'in the loop', Harris points to how apps and sites encourage users to accept continual updates and feeds in order to avoid 'missing something'. This helps breed a culture of needing to be connected and to be online constantly. At the same time, such reminders and interruptions – alerts of the latest news or posts – are designed to grab our attention. It's not just the constant feeds that are designed to grab our attention. A great deal of thought and time has gone into how these alerts also distract us from what we're doing – Google's Gmail notifications are coloured red and placed in the upper right-hand corner of the screen. Both the colour and the location are designed and have been tested to have the maximum chance of making them hard to ignore.[7]

- **'Bottomless bowls' and 'autoplay':** As Harris points out, one way to keep people's attention is to keep feeding them, even when they are no longer hungry. News feeds, suggested links, 'clickbait' and autoplay on YouTube and Netflix keep you engaged. Algorithms suggest what to watch or look at next based on your previous activities, further fuelling and reinforcing attitudes and worldviews.

The point is that we may choose to shop at Amazon, watch YouTube, Tweet or post on any number of social media platforms, but our choice to do so isn't as free as we'd like to think. We may well be reflective and aware that we are the product and that the multitude of 'free' apps and information that

Google and others provide, from maps to word processing, are aimed at harvesting our data and monetising it. James Williams calls these hacks a vast project in industrialised persuasion.[8] Our digital providers seek to play on our vulnerabilities, to persuade us to spend time on their platforms and sites with the aim to make our smartphones as difficult to put down as it is difficult to quit smoking or give up on fast or processed food. And it's going to get more distracting because it *has* to.

> And because of the attention economy, every product will only get more persuasive over time. Facebook must become more persuasive if it wants to compete with YouTube and survive. YouTube must become more persuasive if it wants to compete with Facebook. And we're not just talking about "cheap" amusement (aka cat videos). These products will only get better at giving us choices that make every bone in our body say, "yeah I want that!"[9]

One could respond with a shrug of the shoulders – so what if we're addicted to Facebook or that YouTube manipulates us? It gives us pleasure, it makes our lives easier and provides us with information and services. Fair enough, but there are both individual and societal consequences to this immersion into social media and digital technology that, at the very least, we should be aware of. The Centre for Humane Technology sets out a number of consequences of digital persuasion as a first step in seeking to counter it.[10] These include:

- **Digital addiction and distraction:** The first repercussion is the most obvious, the extent to which we are addicted to and distracted by our smartphones, social media and digital existence. Half of teenagers and a quarter of adults feel addicted to their mobile phones. With the stakes in terms of revenue so high, it is hardly surprising that Big Tech uses every trick it can to keep us engaged.

- **Mental health:** At one level, social networking and the quantity of our relations have been greatly enhanced by digital technology. On the other hand, there is growing evidence that too much use of social media leaves people feeling isolated, depressed and lonely. One reason seems to be that we see superficial highlights of others' lives without the challenges and complications that we all face. Our own complex and messy lives will always fall short of such ideal and seemingly perfect existence. This shortfall also applies to our appearance. The term 'Snapchat dysmorphia' is used by doctors to describe the condition when patients seek plastic surgery to make their actual appearance closer to their modified or filtered online photos and selfies.[11] 'The pervasiveness of these filtered images can take a toll on one's self-esteem, make one feel inadequate for not looking a certain way in the real world, and may even act as a trigger and lead to Body Dysmorphic Disorder', claim researchers in *JAMA* (*Journal of the American Medical Association*).[12]

- **Fuzzying of facts and truth:** The Center for Humane Technology is by no means alone in highlighting that the huge advances in online communication and information have also spawned a corresponding increase in fake news, misinformation and downright lies. A study of videos hosted on YouTube concerning climate change found that 89 videos of the 200 in the sample supported scientific consensus views about anthropogenic climate change, although the majority of the videos in the sample (107 videos) supported worldviews that oppose scientific consensus views: 16 denied anthropogenic climate change and 91 propagated straightforward conspiracy theories about climate engineering and climate change.[13] In a study of the diffusion of true and false stories on Twitter, it was found that falsehoods diffused significantly farther, faster, deeper and more broadly than the truth in all categories of information, and the effects were more pronounced for false political news than for false news about terrorism, natural disasters, science, urban myths or financial information. The main reason for this faster dissemination was that false news was more novel than true news, which suggests that people were more likely to share novel information. Whilst false stories inspired fear, disgust and surprise in replies, true stories inspired anticipation, sadness, joy and trust.[14] Sites that host views and are a source of information take little, if any, responsibility for content, largely because it would be expensive and time-consuming to do so.

- **Political polarisation:** The promise that the digital age would facilitate debate across the political spectrum, equalise access to information, and expose arguments to evidence and counter-argument has failed to materialise. Instead, social media and the over-abundance of information and views has had another, less desirable, outcome. The accusation backed up by evidence is that we are attracted to groups that share our worldview and opinions that reinforce our own, and that algorithms that select news feeds reinforce and even amplify our online choices, dramatically limiting our exposure to views and information that don't match already-established beliefs. This makes politics and the search for common ground difficult, if not impossible. According to Cass Sunstein, author of *#Republic: Divided Democracy in the Age of Social Media,*[15] the main problem of echo chambers and bubbles of homogeneity is '… group polarization, which means that if you listen to people like you, you'll probably get more extreme and more confident too. If Republicans talk or listen to each other, they'll probably become more extreme, and the same is true for Democrats. We've seen plenty of that, and we're going to see more.'[16]

- **Political manipulation:** There has been a good deal written about how the likes of Facebook, Twitter and other social media platforms were vehicles for election and referendum manipulation, from the US presidential election in 2016 to the UK's vote to leave the EU in the same year. An estimated 150 million Americans were reached by Russian-backed propaganda in the 2016 presidential election, whilst 18.5 per cent of all Tweets from the top 50,000 came from Bots during the election. In fact, one study found that Twitter posted more misinformation, and polarising and conspiratorial content during the 2016 presidential election than real news.[17] Journalists increasingly rely on Twitter for news themselves, further disseminating, reinforcing and legitimising misinformation. As one study of journalism and Twitter found:

> The routinization of Twitter into news production affects news judgment – for journalists who incorporate Twitter into their reporting routines, and those with fewer years of experience, Twitter has become so normalized that tweets were deemed equally newsworthy as headlines appearing to be from the AP wire. This may have negative implications, such as pack journalism, but we also see positives, as Twitter may conduit a wider array of voices into the mainstream news agenda.[18]

- **Superficiality:** Whilst the overall levels of communication and connectivity have increased through digital technology, the impacts have not been entirely positive at the level of personal interaction. The shift to electronic and text-related exchanges and communication inevitably reduces face-to-face human interaction. Actual, as opposed to 'at a distance', interaction has been found to be far more effective for understanding opposing viewpoints and creating empathy.[19] Reinforcing this tendency, the various sites that provide platforms encourage binary, superficial interactions – we are encouraged to give something a 'thumbs up' or 'thumbs down'. These immediate, uncomplicated responses provide great 'clickbait' for the platforms and their attempts to get us to interact and spend more time online, but they do not encourage anything beyond the extremes of hate or delight. Understanding different viewpoints and the complexity of different perspectives is discouraged. The upshot of this different, more superficial, form of communication is that although we have never been more connected, we are actually further apart.

Let's be clear, there are huge upsides to social media and personal digital connectivity, benefits that came to the fore during the coronavirus pandemic in 2020 as swathes of individuals, employers and society moved online. Empty offices and full homes had downsides too. But there are also other, more fundamental, issues to be considered. Evidence on the less positive impacts of digital technology and social media on individuals is growing but is overshadowed by the shiny attractiveness of unlimited connectivity. And the attraction isn't hard to fathom:

> If I had to summarize it, it's this: Our phone puts a new choice on life's menu, in any moment, that's "sweeter" than reality. If, at any moment, reality gets dull or boring, our phone offers something more pleasurable, more productive and even more educational than whatever reality gives us.[20]

Yet if there are personal upsides and consequences, do these impacts scale? At one level there would seem to be a clear repercussion: if we are distracted and paying attention to our virtual worlds, there is less time and attention being paid to our physical, real worlds. For the majority of us, those real worlds are cities.

Attention and cities

If we are distracted – consciously or through digital addiction and persuasion – then it would be natural to assume that our attention is in one place and not another, and there are opportunity costs for what we could have done instead. Yet attention is a tricky issue to pin down. At one level we can see how attention is somehow a 'fixed' commodity, with one thing having our attention at the expense of another. However, attention is not always immediate or binary. We can do one thing such as checking our Facebook feed on our smartphone whilst we do another, such as going for a walk. According to Williams, attention and distraction also go beyond the immediate and personal to include our broader capacities that set our goals and values as well as reason and intelligence and the ability to define goals and values. To capture these differences and nuances, Williams proposes a three-tier typology of attention: attention to *knowing*, *being* and *doing*.[21]

- **Attention to knowing:** For Williams, this is the most profound level of attention, one that allows us to define our goals and values, to form general principles and concepts beyond the day-to-day and immediate that would otherwise leave us with only impulses. Knowing is critical for democratic thinking and reflection as it is the basis for longer-term vision and direction, including the need to cede on some matters to achieve others – trade-offs and compromise, the basis of politics. Distraction to knowing can come in many forms, both through the immediate activities of checking our smartphones or news feeds or through the longer-term consequences of fuzzing facts and truth along with the state of superficiality that the digital age brings with it. Another way in which our attention to knowing is undermined is through the blurring of work and leisure, or engagement and downtime. The latter is necessary for us to recover and rest, and it is during this downtime that we think most creatively and constructively. As Williams also points out, 'Leisure also uniquely enables the kind of thinking and deliberation necessary for the thoughtful invention of societal institutions'.[22] Yet we are less 'switched off', and there is little, if any, respite from online reminders as our digital world colonises all aspects of our lives.

- **Attention to being:** If attention to knowing provides us with goals and values – a destination – then attention to being allows us to maintain a course to reach them in our lives. 'Being' is akin to our GPS system, shaping decisions on how we reach our goals. The cumulative impact of distraction on our alignment with our identities and values affects how we come together to agree shared identities and directions. One of the ways in which attention to being is undermined is through the 'compare and contrast' upshot of digital living, discussed above. The constant presence of ideal, perfect lives in our virtual worlds distracts us from our own identities and ideals, whilst the focus on the number of friends or connections is at the expense of the quality or depth of fewer, more meaningful, social relations. Another channel of distraction from being highlighted by Williams concerns what he terms pettiness, or the atomisation of politics; that is, the encouragement to 'like' or 'dislike', 'Twitter wars' of 'flaming' and the disintegration of agreed-on principles and values.[23]

Williams talks of the erosion of shared identity as more than simply political polarisation that could be bridged through argument and debate – essentially, the nature of politics. Instead, he sees a deeper discord emerging as a result of digital and online interaction, one that leads to a loss of political will, of motivation to engage and act. If positions and arguments are incommensurable, then why bother trying to reconcile them? The natural reaction is to withdraw into a smaller, even individualistic position. The other upshot is indecision founded on a surfeit of information and opinions. Williams quotes Charles Taylor to this end: 'the danger is not actual despotic control but fragmentation – that is, a people increasingly less capable of forming a common purpose and carrying it out'.[24] The rise of virtual gated communities will be increasingly reflected in our real world cities.

- **Attention to doing:** Digital technology provides many distractions and alternatives to the 'real world', many far more attractive than what it is we should be doing at that moment. It also feeds us with constant updates and notifications, from emails to posts on social media sites, grabbing our attention even if we choose to carry on with what we were doing before we were interrupted. Such distractions compete not only with our inner tasks and priorities but also with each other to grab our attention and keep it. The lack of attention to actually doing and completing tasks is replaced by a constant state of indecision and fluidity, our focus dispersed from what it is we set out to achieve or do, be it activism on an issue, responding to public consultation or lobbying our political representatives.

Williams' framework provides a really helpful starting point in translating the distracting, attention-grabbing impacts of the attention economy from the personal to the broader city level. As far as cities go we could develop this typology further on the basis that cities require attention at different 'levels' too; for example, at the spatial or physical level (what does this area need and want? What are the challenges?), at the political level (how do we make trade-offs against different needs and meet challenges? How do we pay for them?) and at a longer-term, visionary level (what is a successful city? How do we get there?). Taking this framework and transposing it onto cities is not to suggest that individual-level distractions are somehow unimportant to the city – clearly they are. What I'm suggesting is an approach to link individual attention to the kinds of focus that functioning, successful cities need and the ways in which we can begin to approach this. In other words, in what ways is digital distraction impacting on city planning?

In city planning there is a long-standing and common hierarchical process for managing and shaping change. This common approach to city planning emerged in the 18th and 19th centuries and broadly seeks to separate ends from the means to achieve those ends. In other words, the ends, or desired outcome of a city plan, should be determined through an open, democratic and rational process as far as possible, based on evidence and analysis. The means to achieve these ends could then be developed by a cadre of relevant professionals in consultation with wider stakeholders including the public. Finally, the actions or implementation of the plan are through direct intervention (the city doing 'something' such as building a road or promoting an initiative) or through regulation of the activity of others (what is built and where). The city, therefore, also needs different capacities in order to function and plan. These three capacities, which shape the approaches to city planning in different jurisdictions, map onto Williams' typology, with the 'ends' or goals for the city (sustainable city, smart city, resilient city, etc) corresponding to 'knowing', plans and strategies to achieve the goals being akin to 'being' and the actions or implementations corresponding to 'doing' (see Table 1).

What Table 1 seeks to highlight is how distraction of our individual capacities to know, be and do has wider consequences, in our case, for city planning. However, those consequences could also be seen to have implications for other areas of life,

Table 1: Typology of distraction and city planning

	Williams' typology of individual distraction	City level equivalent distraction	Relevant key issues/ questions for cities in each category
Knowing	Attention economy leads to distraction from our values and long-term vision	Attention economy leads to distraction from city vision, goals and principles, eg, sustainable city, smart city, resilient city, enterprise city, etc	**What constitutes a good city?** What counts as the city? What is the balance between the collective and the individual? Why are things the way they are and what can we do about it?
Being	Attention economy leads to distraction from actions to keep us on course to achieve our values and vision	Attention economy distracts from formulation of city plans and strategies that seeks to move them towards the vision for the city, eg, transport plan, land use strategy, homelessness strategy	**How do we achieve the good city?** What are the social, economic and environmental needs and constraints? How do we reconcile competing demands and needs in the city? What resources and spatial scales are necessary to take forward the city plan?
Doing	Attention economy distracts us from our day-to-day tasks	Attention economy distracts from actions to deliver strategy and plans, eg, provides alternatives to engagement and involvement	**What actions are necessary to ensure we achieve our vision?** How do we make the process of decision-making in cities inclusive and open? How do we build a consensus around actions? What information and data are needed to help inform decisions?

Source: Author's own

such as politics or other policy sectors including climate change or economic growth. The final column in Table 1 highlights some of the questions and key issues that are typically asked as part of the process of planning and management, as I go on to explain overleaf.

Distractions in city planning and management

Cities around the globe are, for the most part, planned and managed. Whilst the approach and mechanisms vary depending on the legal and constitutional framework (for example, federal or unitary systems, common or civil legal codes), and the bureaucratic and political traditions and customs, there is a prevalent underlying approach based around a typical process (see Figure 1). The broad approach flows from the three-tier distinction of distraction set out in Table 1; that is, vision, plan/strategy and action/implementation.

The process outlined above adds three dimensions to the three-tier distinction in Table 1. First, the approach to city planning and management typically involves what is broadly known as the survey–analysis–plan (SAP) process. Whilst evidence-led

Figure 1: Typical city planning process

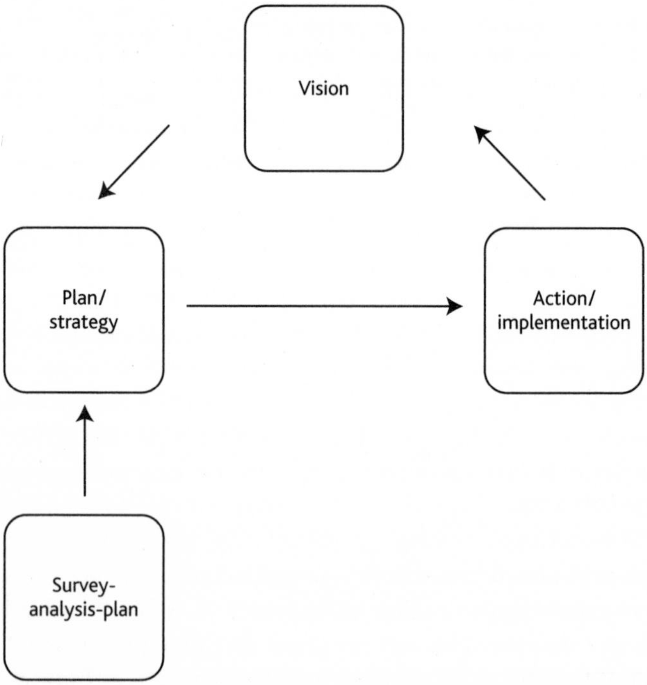

Source: Author's own

policy goes back as far as the Domesday Book, it was Scottish biologist, geographer and town planner Patrick Geddes (1854–1932) who championed this systematic and rational approach in city planning. For Geddes, any intervention in the city needed to put 'diagnosis before treatment', departing from the then dominant design-led view of planning (for example, how to improve cities through the design of buildings and the spaces between them) to embrace a more holistic social, economic and environmental understanding (for example, what factors have led to concentrations of poverty and ill health in some parts of the city). For us it might seem axiomatic that one would need to know how many people lived in a place and how that number had changed and was likely to change in the future in order to be able to address needs such as housing, schools, healthcare and transport.

Yet the dominant understanding of planning at the time was a much narrower conception that focused on the design of buildings or addressing specific issues such as slum clearance and building standards. The comprehensive, whole-place approach to and understanding of planning was introduced by Geddes and has subsequently underpinned city planning around the globe. Collecting and analysing data and information provides the basis for knowing what we are dealing with and allows monitoring of progress towards the vision. A vision for a sustainable city would ideally need to know how much energy is used, how that usage is spread across communities and different uses, and what the future demand is likely to be, for example – the kinds of questions posed in the final column of Table 1. This technical, background work for the plan doesn't provide all the answers, however. Sustainable living can be achieved in a variety of ways that involve trade-offs and choices: one choice would be between a dispersed settlement pattern with energy-efficient public transport or a more compact approach based on a high-density urban form.

Obviously this process is not instantaneous and neither is it entirely linear. A typical city plan will take two to four years to prepare in order to engage individuals and communities fully. There is also the need to reflect and revisit assumptions if, for example, public involvement raises new issues and data needs. The point here is that given the timescale and complexity of the process, there are more than adequate opportunities for distraction.

Distraction and city planning

With this broad heuristic in mind, how is city planning being affected by digital distraction? The first point to make is that the process of city planning is being simultaneously supplemented *and* undermined by digital technology. Online access to information is providing huge opportunities to engage with city planning processes, whilst visualisation techniques and scenario modelling open up opportunities and options. Yet there are other impacts and consequences that are distracting from the process. Two broad trends stand out. The first is the growing movement to standardise data and the SAP process in order to make city planning more suitable for remote, automated data gathering and monitoring and to enable greater use of AI and machine learning techniques. The UK's National Audit Office (NAO), for example, is encouraging standardised collection and analysis of data on climate change and biodiversity as part of the push to meet the UN's Sustainable Development Goals (SDGs).[25] At the same time, research is ongoing at the national Alan Turing Institute on automating population projections and human behavioural responses to different urban simulations,[26] and further AI-related research is looking into what people find to be beautiful or aesthetically pleasing in design.[27,28] The overall direction of travel is to reduce discretion and increase the ability to take the decision-making process into the realm of computation and automation. There are some advantages to this, including speed, reduced costs and consistency. But these upsides sit alongside downsides too. Who decides what factors are included and given weight in the decision-making process, and how can decisions made this way be accountable and explained? Who is accountable, and how can a decision be challenged if it is based on statistics and probability?

In some ways these shifts are a self-fulfilling prophecy for planning, as I discuss further in Chapter 7: if the vision is for a smart city, then digital technology becomes the goal (being) and the means (doing) to achieve it. In other words, we are creating a situation where distraction isn't just a consequence of some external growth in digital technology, but is also baked into the very processes that are being undermined. Like food and tobacco, we are feeding an addiction to digital by narrowing choice and options in how we go about city planning, particularly in what Williams categorises as 'being' and 'doing'.

Looking beyond these more immediate impacts there are wider forces of distraction at work on city planning processes. The timescales involved in preparing a plan, including public involvement and implementation, no longer align with the pace of change and disruption that digital technology is bringing to our cities. As I covered in Chapter 3, there are multiple and fundamental impacts on our cities, from changes in employment and economic activity to housing affordability. The scope of policy interventions is also being diminished as the traditional levers that support city planning and management are themselves being undermined.

Table 2 provides a broad picture of the kinds of levers that have traditionally been employed in cities to help shape decisions and actions. Whilst the detailed instruments will differ from city to city, they broadly fit within these four categories.

As well as supplementing some of the levers of city planning, providing unparalleled access to information and opening up new avenues for engagement, all the tools that cities have at their disposal have also been affected to greater and lesser degrees by digital technology, making them less effective in helping manage our cities. And when something is less effective, we tend to look for alternatives to achieve the impact we desire. This is a search that is helped by the promises of smart cities, particularly the enticement of AI and machine learning doing all this messy, time-consuming and costly stuff for us.

There are, then, two broad upshots from the impacts of digital technology on city planning. First, not only are we distracted by digital technology; we are also losing our faith in city planning too as it becomes less effective. If planning is less likely to be able to make a difference, we are less likely to want to engage with it. Evidence for this is clear, and one only needs to look to the high street for an example of how planning is losing control. City planning seeks to control which buildings

Table 2: Levers of change in the digital age

Traditional city planning levers of change	Impact on levers in the digital age
Information: Support decision-making and actions by collecting data and publishing information, eg, the availability of support to businesses, the extent of air pollution, traffic congestion, etc	Information abundance, fake news, etc reduce effectiveness
Policies and plans: Shape decision-making and actions by coordinating public and private investment and directing change around agreed areas/issues	Slow to adapt and agree compared to the scale and speed of change
Regulating: Directing and controlling decisions and actions through laws and the requirement to obtain permits and permissions	What to regulate? The platform economy has little physical presence in cities. How to control Airbnb, Uber, etc and mitigate their impact is notoriously difficult
Intervening: City authorities can intervene directly through, for example, investing in housing developments and improvements, shifting taxation to change behaviour, supporting public transport and providing startup accommodation for businesses	Seismic shifts in economic and social foundations of cities raising existential questions about what to intervene in – how can cities reverse the decline of bricks and mortar shopping and should they bother? How can they tax online activity?

Source: Author's own

in the high street are shops, fast food takeaways, homes, and so on in order to provide a balance and to avoid too many negative impacts such as traffic generation or noise impacting on residents. Changes to these uses are being driven not by planning but by disruption wrought by digital technology, with shops closing as we move online, takeaways delivering directly through Deliveroo and homes being rented out through Airbnb. Cities and city planning are left with few levers to effect change, so why engage with it? Second, many see the very cause of this distraction and disinterest not as the problem but as the solution, creating a vicious circle of distraction and decline. For some cities the tipping point has been reached, and smart is now taking on city planning with the enthusiastic support of planners, city managers and politicians, as I discuss in Chapter 7.

Why distraction is bad for cities (and planning is good for them)

It is by no means universally agreed that distraction from city planning and management is a 'bad thing'. For some, state-led planning and management is philosophically and practically flawed. Cities emerge through a multiplicity of individual decisions, and attempts at planning and management of cities are not only philosophically wrong-headed but also impractical and impossible – how can planners and others possibly capture, analyse and then predict the decisions and preferences of all those in cities? This is a more libertarian perspective, and one that would assign, if any, a much narrower function for city management and planning in providing information for markets to operate more efficiently. Yet this is a minority view and one that even in the most market-led societies does not prevail when it comes to cities. The simple fact is that successful cities are critical for successful national economies – they're too important to be left to the whims of the market. Successful cities are planned cities.

Putting aside the hype and boosterism around tables and rankings of 'the most liveable cities' or 'the most sustainable cities', there is a broad and strong correlation between those cities that consistently populate the higher end of such indices and a commitment to city planning and management. Cities such as Vienna, Melbourne, Sydney, Osaka, Calgary, Vancouver, Toronto and Copenhagen consistently populate such indices, which use a range of indicators including safety, architecture, public transport, urban design and what is broadly termed a proactive policy appetite – in other words, city planning and management. But not just any city planning and management. These are also cities that approach these issues in open and inclusive ways, using digital technology as a tool to support liveability. They have another characteristic too: they don't pretend that difficult choices do not exist but face up to them rather than running to digital as the solution.

There are many examples of what happens when cities attempt to 'smooth over' difference and instead seek ways forward that sideline necessary 'friction'. In Stuttgart the decision to redevelop the central railway station without a full discussion and public mandate led to riots. In Aalborg a major redevelopment of the city centre led to the breakdown of trust with the city council and was compared to something that Machiavelli would have been proud of.[29] These are not examples taken from the digital age but a warning of what happens when we seek to 'flatten' our cities, take away the sharp edges and treat citizens like children – you can have everything rather than having to choose. Distraction feeds this condition, taking away our attention whilst shifting the responsibility of making difficult and necessary choices (cars versus bikes, housing versus jobs, schools versus tax cuts) to the smart city where such decisions magically disappear. It's a short-term palliative rather than long-term investment.

What successful cities need is engagement, not transactional options, because city planning takes time. Swiping left to decide between one thing and another misses the deeper immersion and understanding necessary for the kinds of issues that planning needs to focus on, particularly the climate emergency and carbon reduction. These are political as well as technical challenges that require trade-offs and compromise.

Paying attention to the city

If we want our cities to thrive and be successful, we need to give them attention. Right now our focus is elsewhere and cities are being overtaken by a multitude of digital challenges and disruptions that we are indifferent towards. It's this indifference and neglect that represents the greatest challenge our cities face. Traditionally, one could look at this issue as a supply or demand-side challenge: is the lack of attention because we are not competing in the marketplace, making it attractive and persuading people to engage, or is it a demand-side issue where people simply prioritise other ways to spend their time regardless of how important the future of the city is? But this is to ignore the ways in which the market is being fixed. When society faces a problem of addiction with clear consequences for the individual and the wider community, then the usual course of action is to step in and seek to level the playing field, with health warnings on packets of cigarettes and high taxation or the 'sugar tax' on junk food. In the case of digital, we are actually facilitating the rollout through smart cities, highlighting the positives and ignoring the downsides, making smart the vision (the 'knowing', in Williams' phrase) rather than a tool in the means to achieving a successful city.

The question cities need to pose is how does digital support rather than distract from what is needed for cities to thrive? I turn to this question in Chapter 10. First, it's necessary to identify what smart cities should be about and how they can address the problems of cities, not create them.

6

Our disconnected cities:
what 'smart' should be about

For cities around the globe, 2020 was a seismic year, given the various impacts of COVID-19. Whilst some commentators called time of death on the city,[1] others claimed that what we were experiencing was an acceleration of ongoing trends.[2] What was agreed was that cities of the future would be very different in function and composition from those in the early part of the 21st century. But just how different was left very open. Yet the future of cities is unlikely to be one of universal abandonment: cities are the engines of economic growth across the globe, their power and influence increasing in inverse proportion to the decline in significance of the nation states that host them.

In an era characterised by global movements of people, money, goods and services, it is cities rather than countries that have become the primary focus for growth. As a consequence there has been a rush to become a world or global city, to be in the elite club of city-states. Some world cities such as London, Paris, Hong Kong, New York and San Francisco have enjoyed significant economic success in recent years, pulling ahead of the pack, attracting investment, people and attention, and using their clout and influence to good effect. Many other cities have lagged behind. These are our forgotten cities, our cities on the edge. In some of these places there is serious and persistent deprivation and poverty for those out of work and for those in precarious and low-paid employment, places such as Glasgow, Liverpool and Manchester in the UK, and Detroit, Pittsburgh and Baltimore in the US. In the UK's 2019 Index of Multiple Deprivation, Liverpool, Middlesbrough, Kingston upon Hull and Manchester topped the list of places characterised by deprivation, positions that have remained largely unchanged since 2015.[3] Not only are these cities suffering from multiple deprivation – low incomes, poor skills and education, high crime, low employment – they seem unable to break out and improve, falling further behind the leading pack as they surge ahead.

Yet to present a picture in black and white, of flourishing global cities on the one hand, and relative and absolute declining cities on the other, would be an over-simplification. Even in the thriving cities, all is not well. Globally prosperous places are not flourishing for everyone, particularly many of those at the forefront of the digital revolution. The growth in skilled and well-paid jobs in these cities has largely benefited a small proportion of nationally and internationally mobile workers able to take advantage of the opportunities. Many people and communities within successful cities remain disconnected from the connected economy as income and wealth inequalities widen. This can lead to residualisation and a decline in civic engagement as areas become increasingly isolated from growth and opportunities close by. London is the most unequal city in the UK, having the highest per capita income as well as seven out of the top ten areas of highest income deprivation in the country.[4] Growing inequality is a feature of many cities, particularly in the UK and the US. Seven of the ten poorest regions in Europe are in England, and they sit alongside the richest region in Europe, inner London. Urban inequality in the US is growing rapidly, increasing in almost two-thirds of metropolitan areas between 2006 and 2012, whilst wage inequality has increased significantly over the past 30 years and is now approaching levels last experienced prior to the Great Depression during the 1930s. To adapt a phrase beloved of the New Right in the 1980s, a rising tide has not lifted all boats. Instead, one could say that it has lifted the yachts, but left the dinghies to take in water.

But disconnection isn't just economic – people are being left behind in terms of health, physical environment, life chances and political influence. Often these issues are themselves multiple, overlapping and connected. Take health. Dr Phil Cumberlidge, a doctor in Liverpool, describes the frustration that he feels when many of his patients tell him about their lives:

> Imagine being a single parent after finally getting away from your abusive alcoholic boyfriend. Your baby is unwell and frequently in hospital. You have no family support. No money. Your flat is surrounded by drug users and alcoholics.[5]

As Dr Cumberlidge points out, the challenge for our health services is that the array of medical options he can offer cannot address what are deep social and economic issues in our cities, problems of disadvantage and inequality. What doctors can do and are often asked to do by patients is to prescribe antidepressants. Others who are in similar dire situations turn to legal and illegal opioids such as heroin and fentanyl, whilst alcohol remains an option for many. What Angus Deaton calls 'deaths of despair'[6] and others label 'shit life syndrome' captures the reality of poverty and neglect that exists side-by-side with pockets of affluence and plenty. For many, digital technology and social media provide an escape from the real world into virtual worlds, an opportunity to avoid dire conditions. And it is through this same social media that the easy analyses and slogans of blame for these conditions, whether it's immigrants, the 'deep state' or 'fake news media', are also peddled. These, and more, are the actual problems our cities face, problems that digital technology is somehow, vaguely, promising to fix.

If many in our cities suffer from 'shit life syndrome', then the question back to the digital evangelists and smart cities is, 'how will technology make people's lives less shit?' A leading smart city evangelist, Carlo Ratti, Director of the MIT Senseable City Lab, would no doubt point to one of his projects that is concerned with actual shit, where researchers in the Lab are analysing human waste in different parts of Boston in order to map where there has been a jump in opioid use or a contaminated batch of heroin. The idea is that knowledge of such 'hot spots' would allow better and more responsive health planning. The same approach could also be used to monitor the outbreaks of viruses or diseases, the researchers argue.

This is a well-worn and valuable tool in city planning, one pioneered by John Snow in the mid-19th century when he mapped and linked cholera outbreaks to water supplies in London, a process that eventually led to major public health interventions and improvements. Others promoting smart futures for cities also promise digital solutions for social challenges. IBM offers to help address the complex problems of drug addiction, intergenerational poverty, unemployment and homelessness that many cities are grappling with. Yet their 'solution' is one based on bringing together different databases of people and places in order to mine the data for patterns, suggesting that public bodies can then spot fraud, save money by dealing with people more efficiently, whilst also alerting them when individuals do not meet commitments. Clearly, this isn't about helping people or tackling the challenges they face; it won't reduce homelessness or drug dependency; and it certainly won't make people's lives less shit.

The current rollout of smart is a narrow one, focused on making services run more efficiently and, in some cases, more effectively. At present digital technology has very little to say on the social and environmental challenges facing our cities and the many who live in them – the motivation for digital is the opportunity to sell products and services, creating markets and improving market share. At one level this is understandable – (over)-selling products and services is what companies do. Except for three points. First, smart cities and Big Tech are promising and offering much more than simply making services run more efficiently. Smart is the prefix for anything and everything, the vague, attractive, near-future solution to complex, sometime intractable, problems. Why bother understanding never mind addressing knotty, interconnected, individually specific challenges like drug dependency and homelessness that require time-consuming and costly solutions when there is a promise of an easy, digital answer?

Second, smart and digital are capturing the political agenda, shifting the focus and providing answers to questions that they are posing. Under the smart city umbrella the challenge of traffic congestion becomes one of traffic flow optimisation, or how to get more cars into our cities by better management of road junctions, rather than one of reducing access to private vehicles and investment in public transport. These kinds of choices are deeply political and involve trade-offs and difficult, contested decisions that will benefit some and not others. This is the stuff of politics, yet smart is displacing the political, providing incremental, technical, 'everyone wins' solutions that defer such clashes and difficult choices. This leads on to the third issue. No technologies, including digital, are neutral in the sense of being available and beneficial to all. They reflect, reinforce and exacerbate existing inequalities in society. In fact, there is a growing body of opinion that argues that digital technology is *increasing* inequality both between developing *and* developed nations and within nations and cities. As Tim Unwin, UNESCO Professor at Royal Holloway, has put it:

> … [digital] technologies can reduce inequalities, but the hidden, ugly secret of "digital development" is that instead of improving the lives of the poorest and most marginalised, such technologies have actually dramatically increased inequality at all scales, from the global to the local.[7]

The local impacts are, perhaps, the most visible given the contrast between the winners and losers. One Delhi-born resident, Vivek Wadhwa, now resident of Palo Alto, commented on the poverty rate in Silicon Valley, where around one-fifth of residents are classified as poor:

> You have people begging in the street on University Avenue [Palo Alto's main street]. It's like what you see in India. Silicon Valley is a look at the future we're creating, and it's really disturbing.[8]

But it doesn't have to be this way. Some countries, such as the US and the UK, are characterised by high levels of economic growth matched by increasing inequality, whilst there are others, such as Sweden, Finland and Denmark, that manage to achieve high levels of growth but that are characterised by much lower levels of inequality.[9]

Digital technology and smart cannot be held responsible for all the challenges cities face, including inequality: fiscal policy, globalisation, deregulation, education and austerity policies all have their role to play. But digital and smart have not only contributed to challenges; they are promising to solve some of them too – 'governing through code', as it's been put. If smart cities and digital technology are capturing the urban agenda and taking us down a road that not only isn't helping but is actually making matters worse, then what should smart be about?

Disconnection in our connected cities

There is an evangelising zeal around the potential benefits from making our cities 'smarter':

> ... real-time applications are now delivering rich, digitally brewed serendipity, and rather than neutering urban space, networked systems are becoming the new interface with the physical world. Each smartphone communicates in real time with a constellation of phones, businesses, and networks surrounding it.[10]

Whatever the issue or challenge our cities face, digital technology has a solution, a way in which it can somehow make things better, more efficient, more connected. And for some, digital technology and the digital city have been hugely disruptive and beneficial. Advertisers, for example, have moved from casting a wide net to sell us things through printed adverts in wide circulation newspapers and via TV to bespoke, targeted appeals based on a detailed knowledge of individual preferences and choices. We have become the data point of the product, as many have pointed out. Individualising products and services means that car and health insurance can be tailored to us, reducing our premiums as companies better understand and price individual risk. In other areas AI and machine learning are being applied to a wide range of areas including health, with the promise that it will soon out-perform humans in diagnostics.

Transport and traffic are facing their own disruptions as autonomous vehicles are being developed and trialled that will eventually replace human drivers, thereby offering the potential to reduce accidents, injuries and deaths on our roads. As traditional manufacturing industries decline, millions are now employed in the mushrooming web development and IT industries, as well as those finding jobs at the 'front end' of the platform economy, packing and delivering the things we pick online. These current and near-future changes are not science fiction but science fact.

Contrast this with the reality for many who live in cities recorded by Chris Arndale. After working as a bond trader on Wall Street for 20 years, Arndale began to chronicle and photograph the lives of those left behind in US cities, among them the homeless, the sex workers and the drug addicts. His book *Dignity*[11] lays bare the urban reality for many. Visiting Portsmouth, Ohio, he points out that since its peak in the 1940s, when it was a centre for the manufacture of steel, shoes and bricks, it is now struggling to survive, with the factories and jobs mostly gone, and having shrunk to half its former size. In place of the jobs have come drugs. Like many of the cities and towns that Arndale visits it is the local McDonald's that provides the hub, the gathering point for the dispossessed and homeless. As Arndale explains, without a home, they need clean water, a power point to charge a phone and a place to get free Wi-Fi. The fast food chain provides all of these, along with cheap food. The daily routine for the homeless is a midday start in McDonald's, using the bathrooms to clean up and sometimes shoot up, using the wing mirrors of cars in the car park to put on make-up, then spending the afternoon and as much as the evening as possible at a table, avoiding the cold or heat. This is a place where those left behind can still engage with society of sorts, where they can meet and, critically, where they can access the digital world.

How can we reconcile these two contrasting views and experiences of the connected city? To paraphrase Dickens, we have a tale of two *kinds* of city. If we recall the experiences of other stories of the city recounted in Chapter 1, there has always been a dominant, optimistic and partial view of the city, a perspective that favoured certain groups and interests over others. The 'city of the dark night' ditched the city, encouraging those who could leave to relocate, overlooking and leaving behind those who didn't have the means to move. The 'city of bright lights' focused on the winners, boosting the image of the city as a place of opportunity and rewards for those who put in the effort, coaxing those left behind to jump on board and improve themselves. What we are facing right now is another story of the city, one that favours certain groups and interests over others, one that focuses our attention on some issues and not others, and one that promises to solve the challenges if only we embrace the potential of smart.

The first and most obvious point to make is that despite vague and overstated claims, digital connectivity is not the panacea to the challenges our cities face. Digital technology and the smart city promise to connect places and people, compressing time and space, creating and linking data to provide opportunities to improve lives. Yet such glib promises mask the reality of digital linkages, a reality that is more selective, complex and subtle. The networked city brings with it the notion of equality of connection – everywhere and everyone can benefit equally from the smart, digital city. Yet, as I have argued in previous chapters, the digital connected city bypasses some areas that are physically close in favour of other, less proximate, spaces. International financial markets work seamlessly as London, New York and Tokyo exchange information and trade across continents around the clock. Financial or tech workers in New York have needs and experiences that are more similar to those of financial or tech workers over 3,000 miles away in London than they are to those of many who live in the same city as themselves. These new digital 'spaces of flows',[12] as they have been termed, create and reinforce rather than dissipate and rebalance segregation and inequality, splintering the city further.

This unequal impact on people and cities is nothing new but it is being fuelled by a range of factors, including globalisation, although digital technology has a significant role to play. The upshot is that there is an elite club of global cities, sucking in investment and skilled workers and dominating national economies. Ahead of the pack, by some way, are New York and London, followed by a cluster of cities including Paris, Tokyo,

Singapore and Hong Kong.[13] These cities dominate the national and global economies – London accounts for more than 30 per cent of the UK's entire economy, despite representing around 15 per cent of the population. And the gap is growing.

According to the UK Office for National Statistics (ONS), the economy of the capital grew by 19 per cent between 2012 and 2019 compared to less than 6 per cent for the North East of England in the same period. Globalisation – the freeing up of the movement of ideas, people and finance – has fuelled this gap between a small, rarefied group of cities and the rest.

Across Europe, research has highlighted what has been termed a 'big sort' in major cities[14] as experiences of post-industrialisation vary. Some areas and cities have suffered relative and absolute decline, failing to replace lost jobs and industries, whilst others, such as Paris, London and Milan, have more than substituted lost employment with new, service-related jobs including digital. There is also a growing relationship between these elite urban centres as they increasingly look to each other rather than neighbouring cities or national governments for investment and skilled workers, given their common experiences and challenges. If a tech startup needs investment, it is more likely to secure it if it has the 'right address', such as London, San Francisco, and so on, whilst those companies that provide investment and services also locate themselves in these places. The Brookings Institution has highlighted that just five top innovation metro areas in the US – Boston, San Francisco, San Jose, Seattle and San Diego – accounted for more than 90 per cent of the nation's innovation sector growth during the years 2005 to 2017.[15] The majority of cities have been left behind by this growth and success, many characterised by poverty, deprivation and disadvantage, as Arndale chronicles.[16]

There is disconnection in and between our connected cities. So how do we shape digital connectivity and the smart city to help create more equal cities and benefit the lives of those left behind? The answer is to actively focus digital technology on the needs of cities, moving from technology-led to people-led smart cities. The needs of cities and people vary, but there are two pressing issues or disconnections: income and wealth disconnection, and housing disconnection.

Income and wealth disconnection

Cities have always been unequal, but the gap between the wealthy and the rest is widening, a gulf that has been growing over the past three decades.[17] Analysis by the Centre for Cities highlights the disparities in inequality of UK cities. Using the Gini coefficient (a measure of inequality from 0 to 1, with 0 representing equality and 1 extreme inequality), the analysis highlights Cambridge, Oxford and London as the most unequal cities in the UK, with coefficients of 0.460, 0.453 and 0.444 respectively, whilst Mansfield, Bury and Stoke are the most equal, all with the same score of 0.379.[18] For comparison, Mexico, one of the world's most unequal countries, has a Gini coefficient of 0.46. The figures for US cities are more extreme, with coefficients for cities such as New York, Miami and San Francisco of 0.504, 0.496 and 0.475, respectively, whereas San Jose, the tech city at the centre of Silicon Valley, has the highest wage inequality in the US, with someone in the top 10 per cent making more than seven times that of someone in the bottom 10 per cent.[19]

Those cities that have the widest income inequality gaps are the ones that have been the most economically successful – San Francisco, New York, London and Paris in particular. Whilst these cities as a whole have powered ahead, their success has been grabbed by the already wealthy. Since 2008, the top 1 per cent of earners in the US has captured more than 85 per cent of all income growth.[20] At the same time, real wages at the lower end of the income scale have fallen whilst housing costs have risen. This means that widening inequality has been driven by both rising incomes for the wealthy and declining incomes for the majority. Forecasts by the Institute for Fiscal Studies in the UK point to this gap widening up to 2021/22, at which point the UK will have the highest income inequality since comparable records began in 1961. The impacts of COVID-19 are likely to further widen inequalities across nations and within and between cities. Again, widening inequality will be driven by growth in real earnings mostly benefiting higher-income households whilst cuts in the real value of working-age benefits are expected to reduce the incomes of poorer households.

The overall distribution of wealth in society has also widened, largely owing to the ability of higher-income groups to benefit from increases in property prices – property ownership rates are strongly linked to household income.[21] Property-related wealth is also disproportionately greater in London than in other cities and regions of England, largely because of the much higher increases in property values in recent years.

We have been living through an era in which life chances or social mobility have worsened. The US and the UK occupy the unenviable position of having the lowest social mobility of any developed country.[22] Your background – who you were born to – matters more in the US and the UK in predicting where you end up in terms of wealth than anywhere else. And this situation is getting worse.[23]

One upshot is that the long-standing debates around whether the focus of policy should be on equality of outcome or equality of opportunity are misleading – inequality of outcomes determines equality of opportunity. Robert Putnam has written about the 'opportunity gap' as the children of an advantaged minority are almost guaranteed to thrive whilst those in the less advantaged groups and areas struggle to better their starting position.[24] Both inequality of income and inequality of wealth are deepening, but it's not simply that those at the top are pulling away faster than those at the bottom – those at the bottom are slipping behind the position of their parents, with half of those in the US now poorer than their parents.[25]

There is an argument that the most unequal places are the most economically successful and that this is somehow a 'good thing' – booming cities are good for all. But the point is that it is only a small group that is capturing the growth and wealth. In London, 50 per cent of the city's wealth is owned by the richest 10 per cent of its households. The bottom 50 per cent own just over 5 per cent. A person in the top 10 per cent of London's population owns 295 times more than someone just inside the bottom 10 per cent. And the gap is increasing: the least wealthy 10 per cent of people in London lost 32 per cent of their wealth over the last two years, compared to a 2 per cent drop across the UK.[26]

This deepening inequality of income and wealth is having profound consequences for the spatial concentration of poverty within cities. International studies highlight how inequality segregation in cities is a global phenomenon and is closely correlated to city size, economic performance and overall national levels of inequality.[27] In the US, segregation by income has increased since 1990 in 27 of the nation's 30 largest major metropolitan areas. The wealthier parts of cities such as New York, Houston and San Francisco were attracting more wealthy residents whilst the poorer areas were similarly becoming more homogeneous in terms of their residents' socioeconomic background.[28] Residential segregation isn't by any means confined to the city. In London, one impact of rising property prices in the city itself is that social and economic segregation is rippling out to the suburbs. In 2004 Outer London had 32 per cent of London's most deprived wards, but by 2015 the proportion had risen to 47 per cent; 1.4 million people are living in poverty in Outer London – 60 per cent of London's total.[29] A similar picture is emerging in the US where its suburbs are experiencing a demographic shift as they become home to those who cannot afford to live in cities, a group that increasingly includes immigrants and people of colour. One-quarter of suburbanites – 17 million people – in the US are defined as in poverty, 4 million more than in cities themselves.[30] Poverty in cities has not declined as a result, but instead, increased across the board and spread. Richard Florida points to the work of William Julius Wilson, who explored the effects of the spatial concentrations of poverty in the 1980s, including fewer and lower-quality jobs to less developed economic and professional networks and lower-quality schools, higher crime rates, more problematic peer networks and far less exposure to positive role models.[31]

Disadvantage leads to disadvantage across generations.

Housing disconnection

In September 2015 hundreds of people attacked a cafe in Shoreditch, East London, badly damaging it and injuring a police officer. The reason? The Cereal Killer Cafe was seen as a symbol of the gentrification of the area. Local people were feeling the effects of rent rises and property price increases, the loss of local shops and what they saw as colonisation by hipsters. The protest was organised by the group Class War, which justified the attack:

> Our communities are being ripped apart – by Russian oligarchs, Saudi sheiks, Israeli scumbag property developers, Texan oil-money twats and our own home-grown Eton toffs. Local authorities are coining it in, in a short-sighted race for cash by "regenerating" social housing. We don't want luxury flats that no one can afford, we want genuinely affordable housing. We don't want pop-up gin bars or brioche buns, we want community.[32]

London is not alone – protests against gentrification have occurred in many major cities around the globe. From Berlin and Amsterdam to Toronto and Lisbon there have been protests and reactions against the colonisation of parts of the city by those looking for cheaper housing. Local governments often facilitate this process of gentrification – wittingly and unwittingly – through improvement in the physical appearance of an area and investment in infrastructure such as public transport.

Gentrification is the general moniker for the displacement of one set of residents, shops and services by another, usually wealthier, group. It's a process that has been occurring for decades to greater and lesser degrees in cities around the globe. Yet, it is from the 1980s in particular that the term has become more politically charged and aligned with broader growth and inequality arguments.[33] Despite the headline-grabbing actions of groups such as Class War, gentrification of an area isn't necessarily or even ordinarily about wealthy individuals pricing locals out of housing and then creating a demand for high-end shops and services. Often it occurs simply as housing costs generally increase to the point that they are out of reach of the poorest in society. Why gentrification has become more politically charged in recent years is that there are fewer, if any, affordable places for the displaced to relocate to other than other, more affordable, cities.

Whilst gentrification provides a rallying point and target for unhappiness and discontent, it reflects much wider and deeper issues, particularly the widespread growth in housing costs amongst middle- and lower-income groups and the role that this plays in inequality. Gentrification is at its heart a problem of housing affordability driven by growing income and wealth inequality. In large parts of London there is no accommodation available that is affordable by anyone on Local Housing Allowance, a payment made to 1.2 million of the nation's poorest families to help support renting privately. In other parts of the South East of England, such as Swindon and Newbury, only 2 per cent of accommodation is affordable, whilst in the wider South East, including Milton Keynes and Cambridge, only 10 per cent of housing is affordable. Research by the national homeless charity Shelter has highlighted the crisis in housing affordability for the lowest-paid workers, pointing out that in parts of the South East families spend up to 60 per cent of their net income on private rent, whereas even in the more affordable parts of London it is up to three-quarters of their income.[34]

The impacts of worsening housing affordability are not simply a sifting of the population across and between cities. According to Shelter, in order to remain, families have to make difficult choices about how they spend their limited resources:

> When housing benefit is so low that people are having to find over £50 a week to cover even the lowest rents, they face grim decisions between food, electric bills and keeping a roof over their head.[35]

The impact of this situation on families is severe, but the consequences for cities are also serious. Those employed in lower-paid public sector and caring jobs – teachers, nurses, cleaners, and so on – struggle to afford to live in cities:

> You can't even contemplate getting into the housing market here. And I don't mean just service workers, I mean highly skilled professionals. The tech elite are having a hard time affording reasonable housing in Silicon Valley. So this is difficult, this makes it very difficult for employers trying to recruit.[36]

People are still moving to places like San Francisco and London, but they are attracted by high-paid jobs in tech or financial services. Many cities face difficulties recruiting service and public sector staff. In San Francisco there is a shortage of teachers as 40,000 left the state between 2013 and 2017, an increase of 22 per cent over the previous five-year period. Some teachers report a two-hour each-way commute in order to find an affordable home.[37] Many restaurants and cafes in the city are closing; others are adapting by putting the onus on customers to serve themselves, scaling down menus and offering simpler dishes that can be prepared by fewer and less skilled staff, a situation that has obviously accelerated under COVID-19.

Other service sector employers are similarly adapting, but even so, they are finding that their staff are holding down two or three jobs simply to make ends meet. Many have given up entirely and moved to other cities where rents and labour costs are more affordable. One upshot of this is that some places are beginning to lose their diversity and distinction. Housing disconnection is feeding a reduction in variety and difference, making places more homogeneous and undifferentiated.

Alongside the disconnection, our cities and their people face a series of other challenges and disconnections including climate change and the growing incidence of extreme weather, an ageing population, air pollution, traffic congestion, outdated infrastructure, and energy and water shortages, among others. Digital technology and smart cities can help address these, but only if they are pointed towards them and their negative impacts are curtailed.

Why does this matter?

There is an argument that cities have evolved and adapted in the past and will do so again, whatever the challenges and disruptions they face – the coal and steam industrial city of the 19th century was disrupted by the growth of the internal combustion engine in the 20th century.

There is another train of thought. In 2008 the Conservative think tank Policy Exchange called for urban policy to be radically rethought through abandoning what it saw as failing cities in the North of England:

> It is time to stop pretending that there is a bright future for Sunderland and ask ourselves instead what we need to do to offer people in Sunderland better prospects.[38]

Although dismissed by many at the time, including by the then Prime Minister David Cameron who said the report was 'bonkers', it represents a stream of thinking around cities, that they are simply functional, temporary containers or arenas for economic activity. This is a view that is not dissimilar to the data-focused perspective on cities that Silicon Valley holds. Others would highlight that whilst there is a mountain of evidence that demonstrates how societies across the globe have become less equal over the past few decades, inequality motivates people to strive and better themselves, and we all benefit from that.

The answer to such a challenge comes from both ideological (inequality and disconnection in society are intrinsically wrong) and selfish (inequality undermines long-term growth and prosperity) sources. There is significant statistical evidence that demonstrates how economic inequality damages growth through hampering social mobility and skill development in society, reducing the number of skilled workers for an economy as well as suppressing opportunities for those who cannot fulfil their potential.[39] As Richard Wilkinson and Kate Pickett pointed out in 2009 in *The Spirit Level*,[40] inequality also leads to social consequences including a lack of social cohesion, crime, ill health, eroding trust and increasing consumption. There is also evidence that more equal societies derive economic benefits, with productivity increasing as inequality reduces.[41]

There is, however, a more fundamental reason why disconnection and inequality in society matters, one that concerns the very future of humankind. Over the past decade, and since 2016 in particular, a grand narrative has emerged that ascribes political outcomes, particularly the vote in the UK to leave the EU and the election of Donald Trump as US president, to the growth of inequality.[42] One must be wary of making a direct, reductionist link between increasing inequality and the rise of what has been termed 'populist' politics. Yet many claim that the impact of post-crisis austerity policies and the perceived scale of immigration played a part in voter dissatisfaction leading to the Brexit vote, whilst in the US the impact of trade with China on traditional industries also contributed significantly in some areas to the vote to elect Trump.

Yet the link is brought into question by the fact that in some countries, such as France and Austria, inequality has not changed significantly and yet there has been a shift to the right amongst the electorate in both countries. Similarly in Poland, economic growth has been more equally shared whilst the electorate has put a populist right-wing government in power. Other issues around this big picture story concern the definition of populist, which is a rather movable, if not ideological, feast, as it seems to include both anti-immigration, anti-EU politicians and those aligned to more environmental and socialist concerns. Studies of the changing pattern of voting have also emphasised the significance of cultural factors, including the backlash from some against progressive values and identity politics.

Notwithstanding the complexity, the overall picture is difficult to deny – support for populist parties across Europe has doubled over the past decade whilst inequalities of wealth and income have broadly increased too. Whilst separating cause and effect in this heady mix of factors that influence voter preference will never be straightforward or unproblematic, a leading thinker on inequality, the French economist Thomas Piketty, has sought to demonstrate the link between rising inequality and populism in the US, France and the UK.[43] According to Piketty, the 1950s and 1960s were characterised by education and wealth-based voter alignments – those with lower educational attainment and wealth tended to vote for left-wing parties whilst the more educated and those with a higher income tended to vote for more right-wing parties. Left-wing parties tended to pursue redistribution policies whilst right-wing parties supported policies that benefited business. However, this pattern began to change and reverse during the 1980s, as the more educated began to align themselves and vote more with left-wing parties whilst the wealthy stuck with the right. The elite, according to Piketty, now dominate left and right – the educated because the left is more pro-migration and internationalist, and the wealthy because the right favours policies that benefit them, such as lower taxation. This leaves the lower-educated and less well-off with no natural party affinity. There are a number of conclusions that can be drawn from this analysis. The first is that economic growth per se has not benefited lower-income groups as there is no mainstream party on the left or right that reflects or fights for their interests. This also goes some way to explain the rise in more populist politics and the emergence of politicians that provide explanations (immigration has taken your jobs; climate change is a hoax) and solutions (take back control by withdrawing from multilateral bodies such as the EU). Political instability and the rise of isolationist politicians and parties resulting from unequal growth, and the lack of options, has come at a time when we need political cooperation and coordination to tackle the greatest threats to our cities.

How tech could and is helping cities

Cities are unequal and always have been, but as urban analyst Richard Florida puts it:

> There can be no doubt that the recent influx of the very rich, of tech startups and their employees, and of financial and other professionals into cities is generating real challenges and prompting highly charged conflicts.[44]

Despite this view, Big Tech and digital startups can't be blamed for everything that is going on in cities. Digital technology, the smart city and Big Tech are fuelling and adding to what is in many places an existing urban crisis, particularly if one takes a wider perspective that includes the digital economy. Yet the traffic is not just one way. There are many examples from around the globe of how tech and digital are being used to help and support cities. Specific cities such as Eindhoven are seeking to develop people-led smart city initiatives. Barcelona has led the way in what has become termed 'digital sovereignty' with a wide range of initiatives that seek to use digital technology for social good, including re-use and recycling, free software and digital services, and community education and information.[45]

At another level there are more general, social-tech initiatives. For example, Moyee Coffee uses blockchain technology to help farmers get fairer prices and negotiate supply chain costs, providing coffee directly to consumers. In many places in the Global South digital technology is also being used to support better and fairer deals for workers as well as seeking to deliver on the original promise of Google to not 'do evil'. FairBnB, for example, is a workers' cooperative that provides an alternative to Airbnb. FairBnB partner Sito Veracruz is clear about the difference from its namesake: 'The first difference is transparency and legality. We're not just transparent; we foster transparency and we actually want to work with governments.'[46] FairBnB has a strict 'one host, one home' policy, and all properties are checked to ensure that it is legal to be rented in that city. Finally, half of the commission is used to fund community projects. FairBnB won't exclude for-profit rentals and models, but leaves it up to individual cities to decide what their needs are.

Other alternative platform services are emerging that seek to address the negative consequences of the dominant providers. Ethical Consumer[47] provides advice on a range of alternatives to Amazon, whilst Via[48] provides a ride sharing service that is pitched somewhere between the private car and existing public transport provision, with 95 per cent of its rides being shared. This reduces costs to the riders, pays the drivers more and limits congestion: 'The idea was, can we come up with an intermediate solution that hits that right balance of cost and convenience', says Daniel Ramot, co-founder and CEO.[49] Ramot describes Via as a 'dynamic bus'. Via currently has services in six major cities and has generated more than 70 million rides in 20 countries. It has contracts with some city authorities to provide services to supplement public transport, particularly in hard-to-reach areas. Ironically, much of the interest in and development of tech for social good has arisen because we are more aware of the issues that face the world as a result of digital technology and the availability of information.

And there are cities that are refusing to embrace smart or that have a very different perspective on what constitutes smart. In a widely reported case, the Mexican town of Santa Maria Tonantzintla, designated a *barrio smart* or 'smart city' by the regional governor, resisted the national push for digital colonisation and sought to define what 'smart' meant to them. A number of initiatives within the town raised questions about what kind of change was being packaged under the label of 'smart'. Demolition around the town square to provide more space for an entertainment area was spuriously linked to smart, raising fears in the local community that changes were being introduced without proper consultation and would benefit only tourists and outsiders: 'When politicians ask us what we want, we tell them we want a clinic, parks, things to entertain ourselves, so we don't have to go all the way to *puebla* [city] to go out', one resident commented.[50]

In other nearby towns, some so-called smart initiatives have been removed, including a bike lane that received very little usage. The suspicion was that planners were smart city advocates introducing changes that they had seen in other places, choosing from a 'catalogue' of smart city initiatives from around the globe, without consulting locals. Others felt that 'smart' was being used as a way to force through change that wouldn't be popular. So digital technology can be used for good, and some of the negative dimensions can be controlled – Transport for London (TfL) seeking to regulate Uber, for example.

The race for the future

The issue isn't that tech can be used to help support cities and the challenges they face, but that there is a race between the beneficial uses of digital technology and the tsunami of change that is being wrought by the push from Silicon Valley, our buy-in to this and facilitation by cities. This is a race for how we define and shape the use of smart. It's a race that we all know is going on, even those who are helping the participants. McKinsey & Company define smart cities as 'places where different actors employ technology and data to make better decisions and achieve a better quality of life'.[51] By that measure, many of our so-called smart cities are, at best, partially succeeding and, more likely, failing.

The fear and likely outcome is that cities will lose this race and that digital technology will make parts of the city work harder and more efficiently rather than helping address the fundamental and existential challenges. As it stands, smart will do little to address the current challenges that cities face, never mind those challenges that we know are coming.

7

Yesterday's cities of the future

For better or worse, the smart city has opened up many avenues and opportunities for disruption. One path that is currently being followed around the globe concerns what are commonly known as 'digital twins'. According to one smart city evangelist, digital twins are 'hot':

> Sensors and data analytics, AI, machine learning and drones, are feeding information real-time, giving life to these digital models, which have evolved becoming into more complex representations of their physical counterparts, and no longer of isolated single objects, but full-fledged systems of interconnected things.[1]

A digital twin is a virtual model that replicates an actual city. It allows modellers and decision-makers – politicians, engineers, architects, real estate developers and planners – to pull virtual levers and test 'what happens if' scenarios, posing questions such as what would be the impact of a new shopping centre on traffic congestion in the area, or how would the city's economy react to a change in business taxation?

Such transcendent oversight and power is the Holy Grail for many. That is why cities from Singapore to Newcastle are rushing to develop their digital twin, convinced that they can model, predict and then test interventions without the contested, costly and time-consuming bother of actually talking to and persuading residents and communities. Some greenfield cities like Amaravati, a US$6.5 billion new smart city in Andhra Pradesh, were created or 'born' with a digital twin. According to Michael Jansen, CEO of Cityzenith, a company that develops digital twin software, 'Everything that happens in Amaravati will be scenarioized in advance to optimize outcomes, and adjusted on the fly to keep pace with change. This represents a giant leap forward for cities, how they're designed, built, and managed, and how they optimize their relationships with the private sector and their own citizens.'[2] The superficial appeal of such approaches is not difficult to see:

> What yesterday's greenfield cities took 100 years to do, today's greenfield cities will achieve in under 25 years, and they will do it with the help of the universally-integrative and omni-predictive capabilities of Digital Twin software platforms.[3]

At one level there is much to applaud and welcome in the digital twin and its use as a tool to help support decision-making: the predictive power of AI and machine learning combined with real-time data is allowing us to model the impacts of climate change on the city, helping shape mitigation and adaptation. For many, however, the potential and appeal goes much further. This is city planning as a desk-based exercise, one where people and communities become variables in an algorithm, where reactions of communities and proposals can be foreseen, foretold and factored in.

Digital twins and the attitude that underpins them is not new, however. This is a repackaging of the 'city as a machine' school of thought, a perspective that has a long tradition in urban planning. The computed city attitude has come to the fore at various times, not least in the 1960s, only to be frustrated by public demands for a say in the future of their cities. The reason for this push-back is simple: despite the image and promise of optimisation, modelling and prediction involve deeply political decisions that cannot be computed away. A digital twin might predict that traffic flows and accessibility across the city can be 'optimised' by elevated highways and city centre parking, but this would overlook the individual and community impacts, as many cities, from Bristol to Leeds, experienced in the 1960s when such 'solutions' were imposed on them despite opposition.

The motivation behind the digital twin movement is not, then, *how best* to change the city, as its proponents claim. Instead, it is about *who* changes the city and what interests underpin any change. This struggle over who owns and runs the city is a long-standing one, and throughout history technology has been used as a means to project certain interests over others. In short, technology doesn't just happen to cities – it is actively promoted by advocates and interests and builds on some long-held positions and traditions in city planning, architecture and local politics. Digital twins and other digital planning tools are merely the latest battle in the war to decide who owns the city. This goes some way to explain why digital and smart have been promoted so heavily in cities. To fully understand the smart city one has to therefore step back and appreciate the long relationship between technology and cities in what were yesterday's cities of the future.

From medieval to Metro-Land: technology doesn't just happen to cities

Cities and technology have an abiding and close relationship. Innovations such as sewage systems, electricity, air conditioning and clean water all had massive impacts on the lives of those who lived in cities. Yet the physical form of the city has also been radically shaped by technology. The original compact city, where homes and jobs for all ranks and classes were concentrated in small, dense settlements, persevered because of the lack of choice. Despite industrialisation producing the most 'degraded human environment the world had yet seen',[4] there was little alternative but for people to live in proximity to one another, often in polluted, unhealthy and hazardous conditions. In the early 1700s, Edinburgh was one of the most densely populated cities in Europe. Maze-like multistorey tenements spilled down the Royal Mile from the castle, compacting people into a concentrated urban enclave. Social divisions were horizontal as tradespeople and shopkeepers lived in the cheaper, more accessible, ground floors whilst the wealthier were located in the middle of the buildings and the poorest up high staircases towards the top. The reason for this concentration was partly historic and linked to the walled defences of cities that had constrained development. But once city defence was no longer an imperative, high urban density remained.

The main reason was that up until the mid-1800s, commuting from home to work was limited by the distance a coach and horse could travel. The option of living beyond the confines of the city was a choice limited to the few who could afford it. Another reason was economic necessity. Cheap housing sprang up around the factories, mines and mills of the new industrial settlements, offering an affordable, if low-quality, overcrowded and insanitary place to call home.

The coming of the railways disrupted this necessity, allowing people to live in one place and work in another. One of the earliest examples was in the US in the mid-19th century when the New York to Westchester rail line facilitated commuting to a string of new developments and settlements such as Scarsdale, New Rochelle and Rye. In London the opening of the world's first underground in 1863 was associated with new housing developments, often undertaken by the railway companies themselves as they bought land around planned routes and stations. The demand to flee the city meant that this was a hugely successful business model. As one investor in the London railway companies, the American financier and developer Charles Tyson Yerkes, put it, 'if I build houses near stations people will come'.[5] And he was right. Surrounding land values rose by up to 800 per cent once a station had been built. Those who could afford it couldn't wait to move out of the overcrowded and polluted cities to what became known as 'Metro-Land', a name that more than suggested the expansion of the traditional urban area and one that came from the name of the first underground railway company, the Metropolitan Railway.

Metro-Land became a popular, if manufactured, aspiration, a longing that was fed by the effective marketing of builders, railway companies and banks keen to make money and feed the demand from the growing middle classes for space and clean air. The term itself was coined by the railway company to promote the dream of a modern home in a bucolic countryside with a fast and reliable rail service to London. The main London terminus for the Metropolitan Railway, Baker Street Station, was christened 'The Gateway to Metro-Land'. Walking guides, popular songs and even the novels of Evelyn Waugh featured Metro-Land, a place that didn't actually exist beyond the imagination.

The growth of the suburbs was a common experience in cities across Europe and North America, as rail allowed an exodus of the wealthy and skilled. Around London places like Harrow Weald and Pinner, formerly large villages, grew tenfold or more once connected to the capital by rail. Yet railways worked both ways, allowing people to commute in alongside raw materials to be made into goods and then exported out. They also fed the city with day-to-day material needs, allowing cities to spread and sprawl, creating dynamic places of growth and decline within cities, leading to the segregation of uses as industry located in one area and housing in another. Edinburgh's Old Town tenements were not alone in their decline into slums for those who could not afford to escape, and cities became patterned by areas of wealth and poverty shaped by accessibility.

Rail and railways changed cities dramatically, but it was growing accessibility to another technological intervention, the private car, around a century later that was to revolutionise them, transforming and undermining many. The Model T car, introduced by Henry Ford in 1908, reached sales of more than 250,000 by 1914 and 500,000 by 1916, a growth that was fuelled by falling costs as their price fell over the same period, from US$825 to US$360. By the time production finished in 1927, Ford had produced more than 15 million Model Ts and the company accounted for more than half of all cars in the US. American cities began to restructure to accommodate and facilitate the explosion in car ownership and use, building new and surfacing existing roads, a process that was egged on by property developers and speculators who saw the opportunity to open up space for construction beyond the city.

As with the railways, a powerful alliance of car component manufacturers, property investors and business groups emerged to successfully lobby local and federal government to support car use in cities. In some cases there was more direct action, as when General Motors (GM) undertook a nationwide campaign to remove trolley buses that they felt took up valuable urban road space. GM then used subsidiaries to buy up the street car companies and close them down throughout the 1930s and 1940s in order to create more road space for their cars and buses. At the same time, the US federal government saw an opportunity to invest in roads as part of its response to the Great Depression, pouring US$4 billion into urban road building between 1933 and 1940, further adding 41,000 miles of interstate roads in the 1950s and 1960s that opened up new out-of-town building and development opportunities.

Rail and road enabled cities to grow beyond their boundaries, allowing many to flee, and encouraging segregation and sometimes the ghettoisation of those left behind. But these were not the only technological changes that transformed cities. Whilst better transport spurred expansion outwards, the development of steel, elevators and reinforced concrete allowed cities to grow upwards. Densification edged forward in many cities from the early 20th century. In Chicago the 10-storey Home Insurance Building of 1885 was the first steel-framed skyscraper. Other tall buildings quickly followed as technology evolved and developers realised the economic benefits of high rise. New York's 20-storey Flatiron Building of 1902 led quickly to the 110-storey Empire State Building of 1931. High rise wasn't confined to offices and quickly spread to housing, particularly in the aftermath of the destruction wrought by the Second World War when the need for cheap mass housing combined with advances in prefabrication and reinforced concrete led to the rapid spread of poorly built high-rise housing schemes. In the UK, politicians vied with each other to promise more public housing throughout the 1950s and 1960s, clearing away 19th-century terraces and streets to replace them with clusters of high-rise tower blocks.

The results of these and other successive waves of technological innovation and change were uneven between and within cities. At one level much was achieved as urban motorways and housing schemes spread across cities throughout the world. At another level the outcomes were social and economic segregation in areas such as New York's East Harlem, the Lower East Side and Brownsville.

In echoes of what was to come under the umbrella of 'smart', there was the equivalent of an arms race of technological adaptation throughout the 19th century, as cities competed with each other to accommodate change and embrace technology. Many still bear the scars. Places like Baltimore were hit with the full effects as the (mainly white) middle classes got into their cars and left the city for the suburbs. Services followed, as shopping malls sprang up outside the city on new beltways, taking trade away from city shops. One of Baltimore's main industries, steel manufacture, was hit hard as cheaper steel from other parts of the US became available to a wider market thanks to better transport connections. The overall result was that large parts of the city, and those who could not leave, were abandoned to rising crime, unemployment and poverty.

The alignment of various interests around the promotion of suburbanisation and the creation of Metro-Land highlights how technological change in cities isn't neutral or inevitable. Change is actively promoted, usually to the benefit of those beyond the immediate and obvious beneficiaries – suburbanisation fed the growing demand from the middle classes for space and improved lifestyles but was promoted by banks, land owners and developers. There is obviously a profit motive on the part of those pushing for the smart city, but this does not tell the whole story. Smart and digital provide the latest spur to a long-running battle over who or what defines the future of our cities. Technology and technological change has a range of champions – those who have advanced its cause because it benefits their own.

Why planners love smart

One group of champions for technology and the city are planners. Those involved in city planning, from the professional to the politician, from the community to the corporate, know what a fissiparous and contested activity it is. Any proposition in a city that goes through the planning system inevitably leads to conflict and disputation at a practical as well as an ideological level. In part, contestation derives from the specifics of change – whether a new development enjoys support or disapproval will come down to the actual proposal. But a large part of any reaction – negative or positive – will also come from one's attitude or disposition towards cities and planning. There are many traditions and schools of thought on the purpose of city planning and how to go about it, from Marxists to liberals, and pragmatists to feminists.[6] Some advance people-centred views of the future, some incremental approaches, and some have particular emphasis on and relevance for technology-led approaches to city planning. It is these themes or traditions that smart speaks most loudly to, providing a ready-made and sympathetic foundation from which to build and roll out the digital city. Three, in particular, stand out: technology as ideology, technology as control, and technology and planning by numbers.

Technology as ideology: rethinking the city

There is a long tradition in planning and architecture that advances an ordered, clean-sweep, vertical future for cities, what Peter Hall called the 'city of towers'.[7] This vision of cities emerged from the 1920s onwards, when its evangelical champions saw an opportunity to promote their tabula rasa utopia on the accumulated, evolutionary messiness and disorder of most cities. The call to purge cities and start anew was given added impetus by the continued existence in places such as Berlin, Paris and London of large areas of poor, overcrowded housing, insanitary conditions and poverty, highlighting the failure of piecemeal attempts to address these conditions. But the blame for the persistence of such conditions wasn't only down to half-hearted attempts to fix them. According to the advocates of clean-sweep urbanism, the problem was that measures to address poor housing and poverty were focusing on the symptoms and not the cause of the problem. Cities as a whole needed to adapt and evolve to meet contemporary demands and needs and to improve the lives of their citizens. Technology, in the form of concrete and steel to allow buildings to reach upwards, and the private car that would allow homes and jobs to be separate, were the answer. But new technology was being layered onto old cities that couldn't cope. It was no good tearing up a trolley bus route here and building a new road there. The city itself needed a radical rethink as new technology rendered medieval and industrial cities obsolete. To quote one of the leading lights of the 'city of towers', Le Corbusier, 'the design of cities was too important to be left to the citizens'.[8]

The movement that advanced this clean-sweep approach was termed 'Modernism', a label that suggested that cities were out of step with technology, unfit for the needs of the future. And why wouldn't a city want to be modern? Like 'smart' and its implied opposite of 'dumb', Modernism was an aspiration that everyone could sign up to. Modernism and cities followed the principles originally set out by the Congrès internationaux d'architecture moderne (CIAM), a hugely influential international umbrella organisation founded in 1928. This was architecture and planning as a force for social improvement focused not so much on style as on function, an approach that divorced buildings and cities from their local settings and styles. What counted for Modernism was what worked. The city itself should be ruthlessly planned so as to be functional, clean, safe, healthy and accessible, particularly by the private car.

One of CIAM's founder members and leading lights, the French architect Le Corbusier, summed up this attitude and approach when he described buildings as 'machines for living'. This was an attitude that scaled up to the level of the messy, complex and disordered nature of current cities. Modernism argued that cities should be thought anew with different uses strictly segregated to make them more efficient, more adaptable and liveable. In 1922 Le Corbusier set out his design for an ideal new city of 3 million people composed of identical 60-storey skyscrapers set in wide, open spaces. In Baltimore and many other cities facing typical deep-seated problems of poor housing, deindustrialisation and rising crime, this was an appealing and simple prospect – cities could be remade with the promise that the new city would wipe away the problems of the present.

Lafayette Courts, built in Baltimore in 1955, was envisaged as one of Le Corbusier's 'machines for living', supposedly replacing overcrowded slums with clean, comfortable, affordable, high-rise housing. It was the first of many high-rise public housing projects in the city – 'towers in the park', as Le Corbusier called them. The reality was that they quickly became slums, beset by crime, drugs and miserable living conditions as jobs and opportunities left the city for the suburbs. Lafayette Courts was demolished in 1995 and replaced by housing of a scale and density that had existed before the cult of Modernism took hold of the planners and politicians in the city.

Technology as control: city planning as visionary rebirth

The notion of a top-down clean sweep of the messy city was not confined to Modernism and the 'city of towers'. It also appealed to a wider sensibility across different disciplines charged with city planning. At the turn of the last century Daniel Burnham, master planner of Chicago, set out his ethos for thinking of the future of the city:

> Make no little plans; they have no magic to stir men's blood and probably themselves will not be realized. Make big plans; aim high in hope and work, remembering that a noble, logical diagram once recorded will never die, but long after we are gone will be a living thing, asserting itself with ever-growing insistency.[9]

The notion of the strong man, visionary rebirth for the city was a view that was to prove influential, particularly in many Western cities throughout the rest of the century. Underpinned by a Modernist attitude of planning as something that happened to cities rather than with communities, it encouraged an approach that appealed to the grand, individual vision of massive redevelopment. Nuance, complexity, historic fabric and evolution were replaced by boulevards, high rises, urban motorways and the segregation of homes from jobs.

The moment for the visionary view of city planning came in the post-Second World War era. Wartime had required an expanded and active state, one where government planning in the broadest sense had been necessary. At the same time there had been a growing acceptance of and acquiescence to a state-controlled economy and the restrictions it entailed. When the war ended, this apparatus and momentum continued and turned its attention to the urgent need to rebuild following the physical destruction and economic devastation of the war. Large, urban regeneration projects in the UK sought to replace bomb-damaged cities with new modern housing, made easily accessible by the growth in car ownership. New industrial developments sprang up on the edges of cities and across the country in a conscious attempt to spread growth and avoid future concentrations of targets for aerial bombing. The future spatial pattern was based on the notion of containing existing cities and dispersing homes and development to new locations. A range of new towns – Stevenage (1946), Harlow (1947) and Bracknell (1949) among others – was planned and built that on paper looked remarkably similar to the grand visions of the Modernists.

In the US the car also underpinned this rebirth of the city, no more so than in New York, where Robert Moses, nicknamed 'Bulldozer Bob' by critics and supporters alike, saw himself as the saviour of the city. Moses saw the need to modernise the city and make it fit for the modern age. As a disciple of Burnham, he was convinced that the future city necessitated radical surgery to provide what was needed, to save the city from itself. For Moses and his city of New York, this meant wholesale demolition and the insertion of roads. Lots of them. During a long career that involved holding multiple, simultaneous public offices from the 1920s to the 1960s, Moses reshaped large parts of the city through building 637 miles of highways, 13 bridges and two tunnels, along with 658 playgrounds, 10 public swimming pools (he was a committed swimmer until his death in 1981), 17 parks and many housing projects. This was city planning on a scale that has only recently been matched in China. Compared by some to Baron Haussmann of 19th-century Paris, Moses deployed the argument that he and his staff were experts and knew what was best for the city, drawing on surveys that classified buildings as unfit or slums and backed up by statistics, models and scientific rationalism. Unsurprisingly, this top-down self-confidence and determination received the support of Le Corbusier and other luminaries of Modernist architecture. For them, Moses' approach was the right one – the city needed radical surgery to make it fit for the future, sentiment, public opinion and political sensitivities notwithstanding.

Like Modernism, the big planners such as Moses did not have things all their own way. In the 1960s Robert Moses met his match in the form of community activist Jane Jacobs, someone who dared to take a diametrically opposed view on the future of the city. At the peak of his control in the 1950s, Moses had decided that Lower Manhattan was, as he put it, 'hell's hundred acres', and parts of Harlem were 'a cancerous growth that has to be carved out'.[10] The carving was to be achieved by means of a 10-lane urban expressway that would have involved the demolition of 416 buildings and 365 shops, the relocation of 2,200 families and the loss of parks and open spaces. Rather than radical surgery, Jacobs had a different diagnosis and prognosis for New York. A flyer from a residents group that had come together to oppose the plans drew her attention to them and sparked Jacobs into action. Her activism and organisational skills led to communities opposing the proposals, turning up at public hearings and lobbying through the press. Moses was furious. At a hearing to consider his plan to build a four-lane highway through New York's Washington Square Park in 1958, Moses insisted that:

> There is nobody against this, nobody, nobody, nobody but a bunch of … a bunch of mothers.[11]

Jacobs and her supporters successfully countered with a people-centred vision of organic change and human scale as an alternative to the dominant, top-down, rational view of city planning. Her alternative was set out in her magnum opus, *The Death and Life of Great American Cities*, published in 1961.[12] Taking on everyone from Ebenezer Howard to Le Corbusier, Jacobs argued for diversity and for city planning to embrace and deliver the 'ballet of the sidewalk', where strangers interact in a myriad of ways, and where the human scale of such influences provides for integration and safety. Well–used streets foster civilisation and security, and function as the building blocks of neighbourhoods or communities. In order to foster such communities, Jacobs argued that city planning needed to encourage diversity, not homogeneity. A mix of uses, scales and styles of buildings would help ensure that streets remained vibrant and active.

Technology and planning by numbers

There has always been a strong core belief among many involved in cities and their management that they could and should be conceived of and managed as complex adaptive systems, as places that could be understood, modelled, controlled and improved. Technology was the impulse to betterment, spurring on the belief in progress. Democratic involvement and engagement, on the other hand, was a barrier, thwarting and delaying change and inevitably leading to sub-optimal solutions. When technology or innovation met the reality of existing cities, it was the city that needed to adapt and evolve. Treating cities and city planning as if they were an extension of maths has a long history. The very notion of modern city planning is underpinned by notions of rationality and scientific method, and it is a sentiment that has strong resonance today. But the recent technocratic proclivity within city planning has a more current background. During the Second World War, Heinrich Himmler, Hitler's right-hand man and architect of the Holocaust, needed someone to help plan the Germanisation of newly occupied territories to the east, mainly Poland and Czechoslovakia. He turned to Walter Christaller. In 1933 Christaller published *Die zentralen Orte in Süddeutschland* (*Central Places in Southern Germany*), which postulated a model for the optimal spatial arrangement, size and number of settlements in a region.

Christaller's central place theory sets out a nested, hierarchical settlement pattern with smaller numbers of larger settlements providing more specialised goods and services and a higher number of smaller settlements that would meet more basic needs. According to Christaller, settlements would naturally order themselves into the most efficient spatial arrangement. For Himmler, a rational, efficient settlement pattern would become the model to impose on the conquered lands to the east, and he appointed Christaller to oversee their planning.[13] Christaller's work for the Nazis wouldn't even be a footnote in history if the approach to analysing, modelling and shaping the built and natural environments in a systematic way hadn't subsequently appealed to generations of planners, politicians and geographers the world over, spawning countless studies of places that do and do not correspond to this ideal.

His less obvious legacy has been to provide succour to the idea of an underlying relationship between cities and an unseen ordering hand that reflected a logic and rationality. It appealed for the same reasons that other, heuristic models have shaped the thinking of cities. William Penn, the founder of Pennsylvania, planned a city based on a rational grid layout of ideal size and shape that would be a 'green country towne' comprising 10,000 acres and 10,000 dwellings, each occupying an acre. Ebenezer Howard's Garden City model, first published in 1898, similarly posited a hierarchical settlement model of ideal size and space, advocating what Howard felt was a balance between town and country. Howard's idea directly shaped the UK's Garden City and New Town policy, leading to the development of places like Milton Keynes.

The notion of cities as systems was to re-emerge into the mainstream in the 1960s with the development of computing and the view of people like Brian McLoughlin and George Chadwick that cities should be seen as being composed of multiple, connected parts – employment and housing as different functions of a city but related in that when employment levels rise, so does demand for housing. There would also be other, directly related impacts from changes in employment too, on traffic, demand for health and education services, and retail activity.

Importantly, there would also be feedback loops, so if traffic congestion became too bad, economic activity might be negatively affected as businesses would look elsewhere for locations or seek different transport solutions. In such ways systems evolve and cities change. In the systems view, city planning should seek to understand these changes and then search to shape them to minimise negative effects and maximise city performance. Planners would be modellers, experimenting by tweaking this criteria and twitching that one. The Holy Grail for city planners back then was computing power with which they could create their models and simulations. Cities would look inwards to computers to manage and plan their futures, and city planners would become the high priests of The Model, a role that appealed to many. As one leading advocate of systems planning put it at the time:

> Most planning offices now and in the future will need access to at least a small or medium-sized computer as well as more modest equipment such as automatic electronic calculating machines.[14]

The momentum for thinking about cities as interconnected systems was given a fillip through the work of Jay Forrester, a professor in MIT Sloan School of Management. In 1969 he published *Urban Dynamics*, which turned out to be a highly influential fount of thinking about cities as reducible to modelling and simulation.[15] Forrester played with algorithms and assumptions to simulate what would happen with different combinations of changing population, housing and industry, modelling the impacts on a city's growth and evolution. According to Forrester's model, some interventions such as tax breaks, job training initiatives and the provision of affordable housing actually harmed the long-term economic success of cities through increased demand for services that needed to be paid for by increased taxes on economically active residents. *Urban Dynamics* argued that cities were complex adaptive systems, and that intervening in one area – for example, transport – would have linked and foreseeable consequences in other areas – for example, the demand for land and property in specific locations.

Such models also start with the assumption that economically booming places, like San Francisco at the moment, have got it 'right' and other, less economically successful places need to ape this approach, creating virtuous feedback loops of tax raising that sustains public services, which further fuels economic attractiveness. Growth is the answer to the city's problems, but only a certain kind of growth, one based on crude supply-side interventions. Forrester's assumptions were typical of the 'price of everything, value of nothing' approach to cities and economics, a model that privileges the economy and those policy levers that are easier to control – build more roads to improve accessibility and economic growth – rather than the trickier and more complicated problems of drug dependency or childhood obesity. Yet the abstract systems approach to planning had evolved into a real-world approach, however simplistic and questionable. Systems planning went from a niche sect to a full-scale denomination within city thinking.

Despite its narrow focus and the criticisms of cities and human behaviour as quantifiable and reducible to formulas, Forrester's *Urban Dynamics*, like Christaller's central place theory and Howard's Garden City, was and remains influential. It's still taught in school geography classes and university courses, and is still regarded as a touchstone for those convinced as a matter of faith that cities can be reduced to numbers and understood as systems. One such disciple was a young programmer, Will Wright. Wright had a background in architecture and engineering, and in 1989 he brought these interests together and published SimCity, the hugely popular urban planning simulation game. SimCity has gone through various iterations, but its core appeal remains the ability to develop a city as its mayor, making decisions on everything from investment in transport, hospitals, fire service and police to when and how much land is zoned for housing and employment. It's addictive and open-ended, with feedback on how popular your policies and decisions are. The simulation has as its engine a familiar approach to understanding cities as systems, as its author explains:

> First, it was just a toy for me…. I thought it would be cool to have the world come to life. So I started researching books on urban dynamics, and traffic, and things like that. I came across the work of Jay Forrester, who was kind of the father of system dynamics. He was actually one of the first people I found that actually simulated a city on a computer. Except in his simulation, there was no map; it was just numbers. It was like population level, number of jobs – it was kind of a spreadsheet model.[16]

The combination of underlying models of cities with graphics and the ability to quickly see 'what works' has been hugely popular, but it has also worried many that the 'game' has been taken too seriously, reinforcing a particular view of cities. As Kevin Baker has written:

> Within a few years of its release, instructors at universities across the country began to integrate SimCity into their urban planning and political science curriculums.
>
> Commentators like the sociologist Paul Starr worried that the game's underlying code was an "unreachable black box" which could "seduce" players into accepting its assumptions, like the fact that low taxes promoted growth in this virtual world. "I became a total Republican playing this game," one SimCity fan told the *Los Angeles Times* in 1992. "All I wanted was for my city to grow, grow, grow".[17]

The temptation to see cities and city planning as being akin to a computer simulation was never Wright's intention:

> I realized early on, because of chaos theory and a lot of other things, that it's kind of hopeless to approach simulations like that – as predictive endeavors. But we've kind of caricatured our systems. SimCity was always meant to be a caricature of the way a city works, not a realistic model of the way a city works.[18]

Yet the reductionist lure continues to encourage the rollout of simulations, and modelling cities wasn't the only contribution to urban thinking that Wright made. In 2000 he launched The Sims, a life simulation game that posits the player as a god-like creator and controller of people – sims – directing their lives and sating their desires. Like SimCity, the approach was one of taking complex behaviour and interactions and reducing them to a simulation:

> I was always interested in architecture, and so one of the original things that was a really inspiration for The Sims was this book, *A Pattern Language*, by

Christopher Alexander. He's very much into trying to apply formula. He's a physics guy that went into architecture and was frustrated because architecture wasn't enough of a science. But at the same time, he's got a very interesting humanist side. He felt all the principles of architecture should be clearly reducible back to fundamental principles, which is what he kind of tries to do in that book.[19]

The upshot from these strands of planning thought is that digital technology and smart are pushing at an open door. It might be too simplistic to claim that digital twins arose out of SimCity, but the fact is that there is a warm welcome for this direction of travel from within city planning.

Technology has shaped cities and digital technology has found a receptive audience in its bid to transform them, but how is digital making a difference on the ground, as it were?

Bits and bricks: the computed city revived

These themes of planning provide an important backdrop to the smart city, but they are more than simply historical interest. The digital twin isn't the only way in which digital technology is being used to plan and manage our cities.

In 2017 Santa Monica introduced City Swipe, an online system for helping plan the city, gathering feedback from residents on how their community should develop over a 15-year period. Public involvement has generally benefited from digital technology as information has become more accessible, meetings have been webcast, and residents and businesses encouraged to engage at times that suit them. Yet City Swipe is different because it is a new approach to city planning. In fact, it looks and feels remarkably like a mobile dating app.

Users are presented with images and asked either 'yes' or 'no' questions or which view they prefer. They do this by being invited to swipe left or right, an approach familiar to anyone who uses Tinder, the online dating app. The city authorities are seeking to tap into the zeitgeist and encourage citizens to think of planning in the same way one might choose a date. Santa

Monica underlines this shift in participation in planning through setting out what it sees as the advantages of this approach, benefits that include empowering the end user, avoiding boring meetings, speed (no wasting time trying to understand complex issues if they are boiled down to two photos), a lack of jargon and, as they put it, it's fun.[20]

It could be argued that in order to grab the attention of the distracted online citizen you need to compete with the right tools. Yet, aside from the observation that this is city planning as Tinder, there are some serious issues around reducing complex issues to binary decisions. Who decides on what choices people are given? How could this approach deal with questions and issues that do not easily reduce to 'yes–no' choices? The challenges that cities face are becoming more complex and require trade-offs and difficult choices. In other words, they involve *politics* to determine *policies*.

In 2018 Barcelona introduced a new low emissions zone for the city, seeking to tackle high levels of vehicle-related air pollution by effectively banning non-zero emission vehicles from the centre. In doing so it joined many other cities around the world, including London, Mexico City, Amsterdam, Paris, Athens and Berlin. Air quality in Barcelona has breached acceptable levels for over a decade, with impacts on the health of children and the elderly. To ban or not to ban looks like a binary choice, but the policy came with a wide range of caveats and elements, including how much access residents within the zone with non-zero emissions vehicles should have, how much the city should pay to support delivery companies in replacing older vehicles, how such a policy would impact different groups and different areas, and how those with mobility issues would be treated. Like most city issues there are no easy answers; there is a need for compromise as well as associated costs and consequences. Air quality along with carbon reduction are issues that face most cities and are not easily reducible to binary choices. A newly elected, populist city administration in Barcelona attempted to reverse the decision of the previous administration in 2019 on the basis that the decision hurt businesses, although this was overturned by the courts following a legal challenge.

The 'city planning as Tinder' approach also ignores social learning and interaction as part of the debate as city planning loses its depth and becomes focused on a shallow, transactional approach that seeks to feed our consumer-orientated attitude and one-click culture – don't worry about investing time and energy into understanding complex issues, attending boring meetings and having to actually listen to other points of view! Just swipe left for less housing and right for more freeways! It also bypasses politics and moves straight to policies, minimising meaningful participation and involvement as well as informed decisions.

Planning is not the only area that has been subjected to this transactional approach to public engagement favoured and facilitated by digital technology. So-called 311 apps in the US have been rolled out by municipal governments to allow the public to report issues quickly and easily, overcoming the need for cities to employ people to do this for them. From potholes to broken street lights, 311 apps allow the public to report problems directly. As Ben Green argues,[21] this is part of the belief of many in technology that representative democracy is no longer necessary if we can engage with people directly. Politicians emerged as a necessity to represent the views of constituencies because populations became too large and physically dispersed to engage directly. Digital technology can fix that.

City Swipe fits with this direct, one-click philosophy, making democracy more efficient, as its advocates put it. According to Green,[22] however, app-based engagement is hyper-local and does not encourage people to get involved more deeply and actively in deciding what issues are offered up for a vote. In other words, it is a proxy for politics proper, ignoring distributional issues (how scarce resources are allocated) and inequality (which groups are favoured in getting to decide) and wider, strategic concerns beyond a particular neighbourhood.

There is something else being lost here in the planning of our cities. The very notion of city planning, which, at the very least, hints at something beyond the individual, is being undermined. Planning is looking inwards as it becomes individual, transactional, immediate and very local. At the same time, the actual planning of our cities is being done through a resurgent modelling approach.

Taking back control

The hugely successful film *My Fair Lady* was set in London's Covent Garden, a fruit, vegetable and flower market first built in the 17th century. As the film premiered in 1965, the Greater London Council (GLC) was about to publish plans to redevelop two-thirds of its 96 acres, replacing it with a multilane highway, hotels, a conference centre and high-rise apartments. As with Moses and his plans for New York, it was the local community that rose up and successfully opposed these plans. Other parts of the city – and large parts of many other cities – were not so fortunate. The justification for the wholesale demolition of the area was that the city needed to modernise and be fit for the needs of a contemporary city. The public and community were regarded as a barrier rather than a partner in this.

In 1973 the London Conservative Member of Parliament George Gardiner commented on the community reaction against the GLC's redevelopment plans:

> Any loss of nerve on this [the Covent Garden Development Scheme] by the GLC in face of protest from a small section of London's populace … when the opportunity has presented itself, will go down as a black day in London's history. If the drift of population away from the centre is combined with a retreat from a policy of comprehensive redevelopment in favour of mere site development it is the next generation of Londoners who will be the losers and who will look back on our timid age with scorn.[23]

Look back they did. Not in scorn, but with a mixture of relief and gratitude.

Fast forward to 2006 and a speech to the Regional Plan Association on downstate transportation needs by New York governor Eliot Spitzer, who said that a biography of Moses written today might be called *At Least He Got It Built*. As he went on to say: 'That's what we need today. A real commitment to get things done.'[24] This desire to wrest control away from communities, or at least use digital technology to limit input, is emerging in new, though familiar, forms.

The digital smart city resonates with certain traditions of city planning, approaches that privilege top-down, desk-based development over bottom-up, community-led change. That might be what is desired and needed, but only by a few. Who are the champions? It's the planners, the politicians and those interested in the ideological project who promote the cities as marketplaces. The attraction was always just below the surface, waiting for the opportunity to re-emerge. Never dead, only dormant.

City planning is being colonised, shifted and shaped by the re-emergence of the reductionist attitude of Big Tech. The questions being asked are not the more civic-minded but contested and difficult, from 'how do we create a beautiful place that works for everyone?' to 'how wide should this street be to allow two cars to pass side by side?' The transactional, 'make politics more efficient' approach is moving city planning in the opposite direction to cities and their needs, but is one that cities have been subject to in the past. So the pendulum is beginning to swing again. Moses and his attitude might have been out in the cold for the last few decades, but he's coming back into vogue with some again. And it's reviving the functional, predict-and-provide mentality, always bubbling below the surface of city planning. The other champions of this approach are those who have always benefited, as the experience of cities and technology has not always been one in which the benefits flowed evenly. The rich have often benefited disproportionately, using and abusing their wealth and power to thwart the advantages of the very technology they had championed. The wealthy inhabitants of Long Island who had escaped from the city of New York bought up stock in the Long Island Rail Road in order to thwart any further improvement in the service and therefore development close by.

City planning has often played catch-up with technological-driven change, adapting to the new, seeking to accommodate the advantages and ameliorate the downsides. But at times it has also played a less progressive role, particularly when captured by those who wish to use it to foil rather than facilitate change. The lessons and experiences of technological-driven change in cities are all around us and they provide a sobering counter to the headlong rush into the next wave of smart-led development.

8

Why it's different this time

As discussed in the last chapter, we can learn from the experiences of technological-led change in the past. But this time it's different. Previously, technological disruptions to the city were followed by push-backs and adjustments – high-rise housing and car-designed cities made only partial inroads before public opposition stepped in and balance was restored. Digital and smart are different. Not only are we distracted from the world around us and focused more on ourselves and on the moment, we're also being encouraged to hand over decisions and our destinies to digital technology and those who are behind it. Some claim we no longer need to worry about the future. Thinking about what is needed to make a city better, where to put new infrastructure, how many new homes are required and where they should go are all part of planning the future of cities. Many of these questions and answers involve choices: we could do A but then we couldn't achieve B. The answers also reflect views and values from different groups and interests: the world and the future looks very different if you're living in a sink estate than if you're a commuter from a suburb.

This is the stuff of local politics, but the 'smart city' story says that the answer to these questions and the future of the city don't need politics; they just need lots and lots of data which, of course, companies like Google have. Techno-optimists argue that data speaks for itself. There is no need to debate, discuss and hypothesise any more – just run the numbers and look for patterns and correlations. Data and AI can provide the answers that used to be the concern of City Hall. Except, of course, there is still a need for humans to choose what data, to make sense of the results, and to recommend what we should do once the analysis is done. It's just that the humans who set the questions, choose the data and analyse the results are those behind the screens, those who are adept at grabbing your attention and keeping it. Democracy is becoming technocracy.

Technological change isn't necessarily or even ordinarily a 'bad thing'. Society and cities have evolved and adapted, although the impacts have, at times, been painful and disruptive, even disorderly. Some places have benefited and some have lost out. Changes in agricultural technology in the 18th century increased output and productivity, almost doubling the population of England, although decreased the workforce needed in the countryside. This surplus population migrated to cities, in large part owing to the impacts of the Industrial Revolution and the growing demand for labour in the mills and factories of the 19th century. In the late 20th century computer technology further fuelled economic and social change in our cities as routine tasks were automated and information became a new industry.

The upshot was a shift in employment patterns from manufacturing to services and information services. So technological change has created as well as destroyed jobs, but this creative destruction has not been smooth or even. There have been lags between the loss of old jobs and the emergence of new jobs, leading to periodic crises and social disruption. There have also been uneven impacts on different parts of society: the middle classes created by the 19th-century Industrial Revolution have been hit by more recent technological-led changes as real incomes have been squeezed and professional jobs, such as accountancy and law, are increasingly subject to digital automation. Such disruptions have been traditionally managed by government intervention and support to those affected through welfare and retraining. In our cities the planning system has been the main way in which technological change and the accompanying disruptions have been managed.

City planning has been a critical mediator of change and disruption. This role has been necessary because cities are more than functional places: they are where we work, live and play, where we bring up our children, and where we come together to address common challenges, from climate change to an ageing population, traffic congestion to social exclusion. Managing change and disruption has cushioned and protected people and places, whilst providing a level of certainty around the future. This role for city planning isn't necessarily accepted, however. For some, the city is just a marketplace for people, goods and services, and any form of collective intervention through city planning is anathema. The outcomes of what the 18th-century economist Adam Smith called the 'invisible hand' of the market are made real in the physical fabric of the city, through its appearance and the mix of its buildings, its layout and form. Yet this is a minority view.

Even those who espouse a laissez-faire economic philosophy make an exception for cities. Friedrich Hayek, the doyen of free market liberals the world over, published his influential polemic *The Road to Serfdom* in 1944. Against the backdrop of the rise of national socialism and communism, Hayek railed against their inherent centralised planning and the impacts on personal liberty. For Hayek, markets knew best and were a bulwark against totalitarianism. State planning in any form, he argued, was incapable of understanding, never mind predicting, the complexity of untold individuals' decisions that made up markets. Socialist governments impose the preferences of the few for the many, whilst free markets are a superior mechanism for allocating resources and providing for the needs of people. Except in cities. For Hayek, cities were a special case, places where markets needed to be managed, regulated and shaped. He even dedicated an entire chapter to why city planning was necessary. Common needs, such as clean air and water, cannot generally be easily bought and sold, yet such basic necessities for the many can be disproportionately affected in dense, urban environments by the decisions of the few – a polluting factory poisoning the air or water for homes next door, for example. Common goods and services such as fresh water and sanitation are essential to urban life, yet the huge costs of building and running them is beyond the market, as highlighted by the frequent cholera outbreaks in London in the 19th century or the experiences of millions in developing world cities today.

In his deviation from the primacy of the market, Hayek was working with the grain of history. Athenian, Roman and

Tudor cities were all planned to greater or lesser degrees for the same reasons that Hayek identified. The one takeaway from urban history is that cities need to be managed to succeed, not just economically, but socially and environmentally too. Of course city planning and management aren't perfect – witness the repercussions of servility to the private car in the disaster of urban motorways cutting swathes through our cities and communities. But where cities are allowed to simply grow unregulated and uncontrolled, the results can be more damaging. As someone with more than a passing interest in urban planning, I could be accused of bias here. But don't just take my word for it. The various annual indices of the world's most liveable cities come up with a range of places, although there are some cities that consistently appear, from Melbourne to Vienna, Vancouver to Tokyo. What these cities have in common is that they are managed and planned. Few would hold up places like Houston in Texas as the epitome of a liveable city, and it is renowned for its lack of urban planning. So city planning has provided a filter against disruption. How is planning being affected and why is its role as mediator of change under threat?

The four pillars of city planning

As I have argued in Chapter 7, planning is not simply important for the sake of our cities. The process of collective management that our cities depend on is also critical for the future of the planet. As a species we face a range of existential threats including the impacts of climate change, the pollution of our oceans and decreasing biodiversity. Cities bring people together and require us to figure out how we co-exist, how we manage to live together in close proximity and how to address common challenges. The result is that cities are incubators of democracy and tolerance, places where diversity and proximity require us to work together, putting aside disagreements and focusing on our common needs and interests. These are the traits we need to scale up and apply to our global challenges.

From Shanghai to Sunderland, Melbourne to Mumbai, the vast majority of the world's cities are planned and managed in one form or another. The form this process takes varies, and the mechanisms to manage change reflect the traditions and customs of different places. Yet the desire to plan is independent of whether a city is developed or developing, large or small, or whether it's controlled by political parties of the left or the right. What connects these different and diverse kinds of places is a common belief that successful cities don't just happen. Planning ensures that short-term decisions on the location of housing do not compromise longer-term challenges such as climate change; it seeks to ensure that investment and developments are coordinated with infrastructure; it strives to predict and provide a balance of development, suppressing an oversupply of apartments to ensure that housing is available for the whole population, the wealthy and poorer single people and families. Planning tries to ensure that public services such as schools and hospitals are provided in line with need; it has a critical role in protecting our valuable natural assets as well as in providing public goods such as parks; and, where necessary, planning also stimulates rather than simply shapes the market, overcoming barriers to development and change such as fragmented land ownership, land contamination and lack of market viability, to ensure that cities use their land to greatest effect.

Since the late 1960s there has been another common feature of how we plan our cities: a conviction that making necessary choices is best done in an inclusive and open way. City planning around the world works by giving everyone a voice, by seeking to reach decisions on the basis of consensus. By being inclusive, planning and plans have legitimacy, and those who disagree or have a different view accept the outcome as being fair. This is no guarantee that the direction and choices that cities make will be right, but it does provide a collective intelligence, a smartness, about how cities change.

What I've outlined above encapsulates what I would call the four pillars of city planning. There is a *political* pillar that embodies commitment to a common good – open processes of debate and decision-making that lead to a legitimacy when outcomes are determined that involve winners and losers. There is an *economic* pillar that supports growth and provides and coordinates the provision of public goods for all and a belief in and commitment to a general public interest in the face of narrow, personal need. There is a *social* element that seeks to plan and manage cities in the interests of all, and there is a commitment to the long term, a view that transcends the immediate, looking beyond electoral timescales. And there is a general disposition of *hope* – that the future can be better than the past or present, a belief in the possibility of change, improvement and progress.

Digital technology and social media are threatening all of these pillars, undermining the very notion of collective decisions on common challenges, instilling an individualistic disposition, turning us from citizens of cities into individual consumers in cities. We are unable to think about the future in the same way. Digital technology is replacing hope with a 'hope for the best' attitude. And cities are embracing and encouraging this. The UK government, like many national and local governments around the globe, is looking for solutions to problems from digital technology. In 2013 the Chinese government announced 193 smart city pilot projects whilst in the UK the government introduced a future cities competition in 2012 that funded the development of 30 smart city proposals. In India, Prime Minister Narendra Modi announced a smart cities challenge in 2016 aiming to create 100 exemplars that would inspire other places. This demand is being fed by the promises of Big Tech, academia and consultancies.

MIT Senseable City Lab describes itself as a kind of midwife for the digital city:

> The real-time city is real! As layers of networks and digital information blanket urban space, new approaches to the study of the built environment are emerging. The way we describe and understand cities is being radically transformed – as are the tools we use to design them.[1]

Despite the lofty, Panglossian rhetoric, our cities and the processes of city planning are being eroded, undermined and dismantled. The evidence is all around us on how digital is chipping away at the four pillars.

Living closer but further apart

Consensus in city planning has always been approached more in hope than expectation. Yet reaching broad agreement on the direction of change for any city remains an aspiration. The Future Melbourne 2026 Plan, for example, engaged in a six-month conversation with interest groups, communities and individuals in the city that involved a programme of events and online discussions, inviting the community to share ideas, concerns and aspirations for the city's future. The City of Edinburgh's Development Plan Scheme involved community briefings and workshops, an engagement programme for young people and exhibitions. Neither city's approach is unusual. Despite inevitable disagreements on what each city should focus on, there was consensus on the need for a plan. Yet it is increasingly clear that we agree less and less, not only on the ways forward, but also on what counts as the issues to be addressed. A poll for Hope not Hate, a UK-based think tank, in late 2018 found that 68 per cent of people in the UK felt that there wasn't a political party that spoke for them. This figure had grown from 61 per cent when the same question was asked six months earlier. At the same time there has been a steady rise in traffic to far-right websites and followers of far-right social media accounts.[2]

There is a range of reasons why we disagree more and why political alignments are breaking down, but many point to the impacts of digital technology in general and social media in particular[3] as being part of this story. In 2012 Eli Pariser published *Filter Bubble*, his warning that the popularity and dominance of Facebook and Google would lead us to become more insular and partitioned.[4] Pariser's argument was that the algorithms used by social media platforms feed us information, news and videos that reinforce our existing views, providing the conditions for us to be more suspicious of the attitudes of others and more susceptible to fake news. Whilst his analysis has been vindicated by subsequent events and research, what he highlighted was just the start of how digital technology has transformed the political landscape.

The growth in siloed, irreconcilable opinions has been further fuelled by the changing nature of city economies, in large part a consequence of the impacts of digital technology, including the advent of the gig economy combined with the uncertainty and disruption in a wide range of jobs and professions. One upshot has been the much discussed rise in populist and nationalist politics, a phenomenon that has led to greater engagement by some in politics and activism, in large part dependent on social media for organisation and communication. On the other hand there has been a general disengagement with politics at a general level, a disconnection that is driven by distraction: we check our phones on average every 12 minutes during waking hours, and over 70 per cent of us never turn them off. We are always alert but never fully engaged in anything, constantly absorbed. A lack of concentration and general wellbeing have been shown to result, as has a lack of time to invest in complex issues as we focus, instead, on instant 'clickbait' feeds of headlines and news bites, as I discussed in Chapter 5.

None of this is new and the impacts on society more generally have been well discussed. Yet it is in our cities where the impacts are felt most acutely. More effort is being invested in public involvement in city planning, but to less effect. Clear tensions arise when planning seeks to address issues that cities face – obesity, unhealthy lifestyles, inequality, mental illness, climate change and environmental quality – and the implications of such issues for urban policies on transport, housing, economies, society and energy. Complex issues have always been a characteristic of city planning, but we are losing our shared identities, finding it difficult to share the same social and political spaces, and this has direct implications for how we imagine sharing our physical spaces. Protests have been a common feature of city planning projects, from the massive regeneration of the central railway station in Stuttgart[5] to planned settlements in the West Bank.[6] What is new is the lack of agreement on the need for city planning, an activity that depends on the collective in an era of the individual. Political activism is spreading but becoming more shallow.

Legitimacy of the collective view

The loss of consensus has other implications for the planning of our cities. City planning inevitably involves trade-offs: there are winners and there are losers. The debate over the impact of skyscrapers on London's historic skyline has been taking place for decades, involving local and national government and a range of interest groups, developers and even a member of the Royal family. Here, the planning system has acted as an arena to balance competing demands – the need for economic growth against the historical aesthetics of the capital. It's a familiar scenario for cities across the world and each, in their own way, seeks to manage change, balancing the old with the new. In London certain strategic views such as that around St Paul's Cathedral are protected, focusing development in other areas, mainly in the square mile of the City of London Corporation. As with much of city planning there are no easy or absolute answers – most Londoners would like both jobs and growth whilst maintaining one foot in the past. And so a compromise is reached. Such outcomes are normally accepted because of the realisation that there are competing, legitimate views that need to be accommodated, views that we can understand and even have sympathy for, even if we may not agree with them.

When the latest in a long line of skyscrapers, named The Tulip for its bulbous shape, for the City of London was approved in 2019, the Chief Executive of Historic England commented: 'This building, a lift shaft with a bulge on top, would damage the very thing its developers claim they will deliver – tourism and views of London's extraordinary heritage.'[7] He wasn't denying the need for commercial office space in London, just disagreeing with the location. This cognitive dissonance – the developer who is also keen on protecting the environment, the car driver who is also a keen cyclist – allows us to accept that there are outcomes that are sub-optimal because the issues are not black and white but messy and complex. In other words, city planning is there to balance legitimate, competing interests to derive a common, public good.

What city planning has been experiencing over the past decade or so is a hardening of positions, a breakdown in the acceptance and tolerance of different views. Decisions are contested and options disputed through the city planning process and beyond, into the legal arena. Worse still, there is a growing fragmentation of views that are irreconcilable, threatening the very existence of the search for common answers to common challenges.

City planning is coming up against the rise of what has been termed 'tribal epistemology' or the emergence of truth based not on evidence or reason but on what your group or leader says is true. This post-truth era has similarities with religious cults where we all have access to the same facts or science, such as on climate change, but there is a steadfast refusal to accept it if it does not correspond with the worldview of a particular group. As David Roberts has put it:

> Information is evaluated based not on conformity to common standards of evidence or correspondence to a common understanding of the world, but on whether it supports the tribe's values and goals and is vouchsafed by tribal leaders. "Good for our side" and "true" begin to blur into one.[8]

The impacts and implications of this situation for cities and planning are sombre as we become increasingly implacable around the challenges facing us. City planning is struggling to cope and come to terms with this new reality. At a fundamental level there can be only one plan for a city. Yet if we cannot agree on some of the basic elements of a plan, such as the threat of climate change, or even whether a plan is necessary, then any outcome of the city planning process will be partial and lacking in legitimacy.

A new dark age

City planning is founded on the faith that tomorrow can be better than today. As a future searching activity, planning looks towards the horizon, considering the issues that face cities, evaluating options and proposing change in open and inclusive ways. This forward gaze requires us to go beyond immediate concerns, self-interest and simplistic reactions to consider how complex and sometimes intractable issues can be addressed in the long term.

Traffic congestion could be addressed by banning cars, but this will have serious consequences on businesses and those who cannot afford to live in the city; the answers lie in a combination of supply- and demand-side changes – better and cheaper public transport, congestion charging, more affordable housing, flexible working, and so on.

Much has been written about the emergence of what James Bridle has termed a 'new dark age',[9] or how digital technology is contracting our future gazing and narrowing our outlook, providing information profusion although not adding to knowledge, undermining our ability to come to collective approaches to common challenges. Vision and strategy are being replaced with reaction and prejudice: 'the abundance of information and the plurality of worldviews now accessible to us through the internet are not producing a coherent consensus on reality, but are driven by fundamentalist insistence on simplistic narratives, conspiracy theories and post-factual politics'.[10] Douglas Rushkoff argues a parallel and related point, that digital technology is colonising our lives, constantly feeding us information and demanding our attention, a situation he calls the 'distracted present'.[11] This combination of information overload and an inability to choose on the one hand, mixed with distraction on the other, amounts to the death of the future, a demise that disrupts if not devastates the basis of city planning and management. Many of us are simply focused on the present whilst others are simply focused on their smartphones.

Yet as challenging as this is, it doesn't fully capture what is happening in our cities. The practical implications for city planning and the management of the distracted present concern the difficulties in engaging with communities over the preparation of plans and the growing need to make policies and options vaguer in order to achieve buy-in to any kind of consensus. This vagueness, what some have termed the 'post-political condition', is a technique for city planners and politicians to unite disparate groups through using nebulous phrases in order to generate consensus by allowing competing interests to read into policies what they want.

Everyone can sign up to the notion of sustainable development, but for some it means the environment should come first, and for others it's about the need for economic growth to pay for environmental protection. This 'everything and nothing' approach to planning has obvious consequences, including the lack of ability to implement policies that lack specificity and the breakdown in trust when it becomes apparent that plans are nebulous.

This lack of credibility in planners and others is compounded by a more general attack on 'experts'. City planners, architects, engineers and politicians have been traditionally charged with 'making sense' of the multitude of information and competing claims to knowledge, a role more broadly provided by journalists in the news media. This gatekeeping role provides a filter and makes sense of the superabundance of information. What cities are experiencing now is the rise of the alternative, 'non-political' gatekeepers – the software engineer and Big Tech, experts whose interests are very different from those of the public servant.

The death of theory

A key element of planning as a future-orientated activity is the need to develop theories and assemble evidence to support them – if we introduce a congestion charge, air quality in the city centre will improve; when we restrict new development around the edge of the city, it will encourage more regeneration in the centre as land values rise. These theories are developed in an open and transparent way, transposed into public policy and then tested and refined. Yet digital technology is undermining this open and rational process, shifting us instead into an age of data and algorithms. We no longer have to understand cities, speculate on what might improve them and help address common challenges. Instead, we can look at the data – real-time feedback on what is happening right now – interrogate Big Data and look for patterns and correlations. There are some advantages to this, including the possibility of seeing patterns and relationships in data that previously escaped us. But there are profound implications too. We're shifting deeply political questions and processes to the realm of technocracy.

We're also missing the essential point that all models and theories are 'wrong' – there is no evidence that AI and Big Data are any better at thinking about the future than the collective intelligence of different views, experience and expertise. So what we're doing is replacing one approach or method with another, having been persuaded that the digital alternative is superior. And yet, as has been pointed out, AI and Big Data favour certain kinds of issues and solutions over others, ones for which there is data and those that are susceptible to being examined in this way. AI, machine learning and Big Data may be helpful in managing traffic controls and flows, predicting where police resources should be deployed or organising energy supply to better meet demand, but they have little to say about complex, multifaceted problems such as poverty, homelessness and an ageing population, issues that our cities are facing. The complex challenges also tend to be the ones that are less susceptible to market-driven approaches, which is part of the attraction to digital solutions: the smart city is a neoliberal dream, bypassing bureaucrats and politicians and providing real-time adaptation to markets. City planning becomes akin to a form of SimCity.

Offering an alternative

The possibility of a 'control' room approach to city planning would be less alarming if it didn't already exist. In preparation for hosting the 2014 FIFA World Cup and the 2016 Olympic Games, Rio de Janeiro Mayor Eduardo da Costa Paes commissioned IBM to build a City Operations Centre linking video streams from 900 cameras in the city. The idea was to better 'understand' the city. Real-time video is shown live on the 80-metre wall and multiple screens, and analysed by 30 staff dressed in white boiler suits, in order, the Mayor claims, to give them a sense of common identity. How does the Rio model differ (other than perhaps in scale) from other CCTV monitoring operations found in cities around the world?

Combining real-time data and AI, the Centre is able to predict traffic congestion and natural disasters, providing warnings to residents and coordinating city services, including the police, to respond to natural and human incidents. But as the Centre is using just 15 per cent of its processing power, there is the capacity and desire to move from monitoring and reacting to prediction and control. It's a desire that cities share with Big Tech. In Toronto, Google proposed to take over part of the city and develop its own version of smart, harvesting citizens' data as they moved around, interacting with services and buying goods. As Eric Schmidt, former CEO of Google, put it, think of 'all the things you could do if someone would just give us a city and put us in charge'.[12]

The attractiveness of alternatives comes, in part, from the perceived failure of existing mechanisms, a perception that arises from the indirect (and occasionally direct) impression put out by Big Tech. Offering 'solutions' to issues that are normally dealt with through open, democratic processes supported by professionals implicitly criticises current approaches, however unfairly. Proposals to make efficiency savings, breaking down professional and policy silos, offering new services, and so on all suggest that the ways in which things are currently done are inefficient and ineffective. But recently the digital offer has gone further. As Edward Alden, a senior fellow at the Council on Foreign Relations in the US, puts it:

> They're [Big Tech] really trying to change the narrative. You have stultifying government regulation on one side, and liberation, freedom and consumer choice on the other.
>
> They've done a really good job of framing that. I think it has really restricted the willingness and ability of governments to constrain their activities to a great degree.[13]

Current open and inclusive models of city planning and democracy itself are portrayed as out of touch, slow and unresponsive; democracy is becoming bogged down as agreement becomes increasingly elusive as views diverge, a situation that owes much to the impacts of digital technology itself. So why bother with politics any more, when digital technology provides alternatives?

The enemy within

The four pillars of planning are not only being attacked by Silicon Valley. Whilst managerial and regulatory elements of government including planning seek to address the impacts of the platform economy, companies such as Airbnb and Uber, along with elements of government, seek to encourage them, even changing the regulating framework to facilitate their further rollout. In Australia, for example, whilst local government was seeking to regulate Airbnb in order to address affordability issues, central government was offering cash to homeowners who put their properties on the site.[14] This lack of coordination arises in large part because the 'smart city' narrative appeals to those in government promoting economic growth and development.

There is nothing inherently problematic with this. After all, different professional groups such as transport, health and education all develop and champion their own areas. Yet city planning seeks a broader, more balanced future for cities focused on sustainability, an approach that takes into account environmental and social needs as well as economic growth. This more partial view of smart digital cities as a pathway to growth and economic development puts any attempt at a balanced future for places in the shade because of its compelling narrative, and because it vaguely promises to solve and improve a wide range of other challenges that our cities face, including those in other, traditional, city functions.

Bypassing the focus of regulation

Planning systems vary from country to country, but they are all based on the premise that change can be managed through the control and regulation of the use and development of land. Housing, offices, infrastructure, transport, and so on, are all competing for what is a scarce and finite resource, and the quantum, location and kind of development can all be shaped through city planning. Digital technology and smart solutions largely bypass this framework of land use controls, although there are significant implications.

Amazon and other platform economy operators are replacing land and buildings with people and connectivity. Yet even when there are land use implications of the digital economy, the sheer scale of the disruption and impacts, particularly from the platform economy, mean that effective regulation and control of change is all but removed. Take London's attempts to curb the impacts of Airbnb through a 90-night limit on short-term lets. The information and data needed to monitor and regulate this are only possessed by Airbnb and the company will not share it. The upshot is that London and many other cities find themselves unable to regulate in order to help manage disruption:

> In London ... local governments have to rely on complaints by local residents and triangulate these with Google earth images and information from the Airbnb website itself in order to track down particular properties to fine them. This is not feasible for local governments with limited finances and staff.[15]

This lack of control is reinforced by the willingness of some companies to flout the law, to hide behind the claim that their data are private, and to organise lobbying by users to pressure government to turn a blind eye or even deregulate and roll back what few levers remain. This is part of the 'hacking' and 'hack the city' culture, the feeling that it is the regulatory frameworks that are the problem and that they will catch up and adapt when disrupted enough. In their view, Big Tech isn't destroying the city but saving it.

This self-righteous attitude is reinforced by mobilisation of support by central government, city authorities and regulators for the 'reality' and benefits of the platform economy. Airbnb's parallel platform, Airbnb Citizen, presents a wide range of positive experiences about the individual and community benefits of home sharing, for example. 'Sharers', as they are called, are encouraged to be part of local 'Home Sharing Clubs', swapping stories and experiences. As the website puts it:

> Airbnb is supporting the creation of Home Sharing Clubs to help hosts come together to advocate for fair home sharing laws in their communities. We now have more than 100 Clubs operating in communities around the world. This growing network of hosts, guests, small business owners, and local community leaders is leading the way in demonstrating how

home sharing benefits neighborhoods around the world.[16]

In Berlin, the Club is actively engaged with local politicians seeking to influence changes in the city's regulation of home sharing.

What is replacing the four pillars?

There are obviously benefits from digital technology for planning and managing our cities, and digital technology and the smart city provide many opportunities for people, cities and city planning. However,

> It's one thing to willingly install Alexa in your home. It's another when publicly owned infrastructure – streets, bridges, parks and plazas – *is* Alexa, so to speak.[17]

A local council in London looked at data on the proximity of schools, homeless shelters, food banks, payday loan providers and betting shops, analysis that led them to identify the number of vulnerable people living close to betting shops, leading them to close a number of them.[18]

Social media and the internet have allowed cities to consult and engage more widely whilst Building Information Modelling (BIM), an industry standard 3D design and construction platform, allows communities to suggest changes that can be accommodated quickly and cost-efficiently. City Information Modelling (CIM) expands the approach to whole cities, allowing them to test various scenarios and future threats such as rising sea levels, freak weather events, drought and energy shortages. Yet alongside the benefits come the downsides. City planning is being replaced, seized by a different vision of how cities should be managed. This isn't a coordinated and even conscious movement by Big Tech, but a consequence of the multitude of impacts that digital technology is forcing on our urban areas. The four pillars of city planning, outlined above, are being dismantled, but Silicon Valley isn't stopping there. It's now beginning to rebuild too.

In October 2017 Sidewalk Labs won a competition to develop a 12-acre, publicly owned site on Toronto's waterfront, later expanded to around 800 acres. Announced by Canadian Prime Minister, Justin Trudeau, the winning proposal from Sidewalk Labs drew on the now common 'smart city' rhetoric, promising to develop the waterfront area 'from the internet up', to tackle a wide range of challenges facing the city, including urban sprawl, climate change, traffic congestion, rising house prices and environmental pollution. In part, this smart panacea was to be achieved through what Sidewalk Labs euphemistically called 'centralized identity management'. Each resident would automatically be part of a personal identity scheme that would give them access to public services such as libraries and healthcare as well as, it was suggested, voting. The vision for this smart, data-driven development came from the Chief Executive of Sidewalk Labs' parent company: 'Think of all the things you could do if someone would just give us a city and put us in charge.' That Chief Executive was Eric Schmidt and the parent company was Google.

According to some, Sidewalk Labs/Google was attempting a 'colonizing experiment in surveillance capitalism attempting to bulldoze important urban, civic and political issues'.[19] Concern over the business model underpinning the scheme began to surface early on when it emerged that Sidewalk Labs/ Google would be collecting data from residents and visitors for its own use, intending to become the planning authority for the area, effectively replacing public with private controls. It is the harvesting of personal data that has worried most people: 'I imagined us creating a Smart City of Privacy as opposed to a Smart City of Surveillance', commented Ann Cavoukian, one of Canada's leading privacy experts, in her resignation letter as a consultant on the project.[20] Others concerned with the use of data asked if residents could opt-out of 'centralized identity management'. In the view of Michael J. Bryant, Executive Director of the Canadian Civil Liberties Association, 'Canada is not Google's lab rat. We can do better. Our freedom from unlawful public surveillance is worth fighting for.'[21] The Canadian Civil Liberties Association is suing three levels of government over the Google-backed plan. In terms of Google's proposal to become the planning authority for the scheme, it would be 'as if Uber were to propose regulations on ride-sharing, or Airbnb were to tell city council how to govern short-term rentals. By definition, there is a conflict of interest.'[22] In 2020 Google announced that it wouldn't be proceeding with its development in Toronto but would still explore other opportunities.

Google isn't the only Tech Giant moving from the virtual to the physical world: Facebook, Amazon and Apple are all planning and building new developments. The latest scheme belongs to Microsoft's Bill Gates, who is behind a 25,000-acre smart city development in Arizona.[23] And we can expect more.

Google wasn't proposing to turn into a developer for any other reason than it wanted more data. In 2019 BT, the UK multinational telecoms and internet company, announced its new advertising slogan, 'Technology Will Save Us'. This attitude is a common one in Big Tech where there is a belief that there is literally nothing that digital technology cannot improve or make better. In our cities this attitude echoes and even underpins the 'smart city' narrative. The claims extend to many areas of public policy, from obesity to climate change, and cities are already moving towards partnering with tech companies beyond physical redevelopment, in Toronto and elsewhere, to include infrastructure such as energy, water, telecommunications and, in the UK, the NHS. In 2019 the Google subsidiary Deep Mind signed an agreement with five NHS Trusts to process data. In return for cloud storage Google Health will have access to anonymised data to help develop its AI diagnostic services. The common factor behind all of these moves is data. Google, Facebook, Amazon and Apple all want to gather, analyse and monetise data.

Undermining city planning and then expanding into physical developments, essential infrastructure and public services will eventually lead to a very different kind of city and society. We will move from city planning in the public interest to one that is driven, delivered and controlled by private interests, namely, those of the shareholders of a handful of companies. Yet the lure of consumer-focused technocracy is strong as we experience it on a day-to-day basis through the likes of Amazon. It 'works' at an individual level in that we are presented with choices of goods and services. Yet how this would or could scale to tackle issues such as climate change that are political rather than technical is open to question, to say the least. City planning is by no means perfect, but it 'works' because it combines the political and the technical, and gives everyone a voice, by seeking to reach decisions via consensus. This way plans have legitimacy, and those who disagree or who have a different preferred view accept the outcome. City planning also looks to the longer term, beyond the more immediate focus of consumer-based decisions and timescales. It's not easy to see how one-click ordering and next-day delivery help us plan and manage our cities over the medium to longer term.

9

Why bother to save the city?

As James Williams puts it, in order to do anything that matters, we must first be able to give attention to the things that matter.[1] The purpose of this chapter is to argue that cities matter, and even in the uncertain and challenging times of a global pandemic, they are worth saving. But right now the future of cities is under threat. On the one hand, cities are facing the impacts of digital technology, enabled in part by the Trojan Horse of the 'smart city', as I argue throughout this book. But this isn't the only current threat that cities face. Many are now raising existential questions over the post-pandemic city: if cities bring people together, then post-pandemic they just want to be as far apart as possible. Based on high-density residential and commercial development and a centre for leisure and entertainment, there are growing claims that cities have become the 'plague pits' of the 21st century.[2] Size matters, as by mid-2020 it's the larger cities that have been hit hardest by COVID-19, with around a quarter of all national deaths in the US and the UK being in New York and London, respectively, and around a third of Spain's total deaths being in Madrid.

A world without cities isn't entirely unthinkable as cities are a relatively new phenomenon. They arose for specific reasons to meet certain needs, be it as marketplaces for excess produce or as centres of religion or as military strongholds. Created by humankind they are not immutable. So, if the needs of humankind have changed, then perhaps it's time for cities to change too? It's not as if cities have remained static over the past couple of centuries. In one of his many sweeping historical overviews, Lewis Mumford discusses the rise and the fall of cities, looking for patterns and trends.[3] Taking his cue from ancient Rome, he argues that cities go through a series of stages as they evolve and reflect the needs of wider society. The last stage of city evolution is what he calls 'necropolis', or the city of the dead. Here, cities become physical shells, devoid of purpose.

Obviously, cities as a concept didn't die with the fall of the Roman Empire, but Mumford's point was that there was a life cycle to particular city forms and functions, and we shouldn't assume that cities are a permanent feature of civilisation. There is other evidence to support the claim that cities can come and go. Putting aside the many examples from ancient history, there are also recent examples of cities that are no more. Times Beach, Missouri, was abandoned in 1983 when it became too polluted for its residents,[4] whilst Kolmanskop in Namibia was swallowed up by the shifting desert.[5] Kadykchan in Russia was vacated by its 150,000 inhabitants when the government closed schools and turned off essential services such as water following the collapse of the Soviet Union, whilst many large industrial cities such as Detroit suffered partial abandonment when their economic base collapsed. One of the most interesting cases of abandonment is Kowloon Walled City near Hong Kong. Occupied by Japan during the Second World War and then disowned by the British authorities afterwards, it was taken over by squatters and criminals, soon becoming a lawless city. It was eventually demolished, but not until 1993, when it became ungovernable and a threat to Hong Kong.[6]

Obviously not all cities that face a crisis or challenge are abandoned. Many simply adjust. In the past, when cities have been hit by the plague or public health crises they have adapted, most notably when London built its sewage system following the cholera epidemic in the 19th century, as discussed in Chapter 6. Others have benefited from shocks. New York suffered from global competition as a manufacturing hub in the 20th century, although it then evolved into an international centre for ideas and finance.[7]

Technological change has generally been a key player in contemporary urban change, as discussed in Chapter 3: steam and water were disruptive in the 19th century, steel and the internal combustion engine turned cities upside down in the 20th century, and digital technology is creating turmoil at the moment. Like with the challenges that came from disease and plagues, cities adapted and evolved when faced with technological challenges. As cities changed, humankind evolved with them, benefiting from change through improvements in public transport, water and sewage infrastructure, mass production of goods, and cultural opportunities. Alongside these changes sat other deep issues: poverty and wealth inequality accompanied by precarious work have always characterised cities, and they still do.

So why is the threat of digital technology any different from those events that have driven the evolution of cities in the past? If cities are being disrupted by digital technology, maybe this isn't all bad? Digital technology doesn't just present a challenge to cities; it represents an existential threat to them. Digital infrastructure and services also provide the means by which we could abandon the city if the coronavirus pandemic provides the impetus. Online working, schooling, information, home food deliveries, and so on all demonstrated clearly that the fundamental purpose of the city, to bring people and markets together, was no longer necessary. In the COVID-19 era people didn't need to be in close physical proximity with goods and services because they came to you whether you were in a city, a suburb or a village. There was much discussion about how cities had lost their functional necessity and even allure – people were moving out and redefining their needs. So why is it that cities matter, exactly? If the city isn't an immutable part of society, if it is being undermined by viral pandemics, and if digital technology provides a proven alternative, why bother to save the city?

There are many reasons why we should save the city. Here I offer three. First, cities are vital to how we tackle the pressing issues that face us as a species. Of these challenges, climate change is the most serious and pressing, and cities are the key to addressing it. City living is more resource-efficient, but cities are also places that need to act collectively in order to function, and are politically inclined to do so. These three elements – efficiency, collective attitude and interventionist disposition – are all fundamental preconditions for action in tackling the climate emergency. Second, put simply, cities can make us happier. Some go as far to claim that cities 'are good for you'.[8] The arguments here are that well designed and run cities increase and improve individual wellbeing. It has long been recognised that cities gave individuals the opportunity to 'be themselves', but recent shifts in cities around the globe have begun to seek to balance economic growth as an objective with a broader goal of happiness or wellbeing. Finally, cities are our best hope for the future of democracy and progressive politics. Cities were the birthplace of democracy in ancient Greece. Whilst political positions across many countries have bifurcated and hardened, cities continue to be the home of more tolerant and inclusive values and voting patterns.

Cities and the Anthropocene

The climate emergency is the most significant and pressing danger our cities and humankind face. Since the Cambrian explosion some 540 million years ago there have been five mass extinction events, defined as a sharp decline in the diversity and abundance of multi-cellular organisms.

Since 1900 we have been living through a sixth mass extinction, called the Holocene, driven by human activity, over-population and consumption, with a growing consensus that the current era could be regarded as a distinct epoch, the Anthropocene, an age characterised by the dominance and impact of human activity on the planet, including global warming. Many now regard such impacts as going beyond the biological to wider consequences including civilisation. What is clear is that one victim of the planet's next mass extinction event could be the city.

Cities are at one and the same time the most significant contributor to the problem, our biggest vulnerability to climate change and the silver bullet of attempts to tackle it. Despite occupying around 3 per cent of the earth's surface, cities emit 75 per cent of all carbon dioxide through the energy they consume, whilst large metropolitan urban areas like London import 80 per cent of their food from all corners of the planet, often by air. The resource needs of cities are huge. Their ecological footprint[9] is typically hundreds of times greater than their physical footprint; that is, the resources required to sustain a city – food, energy, water, etc – require an area hundreds of times the size of the city itself. Around two-thirds of consumption-based greenhouse gas emissions in our cities come from beyond the city boundaries. Cities are utterly dependent on global networks of food, energy, and so on to survive,[10] and as such can act collectively to influence how such necessities are managed and supplied to reduce their carbon footprint.

In terms of vulnerabilities, 90 per cent of our cities are coastal whilst approximately 360 million people live in cities that are less than 10 metres above sea level. The Intergovernmental Panel on Climate Change estimates sea level rises of up to 59 centimetres over the next 100 years. In Europe alone, 70 per cent of cities are vulnerable to rising sea levels in that period, whilst in China, 78 million people live in cities that will be affected, a figure rising at 3 per cent per annum. Those most at risk from the impact of climate change on cities are the poor – those who live on marginal land by rivers and coasts, on steep slopes subject to landslides, and in unstable structures that cannot withstand increased storm and wind strength and heat waves. People will be affected in other ways too. The vast majority of our urban infrastructure and services, from energy plants to public transportation systems, healthcare to water treatment, are vulnerable, and these are facilities on which civilisation depends.

Our cities might be the main contributors to and victims of climate change, but they are also our best hope of tackling it. Urban living is far more energy- and resource-efficient than the alternatives. Urban public transport uses about 10 per cent of the energy per passenger kilometre that the private car does,[11] whilst city living uses less energy to heat and run homes. Cities are working together to make our consumption cleaner and more energy-efficient, using more renewable resources and reducing harmful emissions. At a time when some national governments are turning their backs on the global need to address climate change, many cities are stepping up their commitments and their efforts. Surveys highlight that city residents are felt to be doing more to improve people's lives than national leaders. None of this should be a surprise. Cities require us to think communally, to face up to the social rather than turn our backs on each other, forcing us to face common challenges. Cities need common solutions – collective transport, collaborative urban design, communal education, shared waste solutions – to succeed. Proactive city planning and management are strongly correlated with what are commonly regarded as successful cities, as discussed in Chapter 5.

So, rather than decry the resource intensity of urban living, the focus has been on how collective action within and between cities can make a major difference to tackling climate change. Organisations such as C40,[12] an affiliation of 96 global cities, and the Coalition for Urban Transitions,[13] among others, are developing a coordinated approach to help meet the 2015 Paris Agreement and to keep the global temperature rise to below 1.5°C above pre-industrial levels. Given the precarious position of many cities, adaption is also a key element of this coordinated approach, focusing on protecting the most vulnerable and the services on which we all depend. Whilst the measures being taken vary between cities and most starkly between cities in the developed and developing worlds, there is little doubt that the most sustainable form of living for the future is urban.

Broadly speaking, the denser a city, the more efficient it is in terms of household energy consumption, the provision and viability of public transport and infrastructure, and food and water consumption. Because living in close proximity necessitates collective approaches to urban living and the search for common ground, cities have the attitude, disposition and tools (as well as the incentive, given the location of many) to work towards adaptation and mitigation. In many cases, mostly in the US, this work is in the opposite direction of the national governments. I go into more detail on how city planning and management can help save the city and the planet later in this chapter, but the overall message is that we need to be greyer to be greener. Here it is worth repeating the point that this collective mentality and action is being undermined through inequality in cities and the distraction-driven business model of digital technology.

Cities can make more of us happy...

The phrase 'city air makes you free' (*Stadtluft macht frei* in the original German) was a principle or tradition from early medieval Germany where a serf who escaped to a city for a year and a day would earn his freedom. The notion that cities were places of refuge, freedom and happiness has been an enduring one. Whilst putting one's finger on how we measure happiness is difficult, the notion has become a proxy for a range of indicators and a movement to rebalance the direction of cities and policy away from a simple focus on economic growth. As Charles Montgomery argued in *Happy City* in 2013,[14] small changes to big cities can make a significant difference in the extent of happiness – the most dynamic economies of the 20th century have produced the most miserable cities. Fiona Reynolds paints a similar picture:

> In the second half of the twentieth century we became obsessed with materialism, preoccupied by a culture that values consumption more than intangible benefits, and we presided over a period of devastating losses to nature and the beauty of our countryside and heritage, while much of what we built ranged from undistinguished to downright ugly.[15]

As income and wealth in cities grew, so did inequalities. But it wasn't just the poor who felt more miserable – those who benefited from material gains suffered from what Montgomery terms the 'hedonic treadmill', or comparing yourself with others and then shifting expectations of what one feels one needs to reflect 'success'. From the perspective of the individual, increases in material wealth can create a vicious circle as we feel we haven't progressed because everyone else has been fuelling us to want even more. This unhappiness has been particularly felt in our cities.

It is the focus on economic growth at the expense of broader wellbeing or happiness that has driven this rise in dissatisfaction and the perceived need to increase income and wealth to achieve happiness. And this narrow focus on growth isn't just at the individual level. As cities have grown, there has been a corresponding rise in air pollution and associated health problems through increased traffic congestion. Urban sprawl and poor public transport have led to a deterioration in mental wellbeing – those who commute more than 45 minutes to work have a much higher likelihood of divorce whilst people who live in the suburbs and car-dependent neighbourhoods are far less trusting of other people than those who live in walkable, mixed-use neighbourhoods with easy access to shops and services. There are other downsides of focusing on economic growth and the individual above broader happiness too, including higher levels of obesity, as walking and cycling become more difficult because of traffic and pollution.

On the other hand, there are places that have turned this around, cities that have made changes and increased happiness rather than economic growth. Montgomery's argument isn't that we need to create the happy city but recreate it – the city has always been a happiness project. In ancient Athens hedonism was embedded within a drive for broader happiness where civic and personal wellbeing were linked, whilst in Rome civic pride was reflected in architecture and culture. The city as a place of beauty and happiness was championed much later by the likes of Hausmann in Paris and Wren in London. In more recent times there has also been a drive to eschew the material in favour of broader public goals including beauty and happiness. As Fiona Reynolds argues, the Victorians sought to tackle Britain's 19th-century 'city of darkness', discussed in Chapter 1, by promoting a debate around the damaging nature of exploitation of human and natural resources ultimately leading to social and political reforms.[16] In the aftermath of the Second World War, the economic and social reconstruction of society included a commitment to enhance the beauty of the countryside – material wealth alongside cultural development and progress.

This broader disposition may have been eclipsed in some societies, but it is making a strong comeback. In 1979 the young king of a small, poor Himalayan kingdom answered a question from a journalist at Bombay Airport. When asked, 'We do not know anything about Bhutan. What is your gross national product?' His Majesty Jigme Singye Wangchuck said 'We do not believe in gross national product because gross national happiness is more important'.[17] This came as a surprise to his advisers, but Bhutan has subsequently become known for its focus on

GNH, not GNP, as a measure of national wellbeing. Others have subsequently taken up the approach with encouragement from the UN and the OECD's Better Life Index and Social Progress Index. At the global level various country and city happiness indices have emerged, adapting Bhutan's GNH approach at different spatial scales including at the national (for example, the UAE and the UK), state (for example, Victoria, British Columbia) and city (for example, Seattle and Somerville, Massachusetts). Each approach has differed, with some using surveys to directly measure happiness and others drawing on existing and published data. All have sought to develop a more holistic way of measuring growth and directing policy.

At the city level, happiness indices are used to help put the wellbeing of residents at the centre of planning and management. The UK-based Thriving Places Index run by a national charity provides an annual index of wellbeing for cities and regions. Thriving is the new happiness. The Index takes a basket of published data for each city and presents a comprehensive picture. These data include collections of data on equality (for example, health and income), local conditions (such as mental health, education and unemployment) and sustainability (for example, energy use and waste). In all, 30 indicators are blended into three overall scores based on equality, local conditions and sustainability. My city of Cambridge, for example, scores badly on housing and green infrastructure and well on children's education and mental and physical health. There is no actual measure of 'happiness' (the index was formerly called the Happy City Index), but a range of proxies for wellbeing. There is also no indicator on the extent of 'smart'. In fact, the further rollout of digital technology might actually reduce wellbeing through increasing anxiety, as it has in some areas, with a fear of the 'smart city' becoming the 'surveillance city'.

Cities are then encouraged to take on the areas where their residents are 'unhappy' rather than focus on making changes to support further economic development and growth on the basis that this is what will somehow make them 'happy'. The City of Bristol in England's West Country is a place that should have been happy, according to GNH. The economy was strong, the workforce highly educated, and wages were higher than the regional average. Yet, as discussed in Chapter 2, Bristol also suffers from areas of high deprivation, with one in six of its residents being in some of the most deprived neighbourhoods in England in the early 21st century. In parts of the city child poverty is at 50 per cent in 2019.[18] The city's response to being presented with a broader range of indicators of wellbeing has been to focus on improving those areas that contribute to wellbeing, particularly investment in liveability, such as pedestrianisation and traffic restraint, and green infrastructure, including recycling.

...and are our best hope for progressive politics

Cities have long been fertile breeding grounds for a range of liberal and left-of-centre thinking and ideologies. It was in reaction to the dire conditions of the working class in 19th-century Manchester that Friedrich Engels penned his *Conditions of the Working Class* in 1845. With Karl Marx he went on to co-author *Das Kapital* and *The Communist Manifesto*. The Marxist historian Eric Hobsbawm put the relationship between cities and left-of-centre politics down to a combination of density and the proximity of the poor to the levers of power.[19] I'd suggest that cities are politically more left wing and progressive than non-urban areas, in part because they contain a socially and economically diverse population. But city living also exposes people to diversity through a mix of wealths, cultures and backgrounds. Cities require and create a disposition of cooperation, tolerance of difference and openness to change, and these traits are reflected in politics and voting. In Germany, the cities of Munich and Nuremberg are consistently run by Social Democratic administrations, islands of centre-left politics in a Bavaria of Christian-Democrat conservatism. In the US the major cities are more liberal in their voting patterns, particularly the larger, coastal cities. In the 2016 US presidential election the Democrat candidate Hillary Clinton won 88 of the country's 100 largest cities, although still ultimately lost owing to the Electoral College voting system. A major study by two US academics, Chris Tausanovitch and Christopher Warshaw, found that cities with more liberal populations tend to get more liberal policy. Likewise, liberal cities tax and spend more and have more progressive tax systems. And this finding was directly linked to the size of the city: the bigger the city, the more politically liberal it was.[20] Others have highlighted how this relationship is growing stronger and is self-reinforcing. Bill Bishop has talked about what he terms 'The Big Sort',[21] or the ongoing deepening of political segregation in the US. Whilst Bishop's findings have been confirmed by some,[22] they have been challenged by others.[23]

Nevertheless, the evidence from election results is compelling. Over time, suburbs, small towns and rural areas have increasingly voted Republican whilst cities were simultaneously moving in the opposite direction. Bishop and others claim that this situation arises because people move to places that reflect their values and preferences – the Pew Research Center found that liberals are more likely to say racial and ethnic diversity is important in a community whilst conservatives emphasise shared religious faith. Living near art museums and theatres was important to 73 per cent of liberals, although this was of value to just 23 per cent of conservatives. As for actual location, 41 per cent of conservatives preferred to live in a rural area, with a further 35 per cent preferring a small town. Just 4 per cent wanted to live in a city. Liberals took the completely contrary view, with 46 per cent preferring to live in a city and just 11 per cent in a rural area or a small town (20 per cent).[24]

The relationship between political outlook and the urban isn't exclusively a US phenomenon. On 23 June 2016 the UK voted by a narrow margin, 51.9 per cent, to leave the EU. There were many reasons why people decided to vote either way, but there was a clear division between major cities, which largely voted to remain, and other areas. As population density increased, so did the likelihood of voting to remain to be part of a collective organisation, aiming at social, political and economic harmony.

Why, you might ask, is any of this important? Political and cultural silos should be a concern for everyone, left or right. In homogenising views and cleansing difference, be it gender, race, religion, sexual orientation, age, culture, socioeconomic background, etc, society and individuals lose out. Diversity in background and views is important to creating new ideas, solutions, products and services. Diversity is also a vital element in how we view others, helping develop empathy and tolerance and reducing discrimination. But if you're a left-of-centre city dweller like me, there is another dimension to this trend: cities are becoming bulwarks against a number of national policies on immigration, climate change, minimum wages, sick leave and LGBTQI rights. The differences in policy agendas between the cities and states and the federal level in the US have given rise to the so-called 'sanctuary city'. Some US cities have defied President Trump's policies on immigrant rights and withdrawal from the Paris Agreement whilst there is strong evidence that demonstrates that whilst reproductive health services differ between US cities, the difference between cities and rural areas is much starker.

In 2015 the UN published its 17 Sustainable Development Goals (SDGs), and 193 countries signed up. The goals included commitments to clean energy, economic growth and action to tackle climate change.[25] Progress towards the SDGs is being led by cities around the globe, and it isn't simply to SDG 11 that included the commitment to sustainable urbanisation and participatory and integrated city planning. As a consequence it is cities that have taken the lead, individually and acting in networks across national borders. Actions vary from aligning city plans to the SDGs (New York and Helsinki), to changing procurement processes through requiring suppliers to help achieve SDG goals (Malmo and Bristol) and engaging with citizens on changes (Mannheim and Milan).

What is also clear is that cities are acting collectively within and across nations. In the US over 400 mayors from the largest to the smallest cities are part of the Climate Mayors network. The global C40 network of major cities that is developing policies for tackling climate change includes 15 of the largest US cities. Part of those solutions includes increasing urban density and redeveloping previously used land. These cities are not seeing the SDGs as a compliance issue, but as opportunities to make life better for their citizens. And because cities attract like minds and attitudes, there is a broad, positive disposition to make commitments like SDGs real, even when some of the nation states within which cities sit become more lukewarm. The fact is that actions that make a difference are easier to envisage at the city level, because that is where we have to face up to choices and investment to make cities work, be it transport, waste, education, affordable housing, etc. This combination of positive disposition and the necessity of action is joined by an agility: cities are more nimble than nations in effecting changes, particularly those that can shape demand.

What we're up against

Cities are the future for humanity and our best hope of addressing a range of challenges that face the planet. They provide a collective space, the levers to effect change and the political will to do so. Yet digital technology is undermining this through distraction and undermining the levers of city planning and management. There is also another way in which digital more broadly is threatening this solution. If cities are our future, then not everyone has bought into that, as Google, Apple and Facebook are planning and building their own futures, set apart from the communities and escaping the fate of cities.

Even in those cities where Big Tech remains embedded, there is a reluctance to acknowledge the social and economic impacts combined with strong opposition to doing anything about it. In November 2018 voters in San Francisco decided to back Proposition C, a proposal to levy a tax on gross income averaging about 0.5 per cent on companies with an annual revenue of at least US$50 million, raising about US$300 million a year. The tax will be used to help tackle homelessness in the city, which has reached crisis proportions, with nearly 7,500 people sleeping rough every night, including around 5 per cent of school-age children. The reason behind this growth in homelessness is clear: the impact of tech companies likes Twitter, Facebook, and so on, on housing affordability in the San Francisco Bay Area, as discussed earlier. What is also clear is where the main opposition to this Proposition came from. Twitter CEO Jack Dorsey was one of a number of business leaders who argued against it. Dorsey claimed that the tax was unfair because it was levied on turnover, not profit. Many Silicon Valley startups have high revenues but actually lose money, deliberately operating at a loss in order to see off any competition and then become the dominant market player. Think Amazon, which, for years, ran at a loss and now dominates the online retail market.

Some have claimed that this financial model is anticompetitive, as discussed in Chapter 3. Other Silicon Valley companies have also resisted city-based initiatives to address problems that they have, in part, fuelled. Amazon successfully pushed back against a local tax in Seattle that would have been used to help address homelessness, whilst Apple also managed to get a proposed payroll tax in Cupertino taken off the agenda.[26] The lack of commitment to collective solutions to common problems is not confined to local issues. There is a broader reluctance too.

> It's pretty widely accepted that both Google and Amazon are chronic tax avoiders. It's been well documented that Google has shifted billions of dollars of profits out of developed nations and into tax havens.[27]

There is a long history of industrialists looking after themselves and creating a future apart from the rest of society. Yet there is also a fine tradition of industrial philanthropy and engagement between industry and the communities on which it depends. Saltaire in the North of England is a town built in 1851 by the cotton mill owner Sir Titus Salt. It was intended to be a place that balanced work and home, with modern factories accompanied by houses and gardens for the workers and their families, and schools and libraries. New Lanark in Scotland built by cotton industrialist and social reformer Robert Owen in the 18th century, Port Sunlight by the soap magnate Lever family in 1888, and Bournville in Birmingham by the confectionery manufacturing Cadbury family in the 1800s. These are just the UK examples – there are many others around the globe. What are the current tech titans doing for their cities and communities?

How will city planning help save the planet?

So we need cities to help save the planet and humankind to be both happier and more progressive. In short, we need to save cities to save ourselves, and in 2020 that job got more difficult as physical proximity, hitherto the main advantage and raison d'être of cities, became far less attractive. So what can we do to ensure the future remains urban? The success of cities in the abstract rather than as individual places in being able to weather change through time has been relatively straightforward. There is one overarching element that will be critical to the future of cities as the basis for saving the planet: cities need to go back to go forward. They need to densify, even in a time of viral pandemics. As I covered in Chapter 8, the growth in availability and popularity of the private car in the early part of the 20th century, along with the availability of finance, led to an explosion in the suburbanisation of homes and jobs, often leaving behind wretched physical environments and those unable to adapt in cities. This flight out of cities was compounded in many cities by the damage wrought in the Second World War from aerial bombing, which further fuelled relocation and dispersal.

In very different times and for very different reasons many countries took the decision not to abandon their cities. Alongside efforts to limit sprawl and regenerate and rebuild in the post-war era emerged a broader approach of interconnected policy initiatives to support cities. The triad of concepts, as they were known, involved containing further outward growth of the city through what are commonly referred to as green belts, designating a number of planned new satellite towns to focus development pressure, and then regenerating and redeveloping areas within the city. This model has been widely adopted across the globe, with countries from Brazil to New Zealand introducing urban containment policies. Originally such approaches were aimed at protecting open space and improving the environment, but it soon became clear that far from reducing densities, constraining outward development led to increasing densities within cities. This unexpected outcome was less to do with the imposition of green belts and more linked to the lack of progress in developing the satellite towns and cities that would help reduce densities in the cities. In the US, proposals for up to 3,000 'Greenbelt Cities', as they were termed, linked to the New Deal in the 1930s were drastically reduced to a handful.[28]

In the UK a number of New Towns were built, although the number was again reduced because of costs. What didn't directly cost governments was the containment element through green belts, and these began to appear around cities in many parts of the world, from the 1930s onwards.

With limited and partial dispersal to New Towns, the impact of green belt-led containment was twofold. First, demand to move out of the city did not diminish, but with no planned new settlements, people leap-frogged the green belt, moving to dormitory villages. As employment remained in the cities, the outcome was car-based commuting and congestion. Second, land prices in parts of the city began to rise as supply was constrained. The rising cost of land was reflected in the price of developments, notably housing. Green belts were making housing less affordable, further encouraging people to move out of the city. Developments within cities were becoming denser, reflecting the economics of land prices. This has had other environmentally beneficial outcomes too. As land values have risen, restrictions on the supply of greenfield land have led to previously under-developed and contaminated land being brought back into use and redeveloped.

Yet just when voices against the containment of cities began to get traction in government, a further justification emerged. In short, and as argued above, denser cities were more sustainable cities. The green in green belts began to take on a new hue. Not only did green belts maintain open, undeveloped land around cities; they also helped fight climate change. And as developing nations such as China, India and Africa experience massive rural–urban shifts over the coming decades, the aim should be to ensure that compact cities are the norm so that carbon emissions from transport, energy and food are minimised. Whilst green belts have helped ensure that urban areas haven't sprawled at low densities, future demand for living in cities may mean that the policy needs to be revisited. Planned expansion at high density aligned to public transport is likely to be more sustainable in the broadest sense than simply hot-housing cities to ever-higher densities.

None of this is uncontested and there remain a host of voices that question the role and impact of urban containment in helping tackle climate change, but the broad patterns are undeniable: denser cities and living uses fewer resources. And some cities are managing to deliver on this, such as Barcelona and Amsterdam, combining high-density living with high-quality public open spaces.

Yet 'sustainable cities' isn't simply about the environment. There are social and economic dimensions too. There is no point having high-density, resource-efficient living if there are no jobs and people are unhappy. A significant element of sustainability concerns housing affordability. City planning cannot simply restrict development on the edge of cities and then step back to let land values rise and development occur. In many cities there is a severe shortage of affordable housing. There are many ways that city planning can seek to address this, from direct provision to forms of development taxation and requiring proportions of development. The overriding point, however, is that solutions and approaches to city planning need to reflect the needs and characteristics of different cities. This philosophy also allows for experimentation and competition between cities, creating opportunities for new approaches to emerge and be taken on elsewhere.

Density is also less of a silver bullet if the focus is simply on new buildings, ignoring the vast majority of existing building stock. Annual building levels in the UK add far less than 1 per cent to the total building stock. So focusing on existing buildings is also critical, particularly as by 2050 buildings across the globe will need to have 80 to 90 per cent lower emissions than 2010 levels to meet the Paris Agreement targets. What this means is a huge effort in retrofitting on top of the commitment that all new buildings are fossil fuel free and near-zero energy by 2022.[29]

Building upwards as a solution to saving the city isn't quite as obvious as it once was. Whilst densification of cities is a major element in the fight against climate change, the coronavirus pandemic of 2020 has been seen by some to be pushing in the opposite direction – people need and want to stay away from each other. The argument goes that even when the current public health imperative for increased physical space has passed, the legacy for cities may be a tension between two competing yet understandable imperatives. This argument isn't new. During the yellow fever epidemics in the 1800s Thomas Jefferson opined, 'When great evils happen, I am in the habit of looking out for what good may arise from them as consolations to us.... The yellow fever will discourage the growth of great cities in our nation; and I view great cities as pestilential to the morals, the health and the liberties of man.'[30]

Yet cities survived. Threats to their future didn't come from disease or viruses, but from a lack of attention to what cities needed to function, to evolve and to adapt. In short, to what makes cities liveable. The focus on increased density will only work with attention to what is needed to live together, but separately. Far from undermining attention paid to cities, the response to COVID-19 has been to give greater attention to the ways in which cities can manage and adapt, making cities more functional and liveable – restricting motorised vehicles and making more space for cycling and walking, for example. Digital technology has been a key element in this, as I discuss in the next and final chapter.

The future of cities will remain upward, not outward, and the pandemic has actually helped this movement by providing the means and helping turn attention back to what makes cities liveable. Despite the impact of the pandemic, London still has tens of thousands of square metres of new, high-rise office developments in the pipeline alongside residential proposals. As with efficient resource use more generally, cities can make coordinated responses to a range of challenges, including on public health.

Yet it is no longer enough to pursue these key ingredients in the same way, ignoring the existential challenge that digital technology poses to cities. The point is that at the same time that digital is distracting us, cities couldn't be more important for a variety of reasons, which is why we need to save them. This may all come across as dirigiste. It has to be. The time for laissez-faire is over given the imperative to tackle the climate emergency. We need to save the city, and here is where digital technology can have an important role to play, as I explore in the next chapter.

10

Smart for cities: time for a new story

City planning doesn't exist by right. Like any other area of public policy, it needs to prove its worth, add something and make cities better (however defined) than if it didn't exist. City planning in the modern, comprehensive, open and accountable sense is a relatively new phenomenon and some, such as Churchill, preferred the 'old ways'. Some still do. The flip side of the romantic, serendipitous, edgy nature of Churchill's flight of fancy was the disease-ridden, overcrowded, unequal reality for many.

> At 1.00pm Winston Churchill closed his Cabinet folder and lit another cigar. Sir Edward Bridges drew his attention to the fact that there was still one remaining item. It was town and country planning. The determination of those days that we would not go back to the 1930s had inspired Beveridge, the Cabinet White Paper on full employment and also the three basic reports on town and country planning by Uthwatt, Barlow and Scott....
>
> W.S. Morrison had assessed these reports and was presenting his conclusions. Winston was not amused. "Ah yes", said he. "All this stuff about planning and compensation and betterment. Broad vistas and all that. But give me the eighteenth century alley, where footpads lurk and the harlot plies her trade, and none of this new fangled planning doctrine".[1]

Churchill was writing his own story of the city, and it's one that persists today in the views of many who would argue for the state to step back to let the market dictate and decide, a view that characterises the attitude of both left-leaning anarchists and right-wing neoliberals. The 'smart city' story is similar in many ways to Churchill's poetic image. Let the city be the sum of its parts. We don't need to direct cities because digital technology will provide the answers and a route to the future that it will shape. Yet, as I've argued throughout this book, not only is this assurance false, but smart also presents an existential threat to our cities and the future of humanity. It's time to write a new story of the city, one that reclaims a central part for collective, open, inclusive and future-looking management and action.

But with the evidence of such impacts all around us, from boarded-up shops to the zero-hours contract economy, why don't we see the negative impacts that smart and digital are having? In the view of Ben Green,[2] the problem is that we are all wearing tech goggles. According to Green, if we look at a problem or challenge, be it traffic congestion, rising crime, falling voter turnout, childhood obesity or an ageing population, through the eyes of digital, then we will more likely look for digital solutions. These tech goggles filter out alternatives and point us towards a world where if every problem is defined as a nail, then every solution has to be a hammer. It is these goggles that help us filter out our own experiences, and the almost daily headlines and warnings about the growth and influence of Facebook, Google, Amazon, and so on and the downsides of relying on a hammer as the only tool we have to solve a multitude of complex social, economic and environmental challenges in our cities. Perhaps. What such daily alerts highlight is that not everyone is wearing tech goggles. We're not totally unaware of what is happening, and we're not ignorant of the creeping colonisation and power grab going on. So if we are keen to avoid losing city planning to a digital future that we know is harmful, then why aren't we doing more? If our 21st-century cities are to avoid reverting to Churchill's 18th-century 'footpads and harlots', we need to understand why we are still moving down a smart city future.

There are three main reasons why we don't perceive the need to rewrite the story of the city. The first is simple: there are undoubtedly clear advantages and benefits to the rollout of digital technology and smart to both society and the individual. We *are* more connected, digital *does* improve our cities in some ways, and our personal lives and city planning *do* benefit from the costless duplication and dissemination of information and data. I recall being a planner in the early 1990s, long before smart and digital were on the scene. One major challenge was to get people involved in discussions and decisions. If something was happening – a new development proposal, a new challenge that needed to be faced or a discussion on the direction of a new plan – we put up notices on lampposts and in local newspapers, and sent letters. It was far from perfect and people were asked to come to see what was happening and get involved, often miles away and at times that were convenient to us, not them. It was costly, time-consuming, inefficient, and not very effective. We couldn't do it regularly because of the effort and cost. So power and influence largely lay with people like me, the planners. Now you can go online at your convenience, interrogate data, provide input and comments, lobby, disseminate and network with others. The internet and digital have democratised and vastly improved decision-making, crowd sourcing views and opening up discussions. Planners can see what other cities are doing and how they've approached issues with a few keystrokes and clicks.

At a personal level, our lives are in many ways enriched too. Digital technology and the likes of Google, Facebook, Amazon, and so on are giving us direct and immediate control and influence, a one-click culture of goods, services, connectivity and information. I'm now involved in a government-funded local body with three local authorities and business, investing hundreds of millions of pounds in transport infrastructure and affordable housing to support the city of Cambridge. It's a far cry from the concentrated model of knowledge and power in the early days of my career. Information and consultation is frictionless and virtually costless. Meetings and information are available online, and coordination between communities and other bodies ensures that even when there is disagreement, there isn't exclusion. The issue now is analysing the sheer amount of information and data. So we buy into the benefits and accept that few, if any, technologies come without any downsides. We might be addicted, but we're conscious of what's happening and choose to wear tech goggles. Even if we wanted to there's no going back: we can't uninvent the internet and live in a Faraday cage. We have to want to rewrite the story of the city, and at the moment not enough of us are sure we do.

The second reason why we don't perceive the need to rewrite the story of the city is that smart has become a cult. It's a matter of faith: there is no alternative to a digital future and none will be heeded. Smart and digital analyses and solutions are held to be transcendent, applicable to any situation or issue and the basis for any solution. Ben Green quotes Cisco's Urban Innovation Team:

> The debate is no longer about *why* a Smart City initiative is good for a city or *what* to do (which available options to choose), but instead about *how* to implement Smart City infrastructures and services.[3]

Finally, we're promised even bigger returns and changes at some point in the future – autonomous vehicles, better health diagnostics, more efficient energy use, etc. The promise of a better future, at no extra cost and with conflict and difficult decisions smoothed over is compelling. Some of the promises may well come to pass; after all, 20 years ago who could have envisaged that we could hail a ride, order our groceries and have them delivered, plot a route from home to work avoiding congestion, meet with colleagues and keep up to date on world news, all from a pocket computer?

So we've got a fight on our hands and the 'smart city' story is not going to be easy to displace. It's not us versus them, as we're part of the 'them' in many ways. And there's another issue: it's one thing to write *a* new story of the city but it's another to make it *the* story. There are already competing narratives of the role and future of the city, from sustainable cities to entrepreneurial cities. How would another story muscle its way in? Thomas Kuhn may be of help here. A physicist and philosopher of science, Kuhn published *The Structure of Scientific Revolutions* in 1962.[4] Kuhn's widely accepted thesis was that what he termed 'paradigm shifts' in science, such as the shift from Newtonian mechanics to quantum physics, undermine the view that science is a linear, progressive march towards the truth. Instead, paradigms or narratives dominate science at any particular point in time and continue to shape our understanding of the world until a better one comes along. Each paradigm shapes the issues, the evidence, the methods and the outcomes of any inquiry. Once a new paradigm is developed that is better at meeting our needs and fitting the evidence and data, there is an abrupt, seismic shift from the old to the new. Yet it's not enough to simply offer an alternative paradigm; one also needs to show how and why the alternative is a better 'fit' than the existing paradigm if followers are to switch. Sometimes, as with Galileo's evidence of a heliocentric model of the solar system, even that is not enough.

For our purposes, Kuhn provides a framework of how we might attempt to replace the 'smart city' paradigm: a new story of the city needs to be a better fit for what we want to achieve. We also need to point out that the Panglossian take on how smart will solve all our problems isn't the only direction that this story goes. Yet even with a new paradigm or narrative there's no guarantee of success. Smart and the digital city are already here, well established, and growing in influence.

Those behind smart are not going to simply roll over and give in to the force of better argument. It's not going to be a fair fight unless and until there are other changes too. There are two other, necessary elements to change the story of the city alterations that will also be necessary. First, there has to be a levelling of the playing field so that alternative stories of the city have a chance to disrupt, in the phrase beloved of Silicon Valley, the 'status quo'. Second, changing the story and curtailing the power and impacts of Big Tech won't address the final step in saving the city, the need for city planning to step up and meet the challenge of what cities currently face. So the new story for the city involves four related steps:

- Challenging the faith and highlighting why smart won't make everything better.
- Creating a new story that fits the challenges and needs of the city.

- Levelling the playing field to make it a fair fight.
- Reforming city planning to meet the needs of new times.

Smart isn't the answer to everything

As I have argued throughout this book, the digital future is painted as being very bright. Lucie Green talks about this level of ambition, confidence and hope as being necessary to Big Tech, not simply from the perspective of securing business, but also to secure the best talent.[5] What Silicon Valley calls 'moonshots' – ambitious goals from space travel to solving world problems – help persuade idealistic and talented staff to work for them: 'come work at Google because we do no evil' (a motto that was dropped a while ago). In cities the moonshots are the familiar digital dream of frictionless, efficient, effective and low-cost living – we can have everything, from driverless cars to takeaways delivered to our doors. In fact Google, Amazon and others know so much about you and your habits you don't even need to ask: we'll just know what you want before you do.

But what would a smart future for the city actually look like? Look at the business models and project them into the future and we may well see:

> Task Rabbit-style platforms replacing emergency services, or on-demand fire services powered by contractors, or social media regulating services such as water or roads. (What happens when there's surge pricing, not enough Uber fire-fighters, or no background checks?)[6]

The business model and framework of Big Tech doesn't translate well into public services. In fact, it looks downright scary. If this is a dystopian vision of the future, then how do we create an alternative one that uses digital technology in ways that support the city? Despite the seeming inevitability, there has been resistance to aspects of the digital city. In September 2017 Transport for London (TfL) informed Uber that it would not be renewing its licence to operate vehicles for hire because it was not a 'fit and proper' company. A temporary licence was approved in 2018 subject to changes in how Uber operated, including training for drivers, complaints procedures and data security. In September 2020 TfL granted Uber its licence after its conditions were met. Many cities are now regulating Airbnb and other home-sharing services, placing caps on how many nights properties can be rented out in order to help tackle rising housing costs that hit locals. Yet not everyone is optimistic that Big Tech can be reshaped to support cities. According to my colleague, John Naughton:

> ... the only states that now have the capacity to tame or control tech giants are authoritarian ones. Liberal democracies are no longer up to the job because they have to stay within the bounds of the neoliberal legal frameworks they have been assiduously constructing over half a century. Large corporations have the resources to spin things out for years or even decades, while governments and their elites are increasingly trapped in the attention-deficit syndrome brought about by five-year electoral cycles.[7]

We may have gone too far down the road of free markets and global trade to row things back, but despite protests organised by the operators against any kind of restraint, the successful examples of some cities highlight that where the private has consequences for the public, we can and should act.

In a speech in Pittsburgh in 2016, former US president Barack Obama pushed back on the idea that Big Tech could apply its business model and operations to government. It's worth quoting at length here:

> The final thing I'll say is that government will never run the way Silicon Valley runs because, by definition, democracy is messy. This is a big, diverse country with a lot of interests and a lot of disparate points of view. And part of government's job, by the way, is dealing with problems that nobody else wants to deal with. So sometimes I talk to CEOs, they come in and they start telling me about leadership,

and here's how we do things. And I say, well, if all I was doing was making a widget or producing an app, and I didn't have to worry about whether poor people could afford the widget, or I didn't have to worry about whether the app had some unintended consequences – setting aside my Syria and Yemen portfolio – then I think those suggestions are terrific. That's not, by the way, to say that there aren't huge efficiencies and improvements that have to be made.

But the reason I say this is sometimes we get, I think, in the scientific community, the tech community, the entrepreneurial community, the sense of we just have to blow up the system, or create this parallel society and culture because government is inherently wrecked. No, it's not inherently wrecked; it's just government has to care for, for example, veterans who come home. That's not on your balance sheet, that's on our collective balance sheet, because we have a sacred duty to take care of those veterans. And that's hard and it's messy, and we're building up legacy systems that we can't just blow up.[8]

Rather than buying into the vague, always just around the corner promises, we need to be clear about what *will* benefit cities from the Silicon Valley approach and which issues, as Barack Obama points out, are too complex, too sensitive and too political to be reduced to algorithms and demand-led pricing models. So what we need to do is rebalance smart, let it disrupt and replace where appropriate, but at the same time reclaim the political and the collective balance sheet. The first step in taking back control is to understand that a significant element of the political isn't simply about the issues and challenges that cities face; it's about time and the future, perhaps the most political dimension of cities that are being colonised by Silicon Valley. City planning is concerned with hope and a belief that the future can be better than the present and the past. But the future is being subjected to two pressures at the moment. On the one hand, it is being compressed, made more immediate in our focus on 'now', our one-click culture and expectations. On the other, it is also being kicked down the road, deferred to longer and vaguer aspirations, objectives and timescales that are difficult to disagree with. This poses problems for cities and for their management given that plan and strategy making typically exist in a rolling 5- to 10-year timescale, what we might term the 'imminent future'.

Writing a new story for the city: time for an urban renaissance

Pointing out that the digital emperor has far fewer clothes than believed won't be enough. Smart is presenting cities with a positive story for the future, one that sells the idea that society's problems can be solved by embracing digital. But that is by no means the only take on how smart will change our cities. If D.H. Lawrence and Henry James spoke to the story of the 19th-century city, then it's J.G. Ballard who best opens the lid on the age of the smart city and looks to the future.

Ballard wrote three books about gated communities – *Cocaine Nights* (1996), *Super-Cannes* (2000) and *Millennium People* (2003) – with *Super-Cannes* set in a fictional, walled and private city called Eden-Olympia, home and work for tech and business elites. Eden-Olympia is a Saltaire or Bournville for the digital age, but with a nod to E.M. Forster's dystopian Machine. Echoing the positive yet empty rhetoric of Big Tech, Ballard describes Eden-Olympia as an 'ideas laboratory for the new millennium', a place to 'hothouse the future'. In this gated city the executives' lives are fully catered for. Chauffeur-driven visits to the outside world provide thrills:

> At Eden-Olympia there were no parking problems, no fear of burglars or purse snatchers, no rapes or muggings. The top-drawer professionals no longer needed to devote a moment's thought to each other, and had dispensed with the checks and balances of community life. There were no town councils or magistrates' courts, no citizens' advice bureaus. Civility and polity were designed into Eden-Olympia, in the same way that mathematics, aesthetics, and an entire geopolitical world-view were

designed into the Parthenon and the Boeing 747. Representative democracy had been replaced by the surveillance camera and the private police force.[9]

Ballard's story is about how such closed communities are simply replacing the problems of the outside world with others, creating their own morality and barriers between the haves and the have-nots in a world where competition and capitalism remain truly global. Within this world the tech and business class sit in their enclaves, places that have no common future with the world outside.

Ballard's 'smart city' fiction isn't far from the dream of some in Silicon Valley. There is a strong and growing movement of what has been termed 'crypto-anarchy' within parts of Big Tech. The founder of crypto-anarchy, Tim May, set out a manifesto in 1992 that put forward a series of proposals based on emerging technology that provides for the economic and political freedom of individuals from government. According to May:

> Some of us believe various forms of strong cryptography will cause the power of the state to decline, perhaps even collapse fairly abruptly. We believe the expansion into cyberspace, with secure communications, digital money, anonymity and pseudonymity, and other crypto-mediated interactions, will profoundly change the nature of economies and social interactions. Governments will have a hard time collecting taxes, regulating the behavior of individuals and corporations (small ones at least), and generally coercing folks when it can't even tell what continent folks are on![10]

Much of this manifesto has now come to fruition, from blockchain technology and bitcoins that allow financial transactions without government knowledge to cryptographic software that permits the distribution of prohibited goods, including drugs and illegal pornography, as well as tax evasion through the dark web. At some point the regulated will become the regulators, able to operate with impunity, setting their own rules. That's a point that the likes of Amazon and Google are now close to achieving as they can move income and profits from one country to another to avoid taxation and regulation. This is a dark-side conclusion to the story of smart, and one that isn't widely discussed. That some involved see it as desirable rather than simply possible and that we are getting closer to this dystopian ending should make us sit up and take notice. So we have to highlight not only that Big Tech can't and won't solve all the challenges of our cities, but also that it is actually seeking to dismantle them.

It's time to write a new story of the city, one based on what will help save the planet and make us happy. What that story is will vary depending on how cities see the challenges they face and what is needed to address them. What each story will require is for us to take off our tech goggles and start from first principles, as set out in Chapter 8. The way forward will inevitably include elements of smart and digital technology, but as the means to broader ends, not as ends in themselves. What our new stories of the city will need to do is reclaim the political back from digital.

So what should be the new story of the city? The social, economic and environmental challenges in many cities combined with the importance of cities in tackling the climate emergency all point to the need to reinvest time, energy and resources in making our cities better for all. Whilst each city story will vary, this need to invest attention and time in the future of each city is the common element. This amounts to an urban renaissance, a renaissance underpinned by a commitment to sustainability, making cities that work for everyone, not just those who can afford it.

There is a range of familiar, common elements to this renaissance, including:

- The principle of compact cities, much heralded in the 1990s, as ways to create the kind of densities necessary to support high-quality public transport, schools, health services and housing need. Compact cities also use less energy and fewer resources, making them more environmentally sustainable.

- Focusing development and investment on urban areas, particularly on previously used land, requires constraint over urban expansion in the form of green belts or equivalent. Urban sprawl is wasteful of scarce resources and less efficient for public transport and services.
- An active role for cities in shaping and managing growth and in assembling and decontaminating land to make it suitable for development, and regulating those aspects of digital that impact on the city.

None of this is new. In fact, much of it is very familiar and was the trajectory of city planning prior to the distraction of smart. The contain–densify–redevelop model of city planning is one that goes back even further as an approach to managing cities, as I covered in Chapter 8. Yet this is just one story and it won't be the same story in cities from Los Angeles to Berlin, with each setting out how it balances the need to combat the climate emergency, improve biodiversity and address housing affordability, and do so in ways that are inclusive and open.

New times for city planning

City planning also needs to evolve to help achieve the new story of the city, whatever it might be. Whilst cities have evolved, the model of city planning, as set out in Chapter 8, hasn't. There has historically been a strong link between evolution and physical change in cities – economic change meant factories opening or closing; population change meant new housing and transport. This link between cause and effect has been stretched and broken down in the digital, globalised age. The physical spaces of cities have also been uncoupled from change when the territorial limit of a place no longer captures the full extent of influences that planning needs to shape to make a difference. Extra territorial, networked spaces go far beyond the physical jurisdictions of cities and planning. Finally, how city planning goes about thinking and shaping the future has also come under severe challenge as the time taken to produce plans and make decisions is out of step with the timescales of disruptive change wrought by digital. So there are three fundamental elements of city planning that need to be rethought: regulation (what it controls), space (the area over which it has jurisdiction) and process (how we go about it).

Rethinking regulation

City planning has traditionally shaped the future through regulating the development of land and property – physical space. City planning is not great at managing change that doesn't involve such physical development, such as the growth of e-commerce and the emergence of cloud-based platforms such as Airbnb and Uber that can radically remake cities but have no actual, physical footprint. Cities are faced with the physical consequences of platform players such as Airbnb, including the impact on affordable homes, but cannot easily address the causes. At its most simple, where a factory is located could be regulated in order to minimise the impacts. Those impacts could also be controlled as both cause and effect were one and the same.

The delinking of the future of cities and the challenges they face from the physical space they inhabit is not the only way in which this city-level planning is losing control. Other trends such as the fluidity of capital and people in a more globalised world also disconnect and undermine the link between cities and space.

What planning is being faced with at the moment are new challenges, situations that require cities to face up to intractable and irreconcilable issues with diminished levers to address them. So we need to rethink planning and give it back the ability to shape change in the digital and global age. This will mean shifting the regulatory levers from simply the physical to include the digital.

The ability of cities to challenge behemoths such as Amazon is not beyond the realms of possibility, only currently beyond political will. Levies or taxes on online retail or the ability to look beyond their territorial borders to control the size and scope of Amazon fulfilment centres located in other cities would be a good start. For the likes of Airbnb and Uber, the need for platform operators to obtain licences and meet conditions to operate would also help give cities back the levers they need to address cause and effect.

Rethinking process

Planning is slow and linear in a fast, networked and non-sequential world. The survey-analysis-plan process of city planning outlined in Chapter 8 is out of step with the needs and realities of constant, up-to-the-minute data, crowd-sourced analysis, the speed of change and the lack of levers over what residents and cities feel should be the focus of planning. And yet there needs to be a process that is open, transparent and inclusive. The key here is to rethink what constitutes a planning process and shift from the mindset of an end product that comes from a linear process to a constantly 'live' plan, one that can be updated quickly, and in a non-sequential way. The plan would comprise a suite of elements, linked, but independent from each other. If a city faced pressing issues on transport or health, these elements could be focused on, leaving the more long-standing and stable elements as they are. The process of plan making and updates would be more akin to how films are made, with elements being shot out of sequence and in parallel. This might mean constant analysis through live data inputs – traffic, housing developments, energy use – as well as expanding the range of inputs to the plan, the survey elements.

Rethinking space

Digital has reconfigured territorial spaces and scales, opening up new, networked and global spaces whilst fundamentally challenging more traditional, nested hierarchies – some cities, such as San Francisco, New York and London, look to each other and not the nation states they sit within. What does this mean for city planning? As well as the necessity of expanding the kinds of regulation that city planning needs to manage the future, there also has to be new thinking to the spaces that planning oversees. The fundamental issue for our cities comes down to the mismatch between our enduring physical spaces – the high street, homes, communities – on the one hand, and new virtual and networked spaces that include the impacts of online retailing, social media and the attention economy, the dominance of a small number of global tech companies and the lack of innovation and competition on the other. Our virtual spaces are disrupting and reshaping our physical spaces, and there's very little we can do about it at the moment.

Going forward, there are two spaces city planning needs to engage with in addition to the physical spaces of cities. These are the two spaces that Big Tech cares about most: the global and the individual. Firms likes Amazon and Google can hold individual cities to ransom by playing them off against each other in a global competition to attract investment and jobs. Cities therefore need to rethink the spaces and scales of city planning, collaborating with like-minded places across the globe to establish solidarity in the face of divide-and-rule tactics. There are also few, if any, spatial consequences for Big Tech in our cities, no fixed, physical footprint. In effect we, the individual, are the locus. Shaping the future through controlling physical change needs to morph into the individual level, through making clear the consequences of certain trends and decisions or providing and encouraging locally run alternatives to Airbnb, Amazon and the like, for example.

Level the playing field to support cities and city planning

A new story of the city and a reformed approach to city planning will only get us so far. If we are to save the city, we need to ensure that these changes have a fighting chance of succeeding against the prevailing momentum towards a digital city. Across the range of impacts and changes that Big Tech is bringing, we need to level the playing field in four areas.

Democracy and news feeds

Big Tech has not fulfilled the promise of evolution through innovation and ideas that support people, communities and their cities, disrupting the status quo. It was meant to be a force for good, breaking up economic and informational monopolies and providing better alternatives. Instead, Silicon Valley is creating monopolies of its own and thwarting change. As many have pointed out, the concentration of economic power is a threat to democracy. Yet the tide is slowly turning, and there is a growing appetite to take on the increasing dominance of Facebook,

Amazon, Google and Apple and address related issues such as fake news. As Lucie Greene points out,[11] if the US presidential election of 2016 and the UK's Brexit vote in the same year were lessons in the raw power of social media to shape political discourse and the outcome of elections, what if the mountains of data Facebook has collected were used with strategic intent? Robert Mueller's indictment of Russian-backed influence in the 2016 presidential election runs to 37 pages and mentions Facebook 35 times.[12]

Public opinion, backed by advertisers' boycotts, is increasingly shifting the attitude of social media to take responsibility for what is posted on their platforms. This isn't simple: the laws against fake news introduced by Singapore have rightly raised concerns by some that such controls can be used to stifle dissent. What is more concerning for cities is the declining amount of local news and information and the impacts this has on collective understanding and decision-making. Again, the proposal by the Australian government's Competition and Consumer Commission would require Google, Facebook and others to pay for media content from traditional sources such as local newspapers. Despite these moves, a growing amount of disinformation is coming from Big Tech as it strengthens its position, lobbies and pays for supportive research. How do we stop digital platforms from shaping urban policy to their own ends? Here there is also movement. The US Congress and the EU are both investigating Big Tech and their dominance of the market. Unless and until these companies face genuine competition and alternative views and approaches are aired, cities and democracy will continue to struggle.

Gentrification and bifurcation

The displacement of one socioeconomic group by another is a long-standing issue in cities and not one that has emerged with the advent of Big Tech. That said, some places have over-heated and others have gone into steep decline as the disruptions wrought by digital technology are played out. Within cities gentrification is causing significant social, environmental and economic hardship – social hardship as low-paid, key workers like teachers, nurses and others are priced out of an area; environmental impacts as individuals are forced to commute long distances from more affordable areas to their workplaces; economic hardship as families are stretched by high rents and costs of living. This situation is not sustainable and requires intervention on the part of cities, as leaving Big Tech to sort out the problems will not address the scale of the issue. Over-heating and gentrification in a few cities is accompanied by bifurcation of cities within a country as others are forgotten and residualised.

As far as cities and city planning goes, gentrification and bifurcation require a strong, redistributional regional policy, one that involves both carrots and sticks to help support declining cities and regions whilst encouraging what planners term a 'polycentric city structure' – sharing growth and not focusing it on one city at the expense of others. Establishing a number of what used to be called 'growth poles' – cities that have fiscal and regulatory advantages to attract investment – whilst restricting the supply of land and premises in other locations, can help shift demand and spread growth and its consequences.

The gig and platform economy

We can create the physical spaces to host and nurture the digital revolution in ways that can support cities, but what is also needed is genuine competition that can challenge Big Tech and encourage city-supportive innovation. To help achieve this we have to begin to break up their current domination, support new ideas and startups through creating and redistributing a tax on data and e-shopping, hypothecating the revenue to back city- and community-focused digital initiatives. Berlin and other cities host an annual event called Disrupt, a forum for new digital ideas and startups. Here, startups pitch ideas that actually help people and cities, from apps that support the visually impaired, those who are mobility restricted and diabetic to alternative news outlets such as Nuzzera that do not reinforce what we look at online by suggesting more of the same, but use their algorithms to suggest material beyond it.

Various cities around the world have tackled some of the downsides of the platform economy, such as Barcelona requiring permits to offer apartments on Airbnb and London withdrawing the licence for Uber. There are challenges in enforcing such approaches as well as the need to balance the downsides with the benefits. The fact is that these and other such services are not going to disappear, and neither should they. It's all a matter of balance, allowing cities to manage change and disruption whilst benefitting from the improvements that come too. Here, cities need to work with governments, platforms, providers of services and consumers to move to a co-regulatory model. Self-regulation based on feedback and consumer ratings clearly does not address the concerns of cities. Top-down national or city-led regulation similarly raises issues of compliance and monitoring. The missing element in both approaches has been the willingness to include other parties to the platform economy – those who provide the service, those who use it, investors and cities themselves.

A digital retail tax

Some form of 'tech tax' has been proposed by various individuals and organisations over the past few years as a way of avoiding the concentration of wealth in the hands of a few. Others have put forward arguments that the likes of Facebook, Google, Apple and Amazon should be broken up, as the US government did with the Northern Securities Company and Standard Oil, two giant monopolies, just over 100 years ago. Whether or not this happens, what would be more effective, as far as cities are concerned, would be some form of digital retail tax, currently being considered by a number of governments. The playing field between bricks and mortar retailers and online retailers is not an even one: the former pay business rates for their high street locations, making it difficult to compete with high-volume, low-cost set-ups on motorway junctions. A 2 per cent 'Amazon tax', as proposed by some, would allow these business rates to be cut by up to 20 per cent in the UK, helping actual shops to compete. The UK government's digital services tax sought to achieve something similar for online services by levying a 2 per cent charge on the revenues of Amazon, Google, Facebook and others.

Refocus digital technology: it's a means to an end

Cities are dynamic and adaptive, and the motors of our economies. The digital challenges they face and are encouraging are straining their ability to evolve beyond breaking point. At the same time they face new and fundamental issues that require us to work collectively and make choices.

Here, the offer of digital solutions and ways forward is a chimera. Digital needs to serve cities, not run them. The suggestions here are offered as a start to rethinking how cities move forward on a different path, one not directed by the story of smart. This obviously isn't to say that digital technology has no role in making cities better. It is to say that cities – successful cities – need a complex mix of planned and unplanned, order and chaos, in order to successfully adapt. They need long-term thinking and the room to evolve, to experiment and to fail. They also need space for the serendipitous and the unforeseen, the risky and the innovative. The 19th-century city wasn't just the 'city of the dark night'; it was also the 'city of rapid technological change'. The 'city of bright lights' also thrived on managed chaos and complexity, melding the public and the private, managing change and allowing for the new. We need to return to the beauty of disorder, not the homogeneous and off-the-shelf improvements offered by the monopolies of Silicon Valley and their digital 'optimisation'. If smart can help the urban renaissance by offering what it originally promised – disruption, change and innovation – then all the better.

So this book isn't an argument against Big Tech. There have obviously been huge benefits to individuals and society from digital technology. Instead, this book is about making sure that the story of the city works for everyone, a story that saves the city for the sake of the planet, and one that uses the best minds of our generation to think about a better future, rather than finding new ways to keep us looking at our screens.

Notes

Chapter 1

1 Fritz Lang (director) (1927) *Metropolis* [film].
2 D.H. Lawrence (1929/1930) 'Nottingham and the mining countryside', *The New Adelphi*, June–August, 1930, p 14.
3 D.H. Lawrence (1929/1930) 'Nottingham and the mining countryside', *The New Adelphi*, June–August.
4 See, for example, Theo Panagopoulos (2020) 'What a long strange trip it's been', *The Culture Crush*. Available at: www.theculturecrush.com/feature/what-a-long-strange-trip-its-been-1
5 Henry James (1907) *The American Scene*, London: Chapman & Hall, p 5.
6 Quoted in Peter Hall (2002) *Cities of Tomorrow* (3rd edn), London: Blackwell, pp 36–7.
7 Quoted in Leo Hollis (2013) *Cities are Good for You: The Genius of the Metropolis*, London: Bloomsbury, p 4.
8 Christopher Tunnard and Boris Pushkarev (1963) *Man-Made America: Chaos or Control*, New Haven, CT: Yale University Press.
9 Christopher Tunnard and Boris Pushkarev (1963) *Man-Made America: Chaos or Control*, New Haven, CT: Yale University Press, p 22.
10 See Leo Hollis (2013) *Cities Are Good for You*, London: Bloomsbury, p 5.
11 Edward Glaeser (2011) *Triumph of the City*, London: Pan.
12 Edward Glaeser (2011) *Triumph of the City*, London: Pan, p 52.
13 Victoria Turk (2018) 'How a Berlin neighbourhood took on Google and won', *Wired*, 26 October. Available at: www.wired.co.uk/article/google-campus-berlin-protests
14 Richard Florida (2017) *The New Urban Crisis: Gentrification, Housing Bubbles, Growing Inequality, and What We Can Do About It*, London: Oneworld, p 89.
15 Fran Spielman (2020) 'Ald. Patrick Daley Thompson proposes ground delivery tax', *Chicago Sun Times*, 23 November. Available at: https://chicago.suntimes.com/city-hall/2020/11/23/21591819/home-deliveries-amazon-online-orders-city-fee-daley-thompson

Chapter 2

1 Named after the phone number that many cities use for citizens to call them.

2   Siemens (2017) 'The bottom line: The business case for smart cities.' Available at: https://new.siemens.com/global/en/company/stories/infrastructure/2017/the-business-case-for-smart-cities.html

3   IBM (no date) 'The digital era demands modern government technology.' Available at: www.ibm.com/smarterplanet/us/en/smarter_cities/overview/

4   See www.ibm.com/ibm/history/ibm100/us/en/icons/smarterplanet/

5   IBM (no date) 'The digital era demands modern government technology.' Available at: www.ibm.com/smarterplanet/us/en/smarter_cities/overview/

6   See Jonathan Taplin (2017) *Move Fast and Break Things: How Facebook, Google, and Amazon Cornered Culture and Undermined Democracy*, London: Macmillan.

7   Carlo Ratti and Matthew Claudel (2016) *The City of Tomorrow: Sensors, Networks, Hackers, and the Future of Urban Life*, Harvard, CT: Yale University Press, p 28.

8   Julie Snell (2017) 'Smart cities are set to change the landscape of the great West', GW4, 13 November. Available at: https://gw4.ac.uk/opinion/smart-cities-set-change-landscape-great-west/

9   See https://smartcity.wien.gv.at/site/en/the-initiative/smart-simple/

10 https://smartcity.wien.gv.at/site/en/the-initiative/smart-simple/

11 Chris White (2018) 'South Korea's "smart city" Songdo: Not quite smart enough?', *SCMP: This Week in Asia*, 25 March. Available at: www.scmp.com/week-asia/business/article/2137838/south-koreas-smart-city-songdo-not-quite-smart-enough

12 Chris White (2018) 'South Korea's "smart city" Songdo: Not quite smart enough?', *SCMP: This Week in Asia*, 25 March. Available at: www.scmp.com/week-asia/business/article/2137838/south-koreas-smart-city-songdo-not-quite-smart-enough

13 See www.media.mit.edu/groups/city-science/overview/

14 See www.bristolisopen.com/about/

15 Quoted in James Temperton (2015) 'Bristol is making a smart city for actual humans', *Wired*, 17 March. Available at: www.wired.co.uk/article/bristol-smart-city

16 Luke Mordecai, Carl Reynolds, Liam J. Donaldson and Amanda C. de C. Williams (2018) 'Patterns of regional variation of opioid prescribing in primary care in England: A retrospective observational study', *British Journal of General Practice*, 68(668), e225–e233. Available at: https://doi.org/10.3399/bjgp18X695057

17 Performance, Innovation and Intelligence Service, City of Bristol (2015) *Deprivation in Bristol 2015: The Mapping of Deprivation within Bristol Local Authority Area*. Available at: www.bristol.gov.uk/documents/20182/32951/Deprivation+in+Bristol+2015/429b2004-eeff-44c5-8044-9e7dcd002faf

18 Sameer Hasija (2020) 'Smart cities can help us manage post-COVID life, but they'll need trust as well as tech', *The Conversation*, 2 June. Available

at: https://theconversation.com/smart-cities-can-help-us-manage-post-covid-life-but-theyll-need- trust-as-well-as-tech-138725

19 See www.dw.com/en/how-covid-19-could-speed-up-smart-city-visions/a-53654217

20 See https://inequality.org/facts/inequality-and-covid-19/

21 Clare O'Farrell (2020) 'The biopolitics of Covid-19 (2020)', *Foucault News*, 13 June. Available at: https://michel-foucault.com/2020/06/13/the-biopolitics-of-covid-19-2020/

Chapter 3

1 Steven Levy (1984) *Hackers: Heroes of the Computer Revolution*, Garden City, NY: Doubleday.

2 See https://growthhackers.com/growth-studies/airbnb

3 See www.cbinsights.com/research/google-biggest-acquisitions-infographic/

4 Carlo Ratti and Matthew Claudel (2016) *The City of Tomorrow: Sensors, Networks, Hackers and the Future of Urban Life*, New Haven, CT: Yale University Press.

5 See, for example, Nicole Gurran (2018) 'Global home-sharing, local communities and the Airbnb debate: A planning research agenda', *Planning Theory & Practice*, 19(2), 298–304; Daniel Guttentag (2015) 'Airbnb: Disruptive innovation and the rise of an informal tourism accommodation sector', *Current Issues in Tourism*, 18(12), 1192; Dayne Lee (2016) 'How Airbnb short-term rentals exacerbate Los Angeles's affordable housing crisis: Analysis and policy recommendations', *Harvard Law & Policy Review*, 10, 229–53; David Wachsmuth and Alexander Weisler (2018) 'Airbnb and the rent gap: Gentrification through the sharing economy', *Environment and Planning A: Economy and Space*, 50(6), 1147–70.

6 The 10 cities were: Amsterdam, Barcelona, Berlin, Bordeaux, Brussels, Krakow, Munich, Paris, Valencia and Vienna.

7 See www.amsterdam.nl/bestuur-organisatie/college/wethouder/laurens-ivens/persberichten/press-release-cities-alarmed-about/

8 www.amsterdam.nl/bestuur-organisatie/college/wethouder/laurens-ivens/persberichten/press-release-cities-alarmed-about/

9 Gaby Hinsliff (2018) 'Airbnb and the so-called sharing economy is hollowing out cities', *The Guardian*, 31 August. Available at: www.theguardian.com/commentisfree/2018/aug/31/airbnb-sharing-economy-cities-barcelona-inequality-locals

10 See www.airbnbhell.com/airbnb-nightmare-scenario-destroying-communities/

11 Hannah Jane Parkinson (2017) '"Sometimes you don't feel human" – how the gig economy chews up and spits out millennials', *The Guardian*, 17 October. Available at: www.theguardian.com/business/2017/oct/17/sometimes-you-dont-feel-human-how-the-gig-economy-chews-up-and-spits-out-millennials

12 Sarah O'Connor (2017) 'Driven to despair – the hidden costs of the gig economy', *Financial Times*, 22 September. Available at: www.ft.com/content/749cb87e-6ca8-11e7-b9c7-15af748b60d0

13 Neil Craven (2018) 'Tesco chief demands £1.25billion "Amazon tax": Supermarket boss says windfall should aid struggling retailers', *Mail on Sunday*, 7 October. Available at: www.thisismoney.co.uk/money/news/article-6247561/Tesco-chief-demands-1-25-billion-Amazon-tax-Drastic-Dave-boosts-Mail-Sunday-campaign.html

14 Bespoke Investment Group (2017) 'The bespoke "Death by Amazon" indices', BIG Tips, 25 September. Available at: www.bespokepremium.com/wp-content/uploads/2017/10/B.I.G-Tips-The-Bespoke-Death-By-Amazon-Indices-092517.pdf

15 Bespoke (2020) 'Death by Amazon', BIG Tips, 13 October. Available at: www.bespokepremium.com/?s=death+by+amazon

16 OECD (2018) 'Job automation risks vary widely across different regions within countries', Newsroom, 18 September. Available at: www.oecd.org/newsroom/job-automation-risks-vary-widely-across-different-regions-within-countries.htm

17 Centre for Cities (2019) *Cities Outlook 2019: A Decade of Austerity*, London: Centre for Cities. Available at: www.centreforcities.org/publication/cities-outlook-2019/

18 Oxford Economics (2019) 'How robots change the world', 23 July. Available at: www.oxfordeconomics.com/recent-releases/how-robots-change-the-world

19 Oxford Economics (2019) 'How robots change the world', 23 July. Available at: www.oxfordeconomics.com/recent-releases/how-robots-change-the-world

20 Abigail De Kosnik (2014) 'Disrupting technological privilege: The 2013–14 San Francisco Google bus protests', *Performance Research*, 19(6), 99, 2 November. Available at: https://doi.org/10.1080/13528165.2014.985117

21 Quoted in Abigail De Kosnik (2014) 'Disrupting technological privilege: The 2013–14 San Francisco Google bus protests', *Performance Research*, 19(6), 99, 2 November. Available at: www.tandfonline.com/doi/abs/10.1080/13528165.2014.985117

22 See https://boomcalifornia.com/2014/06/19/the-boom-interview-rebecca-solnit/

23 Emily Mibach (2017) 'Protesters target Facebook, Amazon in East Palo Alto protest', *Daily Post*, 31 March. Available at: https://padailypost.com/2017/03/31/protesters-target-facebook-amazon-in-east-palo-alto-protest/

24 Quoted in Alison Bell (2018) 'The anti-Google alliance', *ExBerliner*, 29 March. Available at: www.exberliner.com/features/politics/the-anti-google-alliance/

25 See www.goodjobsfirst.org

26 Robyn Dowling, Pauline McGuirk and Sophia Maalsen (2019) 'Realising Smart Cities: Partnerships and Economic Development in the Emergence and Practices of Smart in Newcastle, Australia', in Andrew Karvonen, Federico Cugurullo and Federico Caprotti (eds) *Inside Smart Cities*, Abingdon: Routledge, Chapter 2.

27 Jeremy Quittner (2016) 'Why states are sending millions of dollars to big players, not startups', *Inc.*, June. Available at: www.inc.com/magazine/201606/jeremy-quittner/state-incentive-subsidies-small-business.html

28 David James (2004) 'Salt, Sir Titus, First Baronet (1803–1876)', in *Oxford Dictionary of National Biography*, Oxford: Oxford University Press.

29 Adam Rogers (2017) 'If you care about cities, Apple's new campus sucks', *Wired*. Available at: www.wired.com/story/apple-campus/

30 Quoted in Adam Rogers (2017) 'If you care about cities, Apple's new campus sucks', *Wired*. Available at: www.wired.com/story/apple-campus/

31 Adam Rogers (2017) 'If you care about cities, Apple's new campus sucks', *Wired*. Available at: www.wired.com/story/apple-campus/

32 Douglas Rushkoff (2018) 'How tech's richest plan to save themselves after the apocalypse', *The Guardian*, 24 July. Available at: www.theguardian.com/technology/2018/jul/23/tech-industry-wealth-futurism-transhumanism-singularity?CMP=share_btn_link

33 Douglas Rushkoff (2018) 'How tech's richest plan to save themselves after the apocalypse', *The Guardian*, 24 July. Available at: www.theguardian.com/technology/2018/jul/23/tech-industry-wealth-futurism-transhumanism-singularity?CMP=share_btn_link

34 See www.change.org/p/supervisor-town-of-schodack-save-schodack-5

35 See www.timesunion.com/opinion/article/Editorial-Amazon-needs-no-break-13022175.php

36 Quoted in Jon Henley (2019) 'Ten cities ask EU for help to fight Airbnb expansion', *The Guardian*, 20 June. Available at: www.theguardian.com/cities/2019/jun/20/ten-cities-ask-eu-for-help-to-fight-airbnb-expansion?CMP=share_btn_link

37 The Economist Intelligence Unit (2016) *Empowering Cities: The Real Story on How Citizens and Businesses Are Driving Smart Cities*, London: The Economist Intelligence Unit. Available at: https://empoweringspaces.economist.com/empowering-cities/

38 Steven Levy (1984) *Hackers: Heroes of the Computer Revolution*, Garden City, NY: Doubleday.

Chapter 4

1   Stephanie M. Lee (2017) 'Here's why people were mad when Apple called its stores "Town Squares"', *BuzzFeed.News*, 16 September. Available at: www.buzzfeednews.com/article/stephaniemlee/tech-and-the-town-square

2   Robert McCartney (2019) 'Amazon in Seattle: Economic godsend or self-centered behemoth?', *The Washington Post*, 8 April. Available at: www.washingtonpost.com/local/trafficandcommuting/amazon-in-seattle-

    economic-godsend-or-self-centered-behemoth/2019/04/08/7d29999a-
4ce3-11e9-93d0-64dbcf38ba41_story.html

3   Quoted in Robert McCartney (2019) 'Amazon in Seattle: Economic
godsend or self-centered behemoth?', *The Washington Post*, 8 April.
Available at: www.washingtonpost.com/local/trafficandcommuting/
amazon-in-seattle-economic-godsend-or-self-centered-
behemoth/2019/04/08/7d29999a-4ce3-11e9-93d0-64dbcf38ba41_story.
html

4   Veena Dubal (2019) 'Who stands between you and AI dystopia? These
Google activists', *The Guardian*, 3 May. Available at: www.theguardian.
com/commentisfree/2019/may/03/ai-dystopia-google-activists

5   Franklin Foer (2017) *World Without Mind: The Existential Threat of Big
Tech*, London: Vintage.

6   Quoted in Erin Durkin (2018) 'Amazon HQ2: Tech giant splits new
home across New York City and Virginia', *The Guardian*, 13 November.
Available at: www.theguardian.com/technology/2018/nov/13/amazon-
hq2-second-headquarters-new-york-city-virginia

7   *Dallas Morning News* (2019) 'Dear Amazon, New York doesn't want you;
Dallas does', Editorial, 8 February. Available at: www.dallasnews.com/
opinion/editorials/2019/02/08/dear-amazon-new-york-doesnt-want-
you-dallas-does/

8   See https://paxtechnica.org

9   Carole Cadwalladr and Duncan Campbell (2019) 'Revealed: Facebook's
global lobbying against data privacy laws', *The Guardian*, 2 March. Available
at: www.theguardian.com/technology/2019/mar/02/facebook-global-
lobbying-campaign-against-data-privacy-laws-investment

10 Cecilia Kang and Kenneth P. Vogel (2019) 'Tech giants amass a lobbying
army for an epic Washington battle', *The New York Times*, 5 June. Available
at: www.nytimes.com/2019/06/05/us/politics/amazon-apple-facebook-
google-lobbying.html

11 See www.techtransparencyproject.org

12 See www.techtransparencyproject.org

13 See www.techtransparencyproject.org

14 See www.cbsnews.com/news/president-elect-trump-says-social-media-
played-a-key-role-in-his-victory/

15 Conservative Party (2017) *Forward, Together: Our Plan for a Stronger Britain
and a Prosperous Future*. Available at: https://general-election-2010.co.uk/
conservative-manifesto-2017-pdf-download/

16 Campaign for Accountability (no date) *Google's Academic Influence in
Europe*. Available at: https://campaignforaccountability.org/work/googles-
academic-influence-in-europe/

17 Nicholas Thompson and Fred Vogelstein (2018) 'Inside the two years that
shook Facebook – and the world', *Wired*. Available at: www.wired.com/
story/inside-facebook-mark-zuckerberg-2-years-of-hell/

[18] Quoted in Franklin Foer (2017) 'Facebook's war on free will', *The Guardian*, 19 September. Available at: www.theguardian.com/technology/2017/sep/19/facebooks-war-on-free-will

[19] Jamie Bartlett (2018) *The People Vs Tech: How the Internet is Killing Democracy (and How We Save It)*, London: Ebury Press.

[20] Peter Elkind and Doris Burke (2013) 'Amazon's (not so secret) war on taxes', *Fortune*, 23 May. Available at: https://fortune.com/2013/05/23/amazons-not-so-secret-war-on-taxes/

[21] BBC News (2020) 'Amazon pays £290m in UK tax as sales surge to £24bn', 9 September. Available at: www.bbc.co.uk/news/business-54082273

[22] See www.dropbox.com/s/dkkgbrv0rvs3ts2/Letter%20to%20Mark%20Zuckerberg%20from%20scientists%20funded%20by%20the%20Chan%20Zuckerberg%20Initiative.pdf?dl=0

[23] See www.dropbox.com/s/dkkgbrv0rvs3ts2/Letter%20to%20Mark%20Zuckerberg%20from%20scientists%20funded%20by%20the%20Chan%20Zuckerberg%20Initiative.pdf?dl=0

[24] Alex Hern (2020) 'Third of advertisers may boycott Facebook in hate speech revolt', *The Guardian*, 30 June. Available at: www.theguardian.com/technology/2020/jun/30/third-of-advertisers-may-boycott-facebook-in-hate-speech-revolt

[25] House of Commons (2019) *Disinformation and 'Fake News': Final Report, Eighth Report of Session 2017–19*, Digital, Culture, Media and Sport Committee. Available at: https://publications.parliament.uk/pa/cm201719/cmselect/cmcumeds/1791/1791.pdf

[26] House of Commons (2019) *Disinformation and 'Fake News': Final Report, Eighth Report of Session 2017–19*, Digital, Culture, Media and Sport Committee. Available at: https://publications.parliament.uk/pa/cm201719/cmselect/cmcumeds/1791/1791.pdf

[27] Peter Suciu (2019) 'More Americans are getting their news from social media', *Forbes*, 11 October. Available at: www.forbes.com/sites/petersuciu/2019/10/11/more-americans-are-getting-their-news-from-social-media/#7639b8a73e17

[28] House of Commons (2019) *Disinformation and 'Fake News': Final Report, Eighth Report of Session 2017–19*, Digital, Culture, Media and Sport Committee. Available at: https://publications.parliament.uk/pa/cm201719/cmselect/cmcumeds/1791/1791.pdf

[29] Quoted in Siva Vaidhyanathan (2020) 'Facebook and the folly of self-regulation', *Wired*. Available at: www.wired.com/story/facebook-and-the-folly-of-self-regulation/

[30] Lucie Green (2018) *Silicon States: The Power and Politics of Big Tech and What It Means for Our Future*, Berkeley, CA: Counterpoint, p 44.

Chapter 5

[1] James Williams (2018) *Stand Out of Our Light: Freedom and Resistance in the Attention Economy*, Cambridge: Cambridge University Press.

[2] Shoshana Zuboff (2019) *The Age of Surveillance Capitalism: The Fight for a Human Future at the New Frontier of Power*, London: Profile Books.

[3] James Williams (2018) *Stand Out of Our Light: Freedom and Resistance in the Attention Economy*, Cambridge: Cambridge University Press.

[4] Yasha Levine (2018) 'Google's Earth: How the tech giant is helping the state spy on us', *The Guardian*, 20 December. Available at: www.theguardian.com/news/2018/dec/20/googles-earth-how-the-tech-giant-is-helping-the-state-spy-on-us

[5] Alexia Tsotsis (2010) 'Eric Schmidt: "We know where you are, we know what you like"', *TechCrunch*, 7 September. Available at: https://techcrunch.com/2010/09/07/eric-schmidt-ifa/

[6] See www.tristanharris.com

[7] James Williams (2018) *Stand Out of Our Light: Freedom and Resistance in the Attention Economy*, Cambridge: Cambridge University Press.

[8] James Williams (2018) *Stand Out of Our Light: Freedom and Resistance in the Attention Economy*, Cambridge: Cambridge University Press.

[9] See www.tristanharris.com

[10] See https://humanetech.com/problem/

[11] See www.vice.com/en_us/article/mby5by/cosmetic-plastic-surgery-social-media-seflies

[12] Susruthi Rajanala, Mayra Buainain de Castro Maymone and Neelam Vashi (2018) 'Selfies – Living in the era of filtered photographs', *JAMA Facial Plastic Surgery*, 20(6), 443–44. doi:10.1001/jamafacial.2018.0486

[13] Joachim Allgaier (2019) 'Science and environmental communication on YouTube: Strategically distorted communications in online videos on climate change and climate engineering', *Frontiers in Communication*, 25 July. Available at: www.frontiersin.org/articles/10.3389/fcomm.2019.00036/full

[14] Soroush Vosoughi, Deb Roy and Sinan Aral (2018) 'The spread of true and false news online', *Science*, 9 March. Available at: https://science.sciencemag.org/content/359/6380/1146

[15] Cass R. Sunstein (2017) *#Republic: Divided Democracy in the Age of Social Media*, Princeton, NJ: Princeton University Press.

[16] Quoted in Christina Pazzanese (2017) 'Danger in the internet echo chamber', *Harvard Law Today*, 24 March. Available at: https://today.law.harvard.edu/danger-internet-echo-chamber/

[17] Philip N. Howard, Bence Kollanyi, Samantha Bradshaw and Lisa-Maria Neudert (2017) *Social Media, News and Political Information during the US Election: Was Polarizing Content Concentrated in Swing States?*, Data Memo No 2017.8. Computational Propaganda Research Project, Oxford: University of Oxford. Available at: https://comprop.oii.ox.ac.uk/research/posts/social-media-news-and-political-information-during-the-us-election-was-polarizing-content-concentrated-in-swing-states/, quoted in James Williams (2018) *Stand Out of Our Light: Freedom and Resistance in the Attention Economy*, Cambridge: Cambridge University Press, p 69.

18 Shannon C. McGregor and Logan Molyneux (2018) 'Twitter's influence on news judgement: An experiment among journalists', *SAGE Discipline Hubs*, 21(5). Available at: https://journals.sagepub.com/doi/abs/10.1177/1464884918802975

19 Juliana Schroeder, Michael Kardas and Nicholas Epley (2017) 'The humanizing voice: Speech reveals, and text conceals, a more thoughtful mind in the midst of disagreement', *Emerging Adulthood*, 28(12). Available at: https://journals.sagepub.com/doi/abs/10.1177/0956797617713798

20 See www.tristanharris.com/

21 James Williams (2018) *Stand Out of Our Light: Freedom and Resistance in the Attention Economy*, Cambridge: Cambridge University Press.

22 James Williams (2018) *Stand Out of Our Light: Freedom and Resistance in the Attention Economy*, Cambridge: Cambridge University Press, p 70.

23 James Williams (2018) *Stand Out of Our Light: Freedom and Resistance in the Attention Economy*, Cambridge: Cambridge University Press, p 70.

24 James Williams (2018) *Stand Out of Our Light: Freedom and Resistance in the Attention Economy*, Cambridge: Cambridge University Press, p 64.

25 National Audit Office (2017) *Environmental Metrics: Government's Approach to Monitoring the State of the Natural Environment*. Available at: www.nao.org.uk/report/environmental-metrics-governments-approach-to-monitoring-the-state-of-the-natural-environment/

26 See www.turing.ac.uk/research/research-projects/synthetic-population-estimation-and-scenario-projection

27 See www.gov.uk/government/groups/building-better-building-beautiful-commission

28 My thanks to Sue Chadwick for bringing these examples to my attention.

29 See Bent Flyvbjerg (1998) *Rationality and Power: Democracy in Practice*, Chicago, IL: University of Chicago Press.

Chapter 6

1 William Fulton (2020) 'Here's what our cities will look like after the coronavirus pandemic', Perspective, 26 March, Houston, TX: Kinder Institute, Rice University. Available at: https://kinder.rice.edu/urbanedge/2020/03/26/what-our-cities-will-look-after-coronavirus-pandemic

2 Norman Foster (2020) 'The pandemic will accelerate the evolution of our cities', *The Guardian*, 24 September. Available at: www.theguardian.com/commentisfree/2020/sep/24/pandemic-accelerate-evolution-cities-covid-19-norman-foster?CMP=Share_iOSApp_Other

3 Ministry of Housing, Communities & Local Government (2019) *The English Indices of Deprivation 2019*. Available at: https://assets.publishing.service.gov.uk/government/uploads/system/uploads/attachment_data/file/835115/IoD2019_Statistical_Release.pdf

4 Ministry of Housing, Communities & Local Government (2019) *The English Indices of Deprivation 2019*. Available at: https://assets.publishing.

service.gov.uk/government/uploads/system/uploads/attachment_data/file/835115/IoD2019_Statistical_Release.pdf

5   See https://workingonthebody.com/what-is-sht-life-syndrome/

6   See https://scholar.princeton.edu/deaton/deaths-of-despair

7   Tim Unwin (2019) 'Can digital technologies really be used to reduce inequalities?', OECD Development Matters, 28 February. Available at: https://oecd-development-matters.org/2019/02/28/can-digital-technologies-really-be-used-to-reduce-inequalities/

8   Quoted in David Rotman (2014) 'Technology and inequality', *MIT Technology Review*, 21 October. Available at: www.technologyreview.com/s/531726/technology-and-inequality/

9   Richard Florida (2017) *The New Urban Crisis: Gentrification, Housing Bubbles, Growing Inequality, and What We Can Do About It*, London: Oneworld.

10   Carlo Ratti and Matthew Claudel (2016) *The City of Tomorrow: Sensors, Networks, Hackers, and the Future of Urban Life*, New Haven, CT: Yale University Press, p 65.

11   Chris Arndale (2019) *Dignity: Seeking Respect in Back Row America*, New York: Sentinel Books.

12   Manuel Castells (1989) *The Informational City: Information Technology, Economic Restructuring, and the Urban Regional Process*, Oxford: Wiley-Blackwell.

13   There are many ways in which this list could be compiled, as the numerous annual world cities indices highlight. However, there is a broad consistency in the results across indices and through time. See, for example, www.atkearney.com/global-cities/2018

14   Christian Odendahl, John Springford, Scott Johnson and Jamie Murray (2019) *The Big European Sort? The Diverging Fortunes of Europe's Regions*, London: Centre for European Reform. Available at: www.cer.eu/sites/default/files/pbrief_eusort_2030_21.5.2019.pdf

15   Robert D. Atkinson, Mark Muro and Jacob Whiton (2019) *The Case for Growth Centers: How to Spread Tech Innovation across America*, Washington, DC: The Brookings Institution. Available at: www.brookings.edu/research/growth-centers-how-to-spread-tech-innovation-across-america/

16   Chris Arndale (2019) *Dignity: Seeking Respect in Back Row America*, New York: Sentinel Books.

17   Jacob S. Hacker and Paul Pierson (2010) *Winner-Take-All Politics: How Washington Made the Rich Richer – and Turned Its Back on the Middle Class*, New York: Simon & Schuster.

18   Paul Swinney (2017) 'Is focusing on inequality the best way to tackle poverty in UK cities?', Centre for Cities, Blog post, 28 February. Available at: www.centreforcities.org/blog/focusing-inequality-best-way-tackle-poverty-uk-cities/

19   Richard Florida (2017) *The New Urban Crisis: Gentrification, Housing Bubbles, Growing Inequality, and What We Can Do About It*, London: Oneworld.

20 Richard Florida (2017) *The New Urban Crisis: Gentrification, Housing Bubbles, Growing Inequality, and What We Can Do About It*, London: Oneworld.

21 ONS (Office for National Statistics) (2018) *Wealth in Great Britain Wave 5: 2014 to 2016*, London: HMSO.

22 Social Mobility Commission (2017) *Social Mobility Policies Between 1991 and 2017: Time for Change*. Available at: www.gov.uk/government/publications/social-mobility-policies-between-1997-and-2017-time-for-change

23 Lee Elliot Major and Stephen Machin (2019) *Social Mobility*, London: Centre for Economic Performance, London School of Economics and Political Science. Available at: http://cep.lse.ac.uk/pubs/download/ea045.pdf

24 Robert Putnam (2015) *Our Kids: The American Dream in Crisis*, New York: Simon & Schuster.

25 Robert Putnam (2015) *Our Kids: The American Dream in Crisis*, New York: Simon & Schuster.

26 See www.trustforlondon.org.uk/data/topics/inequality/

27 OECD (Organisation for Economic Co-operation and Development) (2018) *Divided Cities: Understanding Intra-Urban Inequalities*, Paris: OECD. Available at: www.oecd-ilibrary.org

28 Richard Fry and Paul Taylor (2012) 'The rise of residential segregation by income', Pew Research Center, 1 August. Available at: www.pewsocialtrends.org/2012/08/01/the-rise-of-residential-segregation-by-income/

29 Paul Hunter (2019) *The Unspoken Decline of Outer London: Why is Poverty and Inequality Increasing in Outer London and What Needs to Change?*, London: The Smith Institute. Available at: www.trustforlondon.org.uk/publications/unspoken-decline-outer-london-why-poverty-and-inequality-increasing-outer-london-and-what-needs-change/

30 Scott Allard (2017) *Places in Need: The Changing Geography of Poverty*, New York: Russell Sage Foundation.

31 Richard Florida (2017) *The New Urban Crisis: Gentrification, Housing Bubbles, Growing Inequality, and What We Can Do About It*, London: Oneworld.

32 Nadia Khomami and Josh Halliday (2015) 'Shoreditch Cereal Killer Cafe targeted in anti-gentrification protests', *The Guardian*, 27 September. Available at: www.theguardian.com/uk-news/2015/sep/27/shoreditch-cereal-cafe-targeted-by-anti-gentrification-protesters

33 Edward Clarke (2016) 'In defence of gentrification', Centre for Cities, Blog post, 13 October. Available at: www.centreforcities.org/blog/in-defence-of-gentrification/

34 Robin White (2017) 'The availability and affordability of housing', Shelter Briefing, October. Available at: https://england.shelter.org.uk/professional_resources/policy_and_research/policy_library/policy_library_folder/shelter_briefing_the_availability_and_affordability_of_housing

35 Robert Booth (2019) 'UK housing crisis deepens as benefit claimants priced out by high rents', *The Guardian*, 7 July. Available at: www.theguardian.com/society/2019/jul/07/uk-housing-crisis-deepens-as-benefit-claimants-priced-out-by-high-rents

36 Len Ramirez (2018) 'San Francisco Bay Area experiences mass exodus of residents', CBS SF, 8 February. Available at: https://sanfrancisco.cbslocal.com/2018/02/08/san-francisco-bay-area-mass-exodus-residents/

37 Diana Lambert and Daniel J. Willis (2019) 'California's teacher housing crunch: More school districts building their own', *San Francisco Chronicle*, 22 April. Available at: www.sfchronicle.com/bayarea/article/California-s-teacher-housing-crunch-More-13783401.php

38 Quoted in Tim Leunig and James Swaffield (2016) *Cities Unlimited: Making Urban Regeneration Work*, London: Policy Exchange. Available at: www.policyexchange.org.uk/wp-content/uploads/2016/09/cities-unlimited-aug-08.pdf

39 Federico Cingano (2014) *Trends in Income Inequality and Its Impact on Economic Growth*, OECD Social, Employment and Migration Working Papers, Paris: OECD. Available at: www.oecd-ilibrary.org/social-issues-migration-health/trends-in-income-inequality-and-its-impact-on-economic-growth_5jxrjncwxv6j-en

40 Richard Wilkinson and Kate Pickett (2009) *The Spirit Level: Why More Equal Societies Almost Always Do Better*, London: Allen Lane.

41 Chris Doucouliagos (2017) 'Don't listen to the rich: Inequality is bad for everyone', *The Conversation*, 6 August. Available at: https://theconversation.com/dont-listen-to-the-rich-inequality-is-bad-for-everyone-81952

42 Ronald F. Inglehart and Pippa Norris (2016) *Trump, Brexit and the Rise of Populism: Economic Have Nots and the Rise of Populism*, Faculty Research Working Papers RWP16-026, Cambridge, MA: Harvard Kennedy School.

43 Thomas Piketty (2018) *Brahmin Left vs Merchant Right: Rising Inequality and the Changing Structure of Political Conflict*, WID.world Working Paper Series No 2018/7. Available at: http://piketty.pse.ens.fr/files/Piketty2018.pdf

44 Richard Florida (2017) *The New Urban Crisis: Gentrification, Housing Bubbles, Growing Inequality, and What We Can Do About It*, London: Oneworld.

45 Casey R. Lynch (2019) 'Contesting digital futures: Urban politics, alternative economies, and the movement for technological sovereignty in Barcelona', *Antipode*, 52(3), 660–80. Available at: https://onlinelibrary.wiley.com/doi/abs/10.1111/anti.12522

46 Már Másson Mack (2019) 'FairBnB is an ethical alternative to Airbnb coming in 2019', TNW, 6 December. Available at: https://thenextweb.com/eu/2018/12/06/fairbnb-is-an-ethical-alternative-to-airbnb-coming-in-2019/

47 See www.ethicalconsumer.org

48 See https://ridewithvia.com

49 Quoted in Ainsley Harris (2019) 'Can ride-pooling service Via catch up to Uber and Lyft by being the friendly alternative?', *Fast Company*,

28 February. Available at: www.fastcompany.com/90304594/can-ride-pooling-service-via-catch-up-to-uber-and-lyft-by-being-the-friendly-alternative

50 See https://smartcityhub.com/collaborative-city/be-smart-and-put-locals-first/

51 Paul Nicholas (2018) 'Smart city resilience: Digitally empowering cities to survive, adapt, and thrive', McKinsey & Company, Commentary, 30 January. Available at: www.mckinsey.com/business-functions/operations/our-insights/smart-city-resilience-digitally-empowering-cities-to-survive-adapt-and-thrive

Chapter 7

1 Esther Fuldauer (2019) 'Smarter cities are born with digital twins', 5 April. Available at: www.smartcitylab.com/blog/digital-transformation/smarter-cities-are-born-with-digital-twins/

2 See https://cityzenith.com/customers/amaravati-smart-city

3 Michael Jansen (2019) 'Digital twins for greenfield smart cities', New Cities, 23 July. Available at: https://newcities.org/the-big-picture-digital-twins-for-greenfield-smart-cities/

4 Lewis Mumford (1961) *The City in History: Its Origins, Its Transformations, and Its Prospects*, New York: Harcourt, Brace & World.

5 London Transport Museum (no date) 'Charles Tyson Yerkes: The unscrupulous American businessman who transformed the Tube', Stories/People, Available at: www.ltmuseum.co.uk/collections/stories/people/charles-tyson-yerkes-unscrupulous-american-businessman-who-transformed

6 See Philip Allmendinger (2017) *Planning Theory: Planning, Environment, Cities* (3rd edn), Basingstoke: Palgrave.

7 Peter Hall (1990) *Cities of Tomorrow: An Intellectual History of Urban Planning*, Oxford: Blackwell.

8 Quoted in Peter Hall (1990) *Cities of Tomorrow: An Intellectual History of Urban Planning*, Oxford: Blackwell, p 207.

9 See http://mysteriouschicago.com/finding-daniel-burnhams-no-little-plans-quote/

10 Thomas J. Campanella (2017) 'Robert Moses and his racist Parkway, explained', CityLab, 9 July. Available at: www.bloomberg.com/news/articles/2017-07-09/robert-moses-and-his-racist-parkway-explained

11 Quoted in Oliver Wainwright (2017) 'Street fighter: How Jane Jacobs saved New York from Bulldozer Bob', *The Guardian*, 30 April. Available at: www.theguardian.com/artanddesign/2017/apr/30/citizen-jane-jacobs-the-woman-who-saved-manhattan-from-the-bulldozer-documentary

12 Jane Jacobs (1993 [1961]) *The Death and Life of Great American Cities* (Modern Library hardcover edn), New York: Random House.

13 Mechtild Rösslør (1989) 'Applied geography and area research in Nazi society: Central place theory and planning, 1933–1945', *Environment and Planning D: Society and Space*, 7, 419–31.

14 J. Brian McLoughlin (1969) *Urban and Regional Planning: A Systems Approach*, London: Faber & Faber, p 300.

15 Jay Forrester (1969) *Urban Dynamics*, Waltham, MA: Pegasus Communications.

16 Quoted in Tristan Donovan (2011) 'The replay interviews: Will Wright', *Gamasutra*, 23 May. Available at: www.gamasutra.com/view/feature/134754/the_replay_interviews_will_wright.php?page=2

17 Kevin T. Baker (2019) 'Model metropolis', *Logic*, 6, January. Available at: https://logicmag.io/06-model-metropolis/

18 Quoted in Kevin T. Baker (2019) 'Model metropolis', *Logic*, 6, January. Available at: https://logicmag.io/06-model-metropolis/

19 Quoted in Tristan Donovan (2011) 'The replay interviews: Will Wright', *Gamasutra*, 23 May. Available at: www.gamasutra.com/view/feature/134754/the_replay_interviews_will_wright.php?page=4

20 See https://planningtank.com/city-insight/city-swipe-tinder-cities

21 Ben Green (2019) *The Smart Enough City: Putting Technology in Its Place to Reclaim Our Urban Future*, Cambridge, MA: MIT Press.

22 Ben Green (2019) *The Smart Enough City: Putting Technology in Its Place to Reclaim Our Urban Future*, Cambridge, MA: MIT Press.

23 George Gardiner (1973) *The Changing Life of London*, London: David & Charles Publishers.

24 Eliot Spitzer (2006) 'Downstate transportation issues speech', Regional Plan Association, 5 May. Archived from the original on 27 September 2006.

Chapter 8

1 See http://senseable.mit.edu

2 Hope not Hate (2019) *State of Hate 2019: The People versus the Elite?* Available at: www.hopenothate.org.uk

3 James Williams (2018) *Stand Out of Our Light: Freedom and Resistance in the Attention Economy*, Cambridge: Cambridge University Press.

4 Eli Pariser (2012) *Filter Bubble: What the Internet is Hiding from You*, London: Penguin.

5 See www.theguardian.com/world/gallery/2010/oct/01/protest-germany-stuttgart-21

6 Ali Sawafta (2018) 'Protests erupt at Bedouin village Israel plans to demolish', Reuters, 4 July. Available at: https://uk.reuters.com/article/uk-israel-palestinians-bedouin/protests-erupt-at-bedouin-village-israel-plans-to-demolish-idUKKBN1JU1RB

7 Jim Dunton (2019) 'As City planners meet tomorrow, Historic England dubs Fosters' Tulip "a lift shaft with a bulge"', *Building*, 1 April. Available at: www.building.co.uk/news/as-city-planners-meet-tomorrow-historic-england-dubs-fosters-tulip-a-lift-shaft-with-a-bulge-/5098685.article

8 David Roberts (2017) 'Donald Trump and the rise of tribal epistemology', *Vox*, 19 May. Available at: www.vox.com/policy-and-politics/2017/3/22/14762030/donald-trump-tribal-epistemology

9   James Bridle (2018) *The New Dark Age: Technology and the End of the Future*, London: Verso.

10 James Bridle (2018) *The New Dark Age: Technology and the End of the Future*, London: Verso, p 10.

11 Douglas Rushkoff (2013) *Present Shock: When Everything Happens Now*, New York: Penguin.

12 Quoted in Ava Kofman (2018) 'Google's "smart city of surveillance" faces new resistance in Toronto', *The Intercept*, 13 November. Available at: https://theintercept.com/2018/11/13/google-quayside-toronto-smart-city/

13 Quoted in Lucie Green (2018) *Silicon States: The Power and Politics of Big Tech and What It Means for Our Future*, Berkeley, CA: Counterpoint, p 55.

14 Anna Joo Kim, Anne Brown, Maria Nelson, Renia Ehrenfeucht, et al (2019) 'Planning and the so-called "sharing" economy', *Planning Theory & Practice*, 20(2), 261–87. Available at: https://doi.org/10.1080/14649357.2019.1599612

15 Nancy Holman (2019) 'Regulating platform economies in cities – Disrupting the disruption?', *Planning Theory & Practice*, 20(2), 261–87. Available at: https://doi.org/10.1080/14649357.2019.1599612

16 See www.airbnbcitizen.com

17 Ava Kofman (2018) 'Google's "smart city of surveillance" faces new resistance in Toronto', *The Intercept*, 13 November. Available at: https://theintercept.com/2018/11/13/google-quayside-toronto-smart-city/

18 See www.ukauthority.com/articles/barking-dagenham-uses-data-to-manage-bookies/

19 Ava Kofman (2018) 'Google's "smart city of surveillance" faces new resistance in Toronto', *The Intercept*, 13 November. Available at: https://theintercept.com/2018/11/13/google-quayside-toronto-smart-city/

20 Quoted in Ava Kofman (2018) 'Google's "smart city of surveillance" faces new resistance in Toronto', *The Intercept*, 13 November. Available at: https://theintercept.com/2018/11/13/google-quayside-toronto-smart-city/

21 BBC News (2019) 'Canada group sues government over Google's Sidewalk Labs', 16 April. Available at: www.bbc.co.uk/news/world-us-canada-47956760

22 Nabeel Ahmed, Toronto Smart Cities Forum Member. Quoted in Ava Kofman (2018) 'Google's "smart city of surveillance" faces new resistance in Toronto', *The Intercept*, 13 November. Available at: https://theintercept.com/2018/11/13/google-quayside-toronto-smart-city/

23 Leanna Garfield (2017) 'Bill Gates' investment group spent $80 million to build a "smart city" in the desert – and urban planners are divided', *Business Insider*, 22 November. Available at: www.businessinsider.com/bill-gates-smart-city-pros-cons-arizona-urban-planners-2017-11?op=1&r=US&IR=T

Chapter 9

1   James Williams (2018) *Stand Out of Our Light: Freedom and Resistance in the Attention Economy*, Cambridge: Cambridge University Press.

2   Camilla Cavendish (2020) 'The pandemic is killing the attraction of megacities', *Financial Times*, 15 May.

3   Lewis Mumford (1961) *The City in History*, San Diego, CA: Harcourt Inc.

4   William Powell (2012) 'Remember Times Beach: The dioxin disaster, 30 years later', *St Louis*, 3 December. Available at: www.stlmag.com/Remember-Times-Beach-The-Dioxin-Disaster-30-Years-Later/

5   See https://kolmanskop.net

6   James Crawford (2020) 'The strange saga of Kowloon Walled City', *Atlas Obscura*, 6 January. Available at: www.atlasobscura.com/articles/kowloon-walled-city

7   Edward Glaeser (2011) *The Triumph of the City*, London: Pan Macmillan.

8   Leo Hollis (2013) *Cities are Good for You: The Genius of the Metropolis*, London: Bloomsbury.

9   The ecological footprint is the area of land and water ecosystems required to produce the bio-resources for a population to consume and assimilate the carbon wastes that the population produces.

10 C40Cities (2018) *Consumption-Based GHG Emissions of C40 Cities*. Available at: www.c40.org/researches/consumption-based-emissions

11 Edward Glaeser (2011) *The Triumph of the City*, London: Pan Macmillan, p 208.

12 See www.c40.org/cities

13 https://urbantransitions.global/en/about-the-coalition/coalition-members/

14 Charles Montgomery (2013) *Happy City: Transforming Our Lives Through Urban Design*, London: Penguin.

15 Fiona Reynolds (2016) *The Fight for Beauty: Our Path to a Better Future*, London: Oneworld

16 Fiona Reynolds (2016) *The Fight for Beauty: Our Path to a Better Future*, London: Oneworld.

17 Quoted in Eva Mondal (2019) 'The Happiness Index – Measuring joy across the globe', IndianFolk, 15 November. Available at: www.indianfolk.com/happiness-index-measuring-joy-across-globe/

18 Annie Gouk and Conor Gogarty (2020) 'The Bristol neighbourhoods with "appalling" child poverty levels', BristolLive, 27 April. Available at: www.bristolpost.co.uk/news/bristol-news/dwp-child-benefit-poverty-uk-4078530

19 Red Marriott (2007) 'Cities and insurrections – Eric J. Hobsbawm', 28 April. Available at: http://libcom.org/library/cities-and-insurrections-eric-j-hobsbawm

20 Chris Tausanovitch and Christopher Warshaw (2014) 'Representation in municipal government', *The American Political Science Review*, 108, 3.

21 Bill Bishop (2008) *The Big Sort: Why the Clustering of Like Minded Americans is Tearing Us Apart*, New York: Houghton Mifflin Harcourt.

22 Ron Johnston, David Manley and Kelvyn Jones (2016) 'Spatial polarization of presidential voting in the United States, 1992–2012: The "Big Sort" revisited', *Annals of the American Association of Geographers*, 106(5), 1047–106.

23 Samuel J. Abrams and Morris P. Fiorina (2012) 'The myth of the "Big Sort"', Hoover Institution, 13 August. Available at: www.hoover.org/research/myth-big-sort

24 Pew Research Center (2014) 'Political Polarization and Personal Life', Section 3, in *Political Polarization in the American Public*. Available at: www.people-press.org/2014/06/12/section-3-political-polarization-and-personal-life/

25 See www.undp.org/content/undp/en/home/sustainable-development-goals.html

26 Adam Rogers and Nitasha Tiku (2018) 'San Francisco tech billionaires go to war over homelessness', *Wired*. Available at: www.wired.com/story/san-francisco-tech-billionaires-war-over-homelessness/

27 Adam Rogers and Nitasha Tiku (2018) 'San Francisco tech billionaires go to war over homelessness', *Wired*. Available at: www.wired.com/story/san-francisco-tech-billionaires-war-over-homelessness/

28 Peter Hall (1990) *Cities of Tomorrow: An Intellectual History of Urban Planning*, Oxford: Blackwell.

29 See www.c40.org/programmes/building-energy-2020-programme

30 See www.citylab.com/perspective/2020/05/coronavirus-urban-density-history-traffic-congestion-disease/611095/

Chapter 10

1 Harold Wilson (1976) *The Governance of Britain*, London: Weidenfeld & Nicolson.

2 Ben Green (2019) *The Smart Enough City: Putting Technology in Its Place to Reclaim Our Urban Future*, Cambridge, MA: MIT Press.

3 Ben Green (2019) *The Smart Enough City: Putting Technology in Its Place to Reclaim Our Urban Future*, Cambridge, MA: MIT Press, p 6.

4 Thomas S. Kuhn (1962) *The Structure of Scientific Revolutions*, Chicago, IL: University of Chicago Press.

5 Lucie Green (2018) *Silicon States: The Power and Politics of Big Tech and What It Means for Our Future*, Berkeley, CA: Counterpoint.

6 Lucie Green (2018) *Silicon States: The Power and Politics of Big Tech and What It Means for Our Future*, Berkeley, CA: Counterpoint, p 43.

7 John Naughton (2020) 'Can democracies stand up to Facebook? Ireland may have the answer', *The Guardian*, 26 September. Available at: www.theguardian.com/commentisfree/2020/sep/26/can-democracies-stand-up-to-facebook-ireland-may-have-the-answer?CMP=Share_iOSApp_Other

8 April Glaser (2016) 'President Obama explains the difference between Silicon Valley and the real world', *Vox*, 17 October. Available at: www.vox.com/2016/10/17/13301130/obama-silicon-valley-democracy-messy

9   J.G. Ballard (2000) *Super-Cannes*, London: Fourth Estate.

10   See https://activism.net/cypherpunk/crypto-anarchy.html

11   Lucie Green (2018) *Silicon States: The Power and Politics of Big Tech and What It Means for Our Future*, Berkeley, CA: Counterpoint.

12   Lucie Green (2018) *Silicon States: The Power and Politics of Big Tech and What it Means for Our Future*, Berkeley, CA: Counterpoint.

Index

References to tables appear in *italic* type.

Index

Index